Wordsworth's Philosophical Poetry, 1797–1814

This faculty [Imagination] hath been the moving soul
Of our long labour: we have traced the stream
From darkness, and the very place of birth
In its blind cavern, whence is faintly heard
The sound of waters; follow'd it to light
And open day, accompanied its course
Among the ways of Nature, . . .

. . . .

And lastly, from its progress have we drawn
The feeling of life endless, the great thought
By which we live, Infinity and God.

The Prelude

This leads to a remark in your last, "that you are disgusted with all books that treat of religion." I am afraid it is a bad sign in me, that I have little relish for any other—even in poetry it is the imaginative only, viz., that which is conversant with, or turns upon infinity, that powerfully affects me,—perhaps I ought to explain: I mean to say that, unless in those passages where things are lost in each other, and limits vanish, and aspirations are raised, I read with something too much like indifference—but all great poets are in this view powerful Religionists, and therefore among many literary pleasures lost, I have not yet to lament over that of verse as departed.

To Walter Savage Landor

WORDSWORTH'S PHILOSOPHICAL POETRY, 1797–1814

JOHN A. HODGSON

UNIVERSITY OF NEBRASKA PRESS
LINCOLN / LONDON

Portions of "Wordsworth's Dialectical Transcendentalism, 1798: 'Tintern Abbey,'" *Criticism* 18 (1976): 367-80, are reprinted by permission of Wayne State University Press © 1976 Wayne State University Press

The publication of this book was assisted by a grant from the Andrew W. Mellon Foundation.

Publishers on the Plains

UNP

Library of Congress Cataloging in Publication Data

Hodgson, John A   1945-
    Wordsworth's philosophical poetry, 1797-1814

    Includes bibliographical references and index.
    1. Wordsworth, William, 1770-1850—Criticism
and interpretation. I. Title.
PR5888.H6   821'.7   79-24921
ISBN 0-8032-2310-2

For my parents,
Alfred S. Hodgson
and
Winifred H. Hodgson

Contents

Acknowledgments

I WOULD LIKE to thank Paul Sheats, Gerry Brookes, Michael Cooke, Stephen Barney, and Leslie Brisman for reading and commenting on various parts of this book; James Butler, for graciously guiding me through the Wordsworth manuscripts at Dove Cottage and expertly advising me on a variety of textual matters; Yale University, for the award of a Morse Fellowship to support my research and writing; the Trustees of the Wordsworth Library at Dove Cottage, Grasmere, for permission to consult copies of Wordsworth's manuscripts; Oxford University Press, for permission to reprint portions of "The Date of Wordsworth's 'It is no Spirit who from heaven hath flown,'" which originally appeared in *Notes and Queries* 224 (1979): 228–29; and *The Wordsworth Circle*, for permission to reprint portions of "Wordsworth Teaching: 'To Joanna.'"

Abbreviations

CEY	Mark L. Reed, *Wordsworth: The Chronology of the Early Years, 1770–1799* (Cambridge, Mass.: Harvard University Press, 1967).
CMY	Mark L. Reed, *Wordsworth: The Chronology of the Middle Years, 1800–1815* (Cambridge, Mass.: Harvard University Press, 1975). Except where otherwise noted, all facts concerning dates of events in Wordsworth's life and dates of his manuscripts are taken from Reed's two volumes.
DWJ	Dorothy Wordsworth, *The Journals of Dorothy Wordsworth: The Alfoxden Journal 1798; The Grasmere Journals 1800–1803*, ed. Mary Moorman (London: Oxford University Press, 1971).
HG	William Wordsworth, *Home at Grasmere: Part First, Book First of The Recluse*, ed. Beth Darlington, The Cornell Wordsworth (Ithaca, N.Y.: Cornell University Press, 1977). Citations of line numbers refer to the "reading text" of MS. B; of page numbers, to the textual or critical apparatus.
LEY	William and Dorothy Wordsworth, *The Letters of William and Dorothy Wordsworth: The Early Years, 1787–1805*, ed. Ernest de Selincourt, 2d ed., rev. Chester L. Shaver (Oxford: Oxford University Press, Clarendon Press, 1967).
LMY	William and Dorothy Wordsworth, *The Letters of William and Dorothy Wordsworth: The Mid-*

	dle Years, 1806-1820, ed. Ernest de Selincourt, 2d ed., rev. Mary Moorman and Alan G. Hill, 2 vols. (Oxford: Oxford University Press, Clarendon Press, 1969-70).
Prelude 1799	William Wordsworth, *The Prelude 1798-1799*, ed. Stephen Parrish, The Cornell Wordsworth (Ithaca, N.Y.: Cornell University Press, 1977). All references to the 1798-99 *Prelude* are to this edition.
Prelude 1805	William Wordsworth, *The Prelude; or, Growth of a Poet's Mind (Text of 1805)*, ed. Ernest de Selincourt, 2d ed., rev. Stephen Gill (London: Oxford University Press, 1970). Except where otherwise noted, all references to the text of *The Prelude* are to this edition, which represents a correction of the text given by de Selincourt and Darbishire in *Prelude 1850*.
Prelude 1850	William Wordsworth, *The Prelude*, ed. Ernest de Selincourt, 2d ed., rev. Helen Darbishire (Oxford: Oxford University Press, Clarendon Press, 1959). All references to textual variants and editorial apparatus of *The Prelude* and to the 1850 *Prelude* are to this edition.
Prose	William Wordsworth, *The Prose Works of William Wordsworth*, ed. W. J. B. Owen and Jane Worthington Smyser, 3 vols. (Oxford: Oxford University Press, Clarendon Press, 1974).
PW	William Wordsworth, *The Poetical Works of William Wordsworth*, ed. Ernest de Selincourt and Helen Darbishire, vols. 1, 3-5 (Oxford: Oxford University Press, Clarendon Press, 1940-49), vol. 2, 2d ed., rev. Helen Darbishire (Oxford: Oxford University Press, Clarendon Press, 1952). Except for *The Prelude* or where otherwise noted, I have quoted the earliest text of all poems.
STCL	Samuel Taylor Coleridge, *Collected Letters of Samuel Taylor Coleridge*, ed. Earl Leslie Griggs, 6 vols. (Oxford: Oxford University Press, Clarendon Press, 1956-71).

Introduction

In an early version of his *Prospectus* for *The Recluse*, Wordsworth proclaims the ultimate matter of his song to be

> the individual mind that keeps its own
> Inviolate retirement, and consists
> With being limitless the one great Life.
>
> [*HG*, p. 257]

Bold as it is, the assertion masks in its seeming forthrightness two all-important ambiguities. What is the nature of this one great life, and in what sense or way does the individual mind "consist" with it? The questions are central to Wordsworth's thought and work throughout his artistic prime, and so are they central to this study. I have focused on what F. R. Leavis once called Wordsworth's "religious" preoccupation, his "intent[ness] ... upon ultimate sanctions, and upon the living connexions between man and the extra-human universe";[1] in this sense, my concern is with Wordsworth as a religious poet.

This book pursues its investigation of Wordsworth's poetry on two closely related levels. Its plot, if I may so use the term, is the history of Wordsworth's metaphysical beliefs from *The Borderers* to *The Excursion*. Its counterplot, not always explicit but always a part of the larger scheme, is the correlative history of what I have termed Wordsworth's emblamatizing vision. These two themes are as intimately and inextricably involved with each other as are the comparable (not identical) dualities of philosophy and poetry, content and form. But because they nevertheless have somewhat distinct critical backgrounds, at least within the province of Wordsworth studies, it may be helpful for introductory purposes to consider them separately for a moment here.

i

While Wordsworth's constant metaphysical concern was with how the individual "consists / With being limitless the one great Life," at different times during the period 1797–1814 he conceives of this relationship in markedly different ways; and these differences derive in turn from his changing concept of that ultimate Power of the universe. In the following chapters I have tried not only to identify and distinguish these various metaphysical positions but also to trace the logic of their evolution, to suggest how and why Wordsworth developed each as a modification of its predecessor. For Wordsworth's beliefs at different stages of his career, I would argue, while various, are not discontinuous; and surely it was the continuity of his philosophical quest which helped him in his later years defensively to scant or deny the distinctiveness of the stations through which he had passed.[2]

In a crude sense, Wordsworth's philosophical career can be seen as merely an aging toward conservative Anglican orthodoxy. More specifically and interestingly, however, it would seem to represent a patterned, dialectical progression through his interacting hopes for and anxieties about man's proper relation to ultimate Power, hopes and anxieties particularly centering on notions of godhead and of immortality. The pattern comprises four distinguishable stages: an initial, optimistic embracing of a metaphysical creed which seems to offer a satisfying interpretation of man's nature and fate; a reactive dissatisfaction, as some aspects or consequences of the original creed gradually appear after all to be inadequately consolatory for or unacceptably false to human experience; a defensive, compensatory response, whereby Wordsworth strives to cope as best he can with these limitations of his creed; and finally a revisionary, corrective response, whereby he modifies the very assumptions of his original creed to accord with his new estimate of his metaphysical needs. This last stage may then become the first stage of a subsequent cycle.

The revised *Ruined Cottage* of early 1798, though not at the beginning of my study, affords a convenient beginning for this introductory synopsis, for it marks a pure and optimistic extreme of Wordsworth's belief, characterized preeminently by his notion of the "one life" infusing, linking, and even gladdening all things. With this recognition and celebration of a "sentiment of being" permeating all the world, a spirit of "immortality, revolving life, / And greatness still revolving, infinite," Wordsworth in effect is defining godhead as the great prototype and universal essence of Being itself. And since all existing things are a part of this "one life," all things partake of its immortality; the superficial and "passing shews of being" may change, but the underlying life and soul endures.

All too soon, however, Wordsworth reacts against certain implications of this philosophy. The immortality it promises, he cannot but recognize, comes at the expense of human individuality, awareness, and intelligence. By reducing the concept of godhead to the lowest common denominator of being, Wordsworth finds, he has effectively denied or disregarded the importance of attributes which are uniquely human. As a partial, imperfect response to this inadequacy, he moves to preserve from the consuming flux of being at least some sense and memory of the transient individual's uniqueness: in a series of inscriptive, epitaphic, or otherwise memorializing poems he repeatedly strives to attach to the anonymous immortality of nature some enduring, if not immortal, record of individual life and personality.

Wordsworth's ultimate solution to these metaphysical difficulties, however, is not to endure or compensate for his conclusions but to revise his premises. Already in late 1798 he is developing an awareness that thought, not mere being, is the quintessence of human life. And increasingly after this he comes to recognize how consistently and validly something very like thought seems to be at work in the natural world. His response, therefore, is to reconceive godhead as not merely a type of Being but a type of Mind, a great force whose essential characteristics are not merely existential but intellectual. In line with this revision, he now attributes to godhead a transcendent status, imagining it as a power behind or beneath the presences of nature which acts through and on those presences just as, within the limits of its own capacity, does the human mind.

This revised Wordsworthian metaphysics develops from 1800 on and climaxes in the *Intimations* ode and *The Prelude*. But in these last poems especially, I suggest, we shall need most carefully to observe Wordsworth's distinction of Mind from mind, godhead from man, and honor his generally unrecognized skeptical refusal to attribute either divinity or immortality to the individual mind. As this distinction and refusal inevitably imply, in these very poems Wordsworth also anxiously senses certain continuing limitations of man's destiny: while the "consistency" of the individual mind and the one great life now seems all the more complete, yet man's individuality, if not the general human quality of mindfulness per se, remains vulnerable to his mortality. Wordsworth's defensive response to this liability, like his corresponding response in the preceding cycle of his philosophical development, is to turn toward poetic memorialization. But where in his earlier response he had sought to preserve some memory of the individual's life by associating it with the more enduring presences of nature's life, now instead he seeks to insure some continuity of the individual's mind by recording and preserving its ideas in and as works of thought and imagination.

The Prelude is a great triumph of humanistic thought; but, as events proved, Wordsworth could not long persist in the skepticism which underlies and sustains its human affirmation. The death of his brother John affected him deeply, and the anxious desire for personal immortality became intolerably great. More and more after early 1805, and confirmedly by 1809 or so, he modifies his metaphysical assumptions again. This time, however, the change is not a true revision, a reseeing of the world as it is, but an act of faith: he chooses to believe that the individual mind may indeed be as immortal as the divine Mind it images. He is thus in effect reconceiving godhead once again, this time as something very like the God of Christianity.

While Wordsworth held firmly and outspokenly to Christianity, specifically the Church of England, for the remaining forty-odd years of his life, we may sometimes detect, I think, a certain critical dissatisfaction with it analogous to his reactions against his earlier metaphysical creeds. A bold comment to

Henry Crabb Robinson in 1812 offers a particularly telling glimpse of his reservations. Declaring, as Robinson recorded, that "he could not feel with the Unitarians in any way. Their religion allows no room for imagination, and satisfies none of the cravings of the soul," Wordsworth went on to confirm what should, from his avowed religious beliefs, have gone without saying: "I can feel more sympathy with the orthodox believer who needs a Redeemer." But then, strikingly, he added, "I have no need of a Redeemer." Despite such intimations of unorthodoxy, however, Wordsworth recognized that his religion was an untestable faith, requiring not considered agreement so much as simple assent. Years later, in another religious discussion with Robinson, this one concerning some of the basic mysteries of Christianity ("which," he told Robinson, "I do not feel called upon to solve"), to Robinson's summary personal statement that he himself "tried to believe," Wordsworth replied simply, "That is pretty much my case."[3] He had come to need the consolations of Christianity, it would seem, more than the freedom to question them. There would be no further philosophical revisions from William Wordsworth.

ii

It is doubtless due to the tremendous and continuing influence of Coleridge that readers have always tended to regard Wordsworth's poetry as essentially symbolic rather than allegorical or emblematic, just as under Coleridge's teaching they have found it to be essentially imaginative rather than fanciful. While Coleridge never codified a complete or extensive theory of imagination / fancy and symbol / allegory as innately parallel dualities, such a theory is nevertheless strongly implicit and occasionally fragmentarily explicit in his critical writings, prompting René Wellek, for example, to state quite flatly that "symbol in Coleridge is contrasted with allegory, in the same way that imagination is contrasted with fancy, the organic with the mechanical." And Coleridge's corresponding value judgments are quite clear: imagination is a far higher faculty than fancy, and symbolism correlatively a far higher form of art than allegory.[4]

This apparently forthright valuation of symbol over allegory, however, upon closer examination doubles back all too easily into ambiguity and inchoate paradox. For Coleridge would seem in fact to be criticizing only a certain kind of allegorical writing, while admiring another kind—somehow more vital, more passionate, more unified—as truly imaginative and great. Thus while he at one time alludes to *Don Quixote* as a symbolic work, he also describes the don himself as a "substantial living allegory, or personification of the reason and the moral sense, divested of the judgment and understanding." And he judged that Milton, whom he classed with Shakespeare as a giant of imaginative power, "wrote nothing without an interior meaning. . . . He was so great a Man, that he seems to have considered Fiction as profane, unless where it is consecrated by being emblematic of some Truth."[5] Wordsworth himself, moreover, cites as poetry's "grand store-house of enthusiastic and meditative Imagination" not only, following Coleridge, "the prophetic and lyrical parts of the Holy Scriptures, and the works of Milton," but also the poetry of Spenser; and he values the latter poet not in spite but because of at least certain aspects of his allegorizing:

> Spenser . . . maintained his freedom [from "the bondage of definite form" so limiting to the great classical poets] by aid of his allegorical spirit, at one time inciting him to create persons out of abstractions; and, at another, by a superior effort of genius, to give the universality and permanence of abstractions to his human beings, by means of attributes and emblems that belong to the highest moral truths and the purest sensations,—of which his character of Una is a glorious example. [*Prose* 3:34-35]

Such comments cannot but make us suspect that for Wordsworth and Coleridge allegory is, after all, in some way a mode of great power, value, and attractiveness.

Recently Paul de Man has explored this polemical Romantic (including Coleridgean) preference of symbol to allegory and shown how ambiguous and even misleading it really is. Following Coleridge and his German contemporaries in associating symbol with synecdoche, he observes that in the world of the symbol the relationship of image to substance "is one of simultaneity, which, in truth, is spatial in kind, and in which the intervention of time is merely a matter of contingency, whereas, in the world of allegory, time is the originally constitutive category." And he concludes,

> Whereas the symbol postulates the possibility of an identity or identification, allegory designates primarily a distance in relation to its own origin, and, renouncing the nostalgia and the desire to coincide, it establishes its language in the void of this temporal difference. In so doing, it prevents the self from an illusory identification with the non-self, which is now fully, though painfully, recognized as a non-self. It is this painful knowledge that we perceive at the moments when early romantic literature finds its true voice. . . .
>
> We are led, in conclusion, to a historical scheme that differs entirely from the customary picture. The dialectical relationship between subject and object is no longer the central statement of romantic thought, but this dialectic is now located entirely in the temporal relationships that exist within a system of allegorical signs. It becomes a conflict between a conception of the self seen in its authentically temporal predicament and a defensive strategy [symbolism] that tries to hide from this negative self-knowledge.[6]

Surely this attention to the conflict of synecdoche with analogy, identity with separateness, timelessness with temporality, goes to the very heart of the matter. But what is the field of this struggle; precisely what temptations of identification are at issue? Our answer here, I would suggest, must be multiple, and thus more complex than de Man implies; for the Romantic dialectic can and does in fact engage several different versions of the desire for coincidence.

The Romantic metaphysicians tended to conceive of the world as consisting of two primary, distinct levels or entities of being: self and nonself, subject and object, mind and nature. Allegory can establish itself in the difference between these two entities; and by the same token the collapsing of this difference— the "identification with the non-self" of which de Man speaks— will manifest itself as a synecdochal, "symbolic" assertion. Continually in Romantic literature, however, this metaphysical dualism is complicated by the intrusion of attitudes surviving from an older world view, the traditional conception of the universe as a triad of Man, Nature, and God.[7] The intruding element, of course, is supernaturalism, a perception or postulation of some power in the world unassimilable to the secular premises of a simple mind / nature dualism. And with the reappearance of supernaturalism, the field of the Romantic dialectic between allegory and symbolism significantly expands. For now allegory can further establish itself, as it always has, in the differences between nature and God, man and God; but the collapsings of these differences, too, will constitute synecdochal, symbolic assertions.

Thus the perceived oneness of man with nature—I shall continue to call this, after Wordsworth's and Coleridge's usage, a "one life" vision—while certainly the most characteristically "Romantic" mode of symbolism, is not, after all, the only kind of symbolic thought to figure in Romantic writing. The perceived oneness of nature with God, and that of man with God, are also just such synecdochal and thus symbolic visions, though they have rarely been so labeled. In this study I shall refer to the perceived oneness of nature with God as *iconic* vision, adapting the term directly from its familiar religious sense, whereby an icon of Christ, for example, partakes of His sacredness and even of His power. Thus to Mortimer and Robert in *The Borderers*, to Harry Gill, to the villagers in *The Thorn*, to the shepherd in *Hart-Leap Well*, nature seems iconic in that it appears to function supernaturally as God's representative and agent, purposefully judging and responding to the good or evil behavior of men. More generally, then, iconic vision is superstition. The vision of man's own oneness with God, finally, is none other than "enthusiasm" or mysticism, or in a more measured form simply faith, the most tempting synecdochal assertion of all.

Wordsworth's own allegorizing or emblematizing mode of vision defines and establishes itself during his poetic prime against the antagonism of all these versions of symbolic assertion.[8] Already in 1797 his poetry reveals a strongly emblematic vision refuting a strongly iconic one; and *The Borderers* especially is on one level a struggle between iconic and emblematic readings of the universe, with the latter proving the stronger. Wordsworth's vision at this time is in fact subjectively or egotistically emblematic, and as such is what we customarily think of as emblematic, wherein "a philosophical maxim [is] illustrated by a visual image":[9] the poet or observer begins with an idea, and then illustrates it, or finds it reflected, in the external world.

Thus Rivers in *The Borderers* presents a plant, the nightshade, as an emblem of himself, something both "strong to destroy" and "strong to heal," while the solitary of *Lines Left upon a Seat in a Yew-tree* traces in a desolate scene "an emblem of his own unfruitful life."

With the poetry of early 1798 and the advent of his "one life" philosophy, Wordsworth abandons his earlier epistemology and adopts a genuinely symbolic mode of vision, most purely represented by the Pedlar of *The Ruined Cottage*, who "in all things / . . . saw one life." Gradually during the next few years, however, Wordsworth moves away from this perspective and again develops an emblematic mode of vision. Thus the early two-part *Prelude* shows him reinterpreting childhood experiences of a presumedly iconic world as actually having been his own emblematic projections onto the world; and where in 1798 he had read Margaret's ruined cottage symbolically, he learns in 1800 to read Michael's unfinished sheepfold as an intended emblem, a sign of the old shepherd's covenant with his son. By 1804, with his new recognition in nature of an underpresence and power extensively analogous to man's mind and thought, the reading of emblems becomes the very heart of Wordsworth's philosophical method. Now, however, his readings are not subjectively but objectively emblematic: rather than projecting a significance into nature, he educes an already inherent significance from nature. As Enid Welsford says, "the emblem is used as a means not so much of *illustrating* as of *discovering* truth, and the object of sense-perception leads up to the text, not vice versa."[10] And the skeptical honesty of Wordsworth's new vision, his consistent refusal to read analogy as a sign or promise of identity, produces in the great ode and *The Prelude* neither the transcendental nor the "apocalyptic" poetry we are usually taught to see, but some of the noblest humanistic poetry in the language. Finally, *The Excursion* awkwardly exposes its own essential philosophical weakness as a lapsing into an enthusiast's defensive dishonesty: now the poet does at last try to read analogy as identity, emblem as symbol, and so corrupts his emblematic vision in the deluded hope of transcending it.

PART I: 1797–98

Introduction

W HEN WORDSWORTH first arranged his poems into classes in 1815, he split off *The Borderers*, together with his other work of 1797 and before, as "Poems Written in Youth." His action here, and the critical estimates prompting it, have strongly reinforced the generally received opinion, perhaps justifiable enough in any case, that only in 1798 did Wordsworth find his true poetic voice. This voice characteristically ponders man's spiritual development and his proper relation to nature, and most probably owes a seminal debt to Coleridge, who, Jonathan Wordsworth has joined many others in arguing, "gave Wordsworth a philosophical basis for his response to Nature, and in so doing made available to him the material of much of his greatest poetry."[1]

In a broad sense, however, the mature poetry of 1798 and beyond only renews and extends a philosophical debate already highly developed in the earlier poetry, particularly *The Borderers*. The conflict there between Mortimer and Rivers involves both morality and epistemology: they disagree about both the moral or amoral condition of the universe and, correlatively, the correct ways of interpreting human feelings and external appearances. Mortimer's is what I shall be terming an iconic vision of the world: he believes that morality comes from a supernatural God and that nature has iconic value as God's surrogate, informed by God and able to act for Him in response to human innocence or guilt. Rivers's vision, in contrast, is subjectively emblematic: he believes that the universe is essentially amoral, simply mirroring back in emblems whatever values man cares to create and project. Ultimately, as events demonstrate, the truth seems to lie somewhere in between. The play emphatically rejects iconic in favor of emblematic vision, but it also rejects Rivers's concept of an amoral universe, instead locating the basis of morality not in nature or supernature but in the individual human heart.

When Wordsworth comes to revise and expand *The Ruined Cottage* early in 1798, he turns these earlier conclusions rather topsy-turvy, but continues the internal debate. The Pedlar, first spokesman of Wordsworth's new philosophy, sees all the world as interactingly and inseparably connected, one great and good life or soul. He thus finds moral principles equally present in all things. And with this symbolic mode of vision he not only explicitly rejects the emblematic, but even suggests a revival and redemption of Mortimer's iconic vision. Where Mortimer had anthropocentrically posited God as a force of omniscience and righteousness—indeed, as the great prototype of Mortimer himself, aggressively imposing law and order on an unruly land—the Pedlar instead selflessly conceives of God as Being itself, the universal essence of existence, and thereby naturalizes Mortimer's egotistically flawed mode of vision into something more truly and universally sympathetic.

Tintern Abbey offers a complex and innovative analysis of the rewarding dialectic of mind and nature available to him who, like the Pedlar or Wordsworth himself, learns to see the "one life" and accordingly to attune his "intellectual soul" to "the life of things." But the very thoughtfulness and intellectuality of this investigation, while hardly a murdering to dissect, nevertheless marks a changed attitude from the Pedlar's more spontaneous responsiveness to his world. And with his early work on *The Prelude* Wordsworth begins to revert to his prior emphasis on the autonomy of the individual mind. Recalling episodes of iconic vision from his own boyhood, he yet recognizes these in retrospect as having been emblematic projections and suspects his adolescent vision of the one life as having been similarly subjective. While he continues to conceive of God as "the sentiment of being," this conception becomes decreasingly useful to him as with growing interest he explores "the river of my mind" and the growth of the intellect.

CHAPTER 1
"God Is Everywhere!":
From *The Borderers* to
The Ruined Cottage

i

THE FORCES which threaten the Baron Herbert in *The Borderers* are essentially those against which Wordsworth would warn his sister in the conclusion of *Tintern Abbey*, the cruelties of society and the elemental oppressions of the natural world. But Herbert's rod and staff against these adversaries is not natural but Christian piety; and indeed, his blind-man's staff is inscribed with a pseudobiblical tag: "I am eyes to the blind, saith the Lord. / He that puts his trust in me shall not fail!" (ll. 1413-14; cf. *Job* 29:15). Thus fortified as he is, the unkindnesses and injustices of man do not prevail against him. Blind, dispossessed of his titles and belongings, cast out of his home, he places himself in the hands of his God—

> Like a mendicant,
> Whom no one comes to meet, I stood alone;—
> I murmured—but, remembering Him who feeds
> The pelican and ostrich of the desert,
> From my own threshold I looked up to Heaven
> And did not want glimmerings of quiet hope
> [Ll. 1350-55]

—and is sustained in the harsh world like Elijah in the wilderness.

Where Elijah spoke directly with God, however, Herbert, explicitly an Elijah figure, yet knows Him chiefly through his daughter, Matilda. "Her looks won pity from the world—when I had none to help me, she brought me food—she was a raven, sent to me in the wilderness" (ll. 846-48 app. crit.). As this last allusion would suggest, Matilda seems to her father the prime agent and representative of God's care and mercy:

5

> I heard a voice
> Such as by Cherith on Elijah called;
> It said, "I will be with thee." A little boy,
> A shepherd-lad, ere yet my trance was gone,
> Hailed us as if he had been sent from Heaven,
> And said, with tears, that he would be our guide:
> I had a better guide—that innocent Babe—
> Who to this hour has saved me from all evil
> From cold, from death, from penury and hunger.
>
> [Ll. 1362-70 and app. crit.]

Thus Matilda becomes the very emblem and externalization of Herbert's faith. It is actually she who is his staff; with her own hand she had carved the biblical promise onto her father's staff (l. 1412), and by the beginning of the play she seeks to make herself this staff in fact as she already is in spirit:

> That staff of yours, I could almost have heart
> To fling't away from you: you make no use
> Of me, or of my strength;—come, let me feel
> That you do press upon me.
>
> [Ll. 126-29]

When he is separated from her and led to fear he has lost her, he can no longer sustain himself; in effect, his faith fails to preserve him. In his last days, he is no longer an Elijah, accompanied to his end by a faithful companion and then taken up living into the bosom of his God; he dies alone in the wilderness, separated from kin and friends and abandoned by strangers, and instead of a raven to feed him there comes a crow to feed upon him (ll. 2072-75).[1]

Mortimer abandons Herbert in the wilderness as a test of the old man's virtue and innocence, a trial by ordeal:

> There is a judge above—
> It dawns on me—I see the end for which
> An arm invisible hath led me hither.
> He heard a voice—a shepherd-lad came to him
> And was his guide; if once, why not again,
> And in this desert? If never then he is damned
> Beyond a madman's dream: here will I leave him
> Here where no foot of man is found, no ear
> Can hear his cries—it is a fearful ordeal!
> But God is everywhere!
>
> [Ll. 1381-98 and app. crit.]

As he proclaims to Herbert,

> Thou wilt have many guides if thou art innocent;
> Yea, from the utmost corners of the world
> That Woman will come o'er this heath to save thee.
>
> . . . .
>
>   . . . Repent and be forgiven—
> God and that staff are now thy only guides.
> [Ll. 1409-11 and ll. 1415-16 app. crit.]

Herbert is actually innocent of all crimes, and Mortimer is abused in his suspicions. But God, if all-seeing (cf. ll. 902 app. crit.), nevertheless does not interfere; the wilderness world they inhabit remains a moral vacuum. With God and his staff as his only guides, Herbert cannot survive. A chapel bell, God's Angelus, seems to direct and call him to safety; but the chapel is deserted, and its untended bell, ringing in the stormy wind, with its delusive promise lures Herbert up to a precipice he cannot see to avoid. "Saved" only by collapsing from weakness before he reaches the edge, he lets fall his staff and, now utterly guideless, drops down beside a small pool of water to die.

The assumption embodied in trial by ordeal that God will suspend or manipulate the processes of nature to save the innocent and expose or punish the guilty is deeply engrained in Mortimer's psyche; he is speaking quite literally when he obliquely addresses Herbert just before this as a man "whose crimes / Have roused all Nature up against him" (ll. 1290-91). Yet already he has felt intimations of a contrary truth, as when, upon hearing the "audacious blasphemy" of Herbert's pious and placid reaction to a burst of thunder—

> This is a time, said he, when guilt may shudder;
> But there's a Providence for them who walk
> In helplessness, when innocence is with them

—he thinks that "the spirit of vengeance seemed to ride the air," but must admit,

> Yet nothing came of it. I listened, but
> The echoes of the thunder died away
> Among the distant hills.
> [Ll. 790-94 and app. crit.]

And finally the truth that nature is actually indifferent and arbitrary, a moral cipher, crushingly comes home to him in act 4, when he hears Rivers's life story. In an incident extensively parallel to Mortimer's abandoning of Herbert in the wilderness, Rivers had once marooned on a bare, exposed rock in the middle of the Mediterranean a ship's captain who, as he conceived, had foully conspired against his honor. The island afforded neither food, water, nor even shelter for a man; and here the captain was left to die, never to be heard from again. Mortimer is appalled at the viciousness of this act, but consoles himself with the thought that through such agencies the divine will is done: "But then he was a traitor—these expedients / Are terrible, yet ours is not the fault" (ll. 1745–47 and app. crit.). But Rivers then tells him the captain was after all innocent. Mortimer, incredulous, clings desperately to his two-stranded assumption, first that the man must indeed have been guilty—as he tells Rivers,

> Let not that thought [of the captain's innocence] trouble you.
> His guilt was marked—these things could never be
> Were we not instruments in the hands of heaven
> [Ll. 1750–52 and app. crit.]

—and then, failing this, that the man must somehow have survived: "And the miserable man was heard of no more?" (l. 1754 app. crit.). But Rivers shatters these illusions: the calumny was a plot laid by the crew to rid themselves of a hated master, and the captain never returned. Mortimer's last protest twists painfully in its illogic to obscure the light of self-recognition now breaking in upon him:

> The proofs, the proofs
> You ought to have seen, to have touched the guilt, the heavens
> Have kindly dealt with me, let me be thankful.
> [Ll. 1769–71 app. crit.]

Near the close of the play we once again see the superstition of judgment by nature debunked, this time with Mortimer himself as the defendant. Mortimer enters Robert's hut to view Herbert's body, and Robert, rightly suspecting Mortimer of complicity in the old man's death, approves Matilda's express intention of following Mortimer inside; for she will then be a witness to the viewing:

Lady, you will do well
He has been dead and silent many hours
If you should hear a groan or from his side
He should uplift his hand—that would be evidence.
[Ll. 2128-31 and app. crit.]

But the corpse gives no such sign. Despite Robert's expectations of "plain proofs / Of interfering Heaven" (ll. 2098-99), nature cannot declare Mortimer's guilt; this he must do himself.[2]

Mortimer's criminal error, and the naïveté or superstition of which he must be disabused, is to regard nature as having *iconic* value—that is, as itself sharing and wielding the power of the godhead it veils and represents. This notion of nature as a deliberate, purposeful moral force Rivers has already held up to scorn in an early soliloquy:

—These fools of feeling are mere birds of winter
That haunt some barren island of the north,
Where, if a famishing man stretch forth his hand,
They think it is to feed them.
[Ll. 558-61]

Nature can and does convey moral lessons in *The Borderers*, but not in such a way. Mortimer himself, despite his certainty that "God is everywhere," has no good cause for believing that nature is iconic, that trial by ordeal is a valid test of guilt or innocence. He has, however, directly experienced nature's moral force in a different way, as for example when he was preparing to execute the sleeping Herbert:

Upwards I cast my eyes, and, through a crevice,
Beheld a star twinkling above my head,
And, by the living God, I could not do it.
[Ll. 988-90]

Here we see nature active in its proper moral role—not as divine judge, but as responsive text, or sign. Nature in *The Borderers* is not iconic, but can seem *emblematic*—an assemblage of signs illustrative of man's preconceived moral ideas.[3]

Some phenomena or aspects of nature have become such universal and familiar emblems that they are read almost unthinkingly, like dead metaphors; Herbert's interpretation of the thunder as a sign of God's displeasure with guilty men is a typical example. But the emblematic value of nature is established as an important theme in *The Borderers* long before this, from the moment of the play's first presentation of nature. This moment, significantly, coincides with the first appearance of Rivers. As Mortimer waits alone on stage, Rivers enters to him with "a bunch of plants in his hand" (l. 43):

> *Riv.:* This wood is rich in plants and curious simples.
> *Mort.:* [looking at them]. The wild rose, and the poppy, and nightshade:
> Which is your favourite, Rivers?
> *Riv.:*   That which, while it is
> Strong to destroy, is also strong to heal.
> [Ll. 44-47]

The brusqueness of this interchange veils the richness of its heritage and implications. For Rivers, in the guise of an amateur herbalist, is speaking to Mortimer and to us in one tongue of the language of flowers. He takes his particular cue here from Shakespeare's Ophelia and Perdita and chooses his flowers for the occasion every bit as carefully as they.

Rivers's favorite among the three flowers is the nightshade—specifically, to judge by his comment on its properties, not the common but the deadly nightshade. He makes such a point of gathering it, not because he has any actual need of it, but because it serves so nicely as an emblem: "that which, while it is / Strong to destroy, is also strong to heal." Furthermore, Rivers here clearly intends this emblematic flower as an appropriate figure for himself. He anticipates working on Mortimer's mind in just such a way, poisoning his leader's "thoughtless heart" (l. 1547) but possibly also, in the process, setting that heart free from its sickly and abject bondage to emotions and mores. And in Rivers's final entrance in act 5, an action parallel to this initial entrance in act 1, as he comes on stage he is characterizing himself under his breath by a formula pointedly reminiscent of this floral emblem: "Strong to destroy, strong also to build up" (l. 2245 app. crit.).

Rivers's explicitly emblematic interpretation of the nightshade indicates that the other flowers in his bouquet may have emblematic significance also. It would seem, in fact, that the three flowers he gathers are chosen to represent the three members of the play's strange triangle, Rivers, Mortimer, and Matilda. Matilda, of course, is the wild rose—a rose because a beautiful and loving young woman (traditionally the rose is emblematic of love), wild because reared by nature, in her earliest years an undomesticated child of vagrancy. So the female beggar characterizes her as a matter of course: "a Maiden . . . / lovely as any rose" (ll. 454-55 and app. crit.). And so, approximately, does Mortimer, speaking to Herbert in the mistaken belief that the Baron has conspired to sell Matilda into white slavery:

> Oh villain! damned villain!
> She smelled most sweet, and she was fair, and now
> They have snapped her from the stem—Poh! let her lie
> Besoiled with mire, and let the houseless snail
> Feed on her leaves.
>
> [Ll. 1308-12 and app. crit.]

The association of Mortimer with the poppy, while less overt than these other two associations, acquires force as images of sleep, dreaming, and hallucination increasingly attach themselves to him. Thus as Mortimer relates his failure of will when he first thought to kill Herbert, he says,

> Twice did I spring to grasp his withered throat,
> When such a sudden weakness fell upon me,
> I could have dropped asleep upon his breast.
>
> [Ll. 390-92]

And shortly afterwards, returning from Herbert's bed in the abandoned dungeon following a second abortive executional attempt, he cries to Rivers, "What made you come down and lay your hand upon my shoulder? When I spoke to you, why did you not answer?" (ll. 957-59 app. crit.). But Rivers had remained on stage throughout; Mortimer, we realize, has been hallucinating as he will again frequently in act 5, under the mental pressure of his guilt and remorse (see ll. 1991/7 app. crit., 2245-78 app. crit.).

To say that nature in *The Borderers* is emblematic rather than iconic is simply to recognize that in such a world the significations of the book of nature are established not by God but by man. Nature does not, of itself, express or work God's will. Alone, it speaks only in random and meaningless sounds, as for example through the wind-rung chapel-bell—"a cruel parody," as Frank McConnell notes, "of the aeolian-harp theme."[4] "God is everywhere!" Mortimer thinks, and even a deed done in darkness, as the "twinkling atom's eye" (l. 1220 and app. crit.) of

that watchful star reminds him, is "visible . . . to the eye of God";
but he soon learns that God sees in this world only through the
eyes of men—which is as much as to say that morality, if indeed
it has any real basis at all, comes only from within, not from
without.

It is Rivers's settled conclusion that no ultimate basis for
morality exists within man any more than within nature—that
each man properly creates his own morality regardless of the
would-be "tyranny / Of moralists and saints and lawgivers"
(ll. 1490-91 and app. crit.), and "the only law that wisdom /
Can ever recognize" is the reasoning mind itself as guided solely
by the exigencies of the present moment,

> the immediate law
> Flashed from the light of circumstances
> Upon an independent intellect.
>
> [Ll. 1493-96 and app. crit.]

But Wordsworth himself in *The Borderers* finally rejects such
moral skepticism and nihilism. For however wrongly Mortimer
had originally valued nature, yet he had, after all, rightly valued
the human heart and its sympathies. Despite Rivers's rational-
istic contempt and dismissal of them, nothing in the play under-
cuts the authority of love and benevolence as absolute moral
values; on the contrary, the principles which Matilda, Herbert,
and initially Mortimer espouse are everywhere justified by
events, while Rivers's rejection of them involves him not merely
in suffering but in spiritual and physical ruin, and even, iron-
ically, in mistakes of judgment. As Peter Thorslev observes, "had
[Mortimer] obeyed the intuitions of his heart against [Rivers's]
'proofs' . . . , the tragedy would have been averted."[5] Simi-
larly, had Robert been faithful to the "fervour of [his] heart"
(l. 1670/1 app. crit.), he might have saved Herbert; had Rivers
nourished his heart above his dessicating pride (l. 1701) and so
responded to the cries for mercy which admittedly moved him
(ll. 1732-34), he would never have marooned his captain. It is
thus with unconsciously heavy irony that the deluded Mortimer
is moved to embrace Rivers's moral nihilism as "a creed, built in
the heart of things" (l. 1219); for it is precisely in the heart, in
the heart of man, that man's only valid creed is in fact built.

The question of nature's value as an agent of moral truth
thus becomes a question of the validity of the emblematic use

to which men put it. When men emblematize in nature the true teachings of their sympathetic hearts sensitively and appropriately—Mortimer's externalization of his own watchful conscience as a star's dungeon-probing eye is the play's most important example—then nature indeed speaks to men validly, for it thereby represents a genuinely moral impulse. When, on the other hand, men emblematize moral falsehoods or half-truths, when their emblems are inappropriate or misinterpreted, or, finally, when they renounce their emblematizing and interpreting powers and responsibilities altogether, then nature will necessarily speak to them wrongly, or confusingly, or not at all.

ii

Wordsworth continues to explore these same issues of the dependent, emblematic significance of nature versus the absolute value of the heart's benevolence in the other two poems which we know he read to Coleridge early in the summer of 1797, the *Lines Left upon a Seat in a Yew-tree* and a first version of *The Ruined Cottage.* Here he particularly stresses how man emblematizes his selfless affections in his vision of the world around him or alternatively projects his self-corrupting egotism into a correspondingly distorted view of nature.

As the former poem's lengthy title tells us, a man embittered by failure in worldly affairs built the yew-tree seat "near the Lake of Esthwaite, on a desolate part of the shore, yet commanding a beautiful prospect." The foreground of his view, the "desolate part of the shore"—"barren rocks, with juniper / And heath, and thistle, thinly sprinkled o'er" (ll. 28–29 and app. crit.)—he took as "an emblem of his own unfruitful life" (l. 32); the background, the "beautiful prospect," he regarded by contrast as a type of fanciful, unreal beauty, "visionary views" (l. 45). These emblems, of course, are of his own making and interpreting, even as is that "only monument" (l. 47) and other emblem of his life, the reclusive seat within the "gloomy boughs" (l. 24) of the barren and lonely yew tree.

As in the case of Rivers, so here again there is an intensely egotistical quality to this kind of emblematic perspective. The proud recluse who would gaze so long on the nearer and then the farther scene was in fact, as Wordsworth tells us, simply one

"whose eye / [Was] ever on himself" (ll. 55–56). Even his seem-
ing love of nature is accordingly suspect, for the scene's loveli-
ness thus moves him as he broods upon it, the poet cunningly
suggests, as a self-conceived emblem of his own glorious, unreal-
ized promise. The "visionary views" he cherishes from this seat
are not so much of the present "beautiful prospect" as of a by-
gone prospect in retrospect, the grand hopes and "lofty views"
(l. 15 app. crit.) of his youth remembered.[6]

Clearly the yew-tree solitary's love was not that kind of love
of nature which leads to love of man. The more fundamental
point, however, is, as we have already noted, that *no* emblematic
construct from an essentially indifferent nature can be of such a
kind. For an emblem does not inspire its creator's thoughts, but
simply represents them; the doctrine precedes and shapes the
emblematization. Hence while what the recluse "morbidly" and
"fancifully" (cf. ll. 31, 45) sees in his highly selective view of
nature is inevitably a reflection of his own egotism, yet to
other, more amiable men, "warm from the labours of benevo-
lence," even the larger prospect, "the world, and man himself,"
will seem "a scene / Of kindred loveliness" (ll. 40–42), an image
of their own loving hearts. In effect, this is to say, love of man
leads to love of nature, for the latter affection simply translates
and reflects the former.

By all indications, the 1797 version of *The Ruined Cottage*
was philosophically very much of a pattern with *The Borderers*
and *Lines Left upon a Seat in a Yew-tree*.[7] Particularly note-
worthy is the way in which Margaret egotistically, if pathet-
ically, emblematizes her attitudes in her environment. As Jona-
than Wordsworth observes, "Her garden reflects her decline";[8]
but this reflection, significantly, is of Margaret's own choosing
and making. Abandoned by her husband, she gradually leaves
off tending her garden, her children, and her person, letting
them all become types of her own abandonment. Thus the
pathos of her situation is also poisoned by a bitter irony.

> "I hope," said she, "that heaven
> Will give me patience to endure the things
> Which I behold at home."
>
> [*The Ruined Cottage*, ll. 609–11]

14

What she must pray for strength to endure is her own desolation; but what she beholds at home is a household desolation which she herself has created and which calls for not patience but remedy.

Sometimes Margaret's egotistically emblematizing turn of mind is very apparent indeed. On a visit a year after her husband's departure, the Pedlar surveys her neglected garden and notes that

> a chain of straw
> Which had been twisted round the tender stem
> Of a young apple-tree lay at its root,
> The bark was nibbled round by truant sheep.
> Margaret stood near, her infant in her arms
> And seeing that my eye was on the tree
> She said, "I fear it will be dead and gone
> Ere Robert come again."
> [Ll. 669–76]

She may intend an allusion to her child here; she certainly intends one to herself.[9]

Margaret's decline, then, ostensibly caused by outside events, seems ultimately due to her own attitude. Like the yew-tree solitary, she sees all life in terms of her own plight; and further, like him she makes her little piece of the world an emblem of her plight. Either character will serve equally well as object lesson for the moral which Wordsworth so didactically offers as his concluding *Lines*:

> True knowledge leads to love;
> True dignity abides with him alone
> Who, in the silent hour of inward thought,
> Can still suspect, and still revere himself,
> In lowliness of heart.
> [Ll. 60–64]

From this summarizing admonition all reference to external nature has disappeared as irrelevant. It is only through "inward thought" and from the depths of the potentially loving heart that true morality can arise, only to some fundamental value within man himself that reverence is properly due.

15

Thus in 1797 Wordsworth clearly holds that the foundations of morality lie exclusively within man, while nature, whatever superficial significance man may attribute to it, remains in essence but a neutral presence. By early 1798, however, probably in response to Coleridge's influence, he radically revises these views. Now, as if in great part recanting his beliefs of the previous year, he sets forth a new metaphysics in some ways unmistakably reminiscent of Mortimer's so recently and devastatingly discredited iconic concept of nature.

A curious hint of this change appears early in Wordsworth's new work on *The Old Cumberland Beggar*, a poem begun some time before which he was now rewriting and greatly expanding. In *The Borderers*, as we have already seen, Rivers mockingly likens "fools of feeling" such as Mortimer to the birds in some barren place, "where, if a famishing man stretch forth his hand, / They think it is to feed them." Now, in *The Old Cumberland Beggar*, this image recurs, but with a significant difference:

> He sate, and eat his food in solitude:
> And ever, scattered from his palsied hand,
> That, still attempting to prevent the waste,
> Was baffled still, the crumbs in little showers
> Fell on the ground; and the small mountain birds,
> Not venturing yet to peck their destined meal,
> Approached within the length of half his staff.
> [Ll. 15-21 and app. crit.]

Here, when the hungry old man reaches out his hand, it is indeed with the effect of feeding the birds, despite his directly contrary intent. The incident suggests a new overview of nature as ultimately beneficent even if not benevolent. And as the poem's new conclusion confirms, while nature is not particularly good to the old man—its frosts chill him, its winds beat upon him—it is nevertheless somehow good for him.

The underlying philosophical assumption impelling this new attitude toward nature becomes explicit early in the exhortatory middle section of the poem, as Wordsworth begins to assert the old beggar's essential value:

> 'Tis Nature's law
> That none, the meanest of created things,

Of forms created the most vile and brute,
The dullest or most noxious, should exist
Divorced from good—a spirit and pulse of good,
A life and soul, to every mode of being
Inseparably linked.

[Ll. 73-79]

He is good and valuable, in other words, because all things in
the world are innately good, infused as they are by a universal
soul of goodness—in effect, by God.[10] With this affirmation
Wordsworth returns most emphatically to a version of Morti-
mer's belief, "God is everywhere!" No longer a neutral presence,
nature by this view no less than man contains within itself the
very essence of morality.

Wordsworth explicitly confirms this new sense of a universal,
all-infusing life and soul in several verse fragments also dating
from early 1798, brief drafts which particularly emphasize a
sympathetic love of nature. In one of these his (or his charac-
ter's) advocacy of "sympathy / With nature in her forms inani-
mate" proceeds to a starkly forthright justification: "In all
forms of things / There is a mind" (*PW* 5:340). In another, he
pursues the same theme more elaborately, much in the spirit
and style of the corresponding *Old Cumberland Beggar* passage:

Of unknown modes of being which on earth,
Or in the heavens, or in the heavens and earth
Exist by mighty combinations, bound
Together by a link, and with a soul
Which makes all one.

[*PW* 5:340-41]

Fragmentary as they are, these lines nevertheless suggest Words-
worth's increasing interest in that universal oneness for its own
sake, and not, as may seem to be the case in *The Old Cumber-
land Beggar*, merely for what support it can lend to a tenuously
related argument.

The fragments just cited were probably first intended for
Wordsworth's new version of *The Ruined Cottage*, the poem
which he was currently making over into his first full statement
of his new beliefs. To his original story of Margaret's suffering
and decline he now added a complex philosophical and dramatic
frame, thereby converting the poem as a whole into a great

17

philosophic description and dramatic exemplum of man's proper, moral relation to nature and to society. The main instrument of this transformation is the previously anonymous tale-teller, who is now identified as a Pedlar, fleshed out with a spiritual biography—Wordsworth's "first portrait of the growth of a mind"[11]— and set up, in pointed contrast to Margaret, as a man happily and lovingly attuned to the universal soul. As Dorothy Wordsworth wrote to Mary Hutchinson early in March, "The Pedlar's character now makes a very, certainly the *most*, considerable part of the poem" (*LEY*, p. 199). As a quantitative observation this may be confusing, but as a critical one it is quite true and important, for now the Pedlar has indeed displaced Margaret as the dominant figure of the poem.

The Pedlar's importance, as the emphases of the biography Wordsworth gives him make clear, derives entirely from his sensitivity to what Wordsworth now calls the "one life" (*The Ruined Cottage*, l. 252), his conception of Being itself as godhead, his appreciation of how all modes of being are spiritually joined into one great and good whole. And while the benevolent men alluded to in the *Lines Left upon a Seat in a Yew-tree* are similarly all-encompassing in their love of the world, the Pedlar significantly differs from them in evolving his love of man from a love of nature, rather than the reverse. He is in fact strikingly uninvolved (and apparently unconcerned) with other men in his youth, but "nature was at his heart" (l. 202), incontestably the dominant force influencing his development. Eventually he learns to see through her grand forms into her spiritual grandeur, her essential

> immortality, revolving life,
> And greatness still revolving, infinite;
> There littleness was not, the least of things
> Seemed infinite.
>
> [Ll. 151-54]

And in such insight he finds both the promise and the realization of personal and universal beatitude, a natural revelation of what the Bible can only assert, "the mystery, the life which cannot die" (l. 148):

> He was only then
> Contented, when, with bliss ineffable

He felt the sentiment of being, spread
O'er all that moves, and all that seemeth still,
O'er all which, lost beyond the reach of thought,
And human knowledge, to the human eye
Invisible, yet liveth to the heart,
O'er all that leaps, and runs, and shouts, and sings,
Or beats the gladsome air, o'er all that glides
Beneath the wave, yea in the wave itself,
And mighty depth of waters. Wonder not
If such his transports were; for in all things
He saw one life, and felt that it was joy.
[Ll. 240-52]

In *The Borderers* Mortimer had egotistically conceived of God as a type of supreme reason, a spirit whose dominant characteristic was omniscience; thus he believed that not just his mind, but his God also, stood opposed to the inclinations of his heart. But now, in the Pedlar's selfless vision, the "creed, built in the heart of things" becomes one with the creed built in the heart of man, a universal "sentiment of being"; the values informing the heart equally inform all elements of nature and are equally recoverable therefrom, as God becomes here a type of supreme feeling, a spirit whose dominant characteristic is omnipresence.

iv

Wordsworth would soon after this, in *Tintern Abbey*, claim the Pedlar's vision of the "one life" as his own, and then would even, in his early work on *The Prelude*, appropriate verbatim for himself whole passages which he had originally written for the Pedlar's biography. But however characteristic the Pedlar's philosophy and sensibility are of Wordsworth's own in 1798, they seem remarkably unrelated to Wordsworth's immediately preceding poetry of 1797, appearing on the scene as suddenly and unexpectedly as does the Pedlar himself. Yet a bridge between these two periods does exist, appearing in *The Ruined Cottage* in the person of the poem's second Wordsworth surrogate, the narrator himself, who enacts, during the course of his narrative, Wordsworth's own progression from his 1797 to his 1798 sensibility.

The narrator of *The Ruined Cottage* first presents himself to us as a vexed wanderer who would prefer to be a resting dreamer.

While he is not unappreciative of the scenery through which he is travelling, its prospects require, he thinks, a more comfortable vantage point than his own: they would be

> Pleasant to him who on the soft cool grass
> Extends his careless limbs beside the root
> Of some huge oak whose aged branches make
> A twilight of their own, a dewy shade
> Where the wren warbles, while the dreaming man,
> Half conscious of that soothing melody,
> With sidelong eye looks out upon the scene
> By those impending branches made [more soft]
> More soft and distant.

[Ll. 10-18]

But "other lot was mine" (l. 18), as he notes, and his brief attempt to be himself that dreaming man seems doomed from the start by an unfavorable setting. Lacking the proper bed of "soft cool grass," he can only recline "on the brown earth, my limbs from very heat / [Finding] no rest" (ll. 22–23); instead of a warbling wren to soothe his repose, an "insect host . . . gathered round my face / And joined their murmurs to the tedious noise / Of seeds of bursting gorse which crackled round" (ll. 24–26). Soon, however, he comes to a spot which promises to be far more suitable, a breezy grove of huge elms which cast their dappling shade upon a mossy bench. Here in very fact is a proper spot for dreaming, the actual complement of the one he had previously pictured in his mind. But a disturbing flaw mars this potentially idyllic retreat, "a ruined Cottage—four clay walls / That stared upon each other" (ll. 31–32). The desolate ruin casts a chilling pall upon the spiritual atmosphere of the place, such that, as the narrator judges, even "the wandering gypsey in a stormy night / Would pass it with his moveables to house / On the open plain" (ll. 33–35). So the spot, disappointingly, has been rendered inhospitable to pleasant and tranquil dreaming. Yet on the bench by the ruin's door, incongruously, there does after all lie a proper dreamer, "stretched at his ease" (l. 302). This picture of the dreaming man actualized is our first sight of the Pedlar.[12]

Why does Wordsworth so pointedly and elaborately shape his poem's introduction around the motif of the dreaming man?

His deeper reasons will remain obscure until the poem's close. Yet even at its beginning we may readily sense from the narrator's envious fantasy of this tree-shadowed dreaming man obliquely gazing out "upon the scene / By those impending branches made . . . / More soft and distant" an affinity with the idealizing, reclusive, and fanciful yew-tree solitary. Revealingly, the narrator cannot imagine that the figure resting like a dreamer by the ruined cottage could after all be mentally or spiritually alert: "I guess he had no thought / Of his way-wandering life. His eyes were shut" (ll. 303–4). In fact, however, as the narrator soon learns, the Pedlar is thinking intensely of that life, and particularly of his earlier visits to this very spot to which he seems so oblivious.

While Wordsworth does not dwell on the matter, his effect here is certainly to present the narrator as considering himself sensitive in this place to disturbing presences of which the Pedlar is somehow unaware. From the Pedlar's perspective, however, the situation is actually quite the reverse. "I see around me [here] / Things which you cannot see (ll. 325-26), he announces simply. What he sees are "the spiritual presences of absent things" (Addendum, l. 28), presences to which he begins, as he talks on, to sensitize the narrator.

As a first step in this process, the narrator learns to concentrate on the particulars of the scene "in the relations which they bear to man" (Addendum, l. 25). At this point, the Pedlar's subsequently voiced promise that to the sensitive mind "all things shall speak of man" (Addendum, l. 36) bears a unique application: here all things speak of Margaret, for here all things once related to her. As the narrator listens to the story of Margaret, the objects around him come alive morally (cf. l. 278) as memorials of her life—precisely the light in which the Pedlar presents them: that arbor there is where she would sit idly half the sabbath waiting for Robert's return; from this very bench here she would watch the road; by yon gate she would stand to question passers-by about him. As he becomes newly and intensely aware of these natural things, and, correlatively, as he learns the story of Margaret, the narrator's affections are increasingly engaged: "In my own despite / I thought of that poor woman as of one / Whom I had known and loved" (ll. 460–62).[13] He has learned, under the Pedlar's tutelage, first to see

21

and then to feel intensely. But strikingly, the Pedlar benevolently *rebukes* him for this new grieving sympathy:

> My Friend, enough to sorrow have you given,
> The purposes of wisdom ask no more,
> Be wise and chearful, and no longer read
> The forms of things with an unworthy eye.
>
> [Addendum, ll. 118-21]

The rebuke is very like one the Pedlar had earlier administered to himself, as he broke off his story of Margaret in mid-course:

> "At this still season of repose and peace,
> This hour when all things which are not at rest
> Are chearful, while this multitude of flies
> Fills all the air with happy melody,
> Why should a tear be in an old Man's eye?
> Why should we thus with an untoward mind,
> And in the weakness of humanity,
> From all natural wisdom turn our hearts away,
> To natural comfort shut our eyes and ears,
> And, feeding on disquiet, thus disturb
> [The calm] of Nature with our restless thoughts?"[14]
>
> [Ll. 442-52]

And this earlier disciplining helps explain the later one. The narrator has indeed learned to see things, where before he could not; now he is able to

> trace ...
> That secret spirit of humanity
> Which, 'mid the calm oblivious tendencies
> Of Nature, 'mid her plants, her weeds and flowers,
> And silent overgrowings, still survived.
>
> [Addendum, ll. 112-16]

But he still sees, as the Pedlar says, "with an unworthy eye"; he still shuts his eyes and ears to important aspects of the scene. In effect, his new-found sympathy and grief proclaim both an indulgence in sentimentality and a desolating narrowness of vision, accordingly as his reading of the forms of things is falsely idyllic or falsely gothic.

These linked alternatives, the idyllic and the gothic, reminiscent respectively of the background and the foreground prospects which the yew-tree solitary broods upon, have already appeared in *The Ruined Cottage* in the forms of the dreaming

man and the wandering gypsy, both of them surrogate-figure
creations of the narrator's fancy. Now their increased and unan-
ticipated relevance to him serves to help characterize the nature
of his present "weakness of humanity." The narrator's affec-
tions are as yet unmatured by deeper thought; like the young
Pedlar, like the adolescent self Wordsworth would soon recall
in *Tintern Abbey*, he sees and sees feelingly, but he does not yet
see into the life of things.[15] So, ironically, by the Pedlar's stand-
ards he has been and remains, to his own loss, precisely that
which he thought he had tried but failed to become: a dreamer,
a man alive to fancied scenes but sleepingly oblivious to truth
and fact. The Pedlar first implies this judgment by way of a
comparative self-judgment:

> "we have known that there is often found
> In mournful thoughts, and always might be found,
> A power to virtue friendly; were't not so
> I am a dreamer among men—indeed
> An idle dreamer."
>
> [Ll. 482-86]

While "an idle dreamer" is just what the Pedlar had on first
appearance seemed to be, both his biography and his narrative
have now shown that he is actually quite the opposite. But at
the end of his narrative we learn at last what idle dreaming
really is. "She sleeps in the calm earth and peace is here" (Ad-
dendum, l. 122), he says of Margaret; and then, in a coda to his
story, explains and illustrates his attitude:

> I well remember that those very plumes,
> Those weeds and the high spear-grass on that wall,
> By mist and silent rain-drops silvered o'er,
> As once I passed, did to my mind convey
> So still an image of tranquillity,
> So calm and still, and looked so beautiful,
> Amid the uneasy thoughts which filled my mind,
> That what we feel of sorrow and despair
> From ruin and from change, and all the grief
> The passing shews of being leave behind
> Appeared an idle dream that could not live
> Where meditation was. I turned away
> And walked along my road in happiness.
>
> [Addendum, ll. 123-35]

To be an idle dreamer thus is to see only the surfaces of things, "the passing shews of being." The Pedlar celebrates and advocates a higher, deeper awareness: "Let us rise / From this oblivious sleep, these fretful dreams / Of feverish nothingness" (Addendum, ll. 76–78). Finally, then, the narrator's sensibilities mature thus further, under the Pedlar's tutelage, from the stage of feelings to that of thought and meditation. The Pedlar ends by suggesting how "thus deeply drinking in the soul of things / We shall be wise perforce," how

> Whate'er we see
> Whate'er we feel, by agency direct
> Or indirect, shall tend to feed and nurse
> Our faculties, and raise to loftier heights
> Our intellectual soul,
>
> [Addendum, ll. 92-93, 95-99]

and this process begins to occur in the narrator even with these very words, which, he finds, "had sunk into me," "for while he spake my spirit had obeyed / The presence of his eye, my ear had drunk / The meanings of his voice" (Addendum, ll. 101, 103-5). As "the sweet hour" of twilight approaches (Addendum, l. 140), he realizes that now he too appreciates the beauty of this spot. He sits with his teacher on the bench beneath the trees and the setting sun sends "a slant and mellow radiance" (Addendum, l. 137) upon him;

> A linnet warbled from those lofty elms,
> A thrush sang loud, and other melodies
> At distance heard, peopled the milder air.
>
> [Addendum, ll. 141-43]

Now the beauties and pleasures he once attributed enviously to the situation of some fancied "dreaming man"—the soothing melody of a warbling bird, the shadows with beams of pleasant sunshine interspersed, the comfortable seat beneath tall trees—have come to characterize his own; now, himself awakened from idle dreaming, he finds in the world around him the reality of which his dreams had provided only a frustratingly elusive image; now, having learned how to see truly, he gazes out from his elm-shaded station not like the solitary from his yew-tree seat but like the *Tintern Abbey* poet from his sycamore-shaded repose.

Thus the completed *Ruined Cottage* of 1798, within its new narrative frame, offers a perspective on Margaret greatly clarified, but not changed, from that of the original, 1797 poem. Wordsworth continues to regard his solitary sufferer with a quietly critical if deeply sympathetic eye. His judgment of her becomes especially clear in a subtle vignette the Pedlar presents near the end of his narrative:

> In that broken arbour she would sit
> The idle length of half a sabbath day
> There—where you see the toadstool's lazy head,
> And when a dog passed by she still would quit
> The shade and look abroad. On this old Bench
> For hours she sate, and evermore, her eye
> Was busy in the distance, shaping things
> Which made her heart beat quick.
>
> [Ll. 700–707]

She strikes, unconsciously, a pose we are now quick to recognize, that of the idle dreamer; like the yew-tree solitary, if with differently focused desires, her fancy feeds "on visionary views." Confessing to the Pedlar that "I have slept / Weeping, and weeping have I waked" (ll. 604–5), she becomes the archetypal exemplum provoking the Pedlar's exhortation, "Let us rise / From this oblivious sleep, these fretful dreams / Of fevered nothingness."

Margaret's weakness, we are now given to understand, is no more or less than the symptom and fate of all idle dreaming: she could not, or would not, see into the life of things, see the "one life" and know herself a part of it. Able to perceive only "the passing shews of being," she abuses her inner self and its potential, and in her essential blindness wills and works her own decline. To a degree she senses this: "'I am changed, / And to myself,' said she, 'have done much wrong, / And to this helpless infant'" (ll. 602–4). But her hopes for improvement are misplaced, her better intentions futile, so long as she regards herself as victimized rather than self-victimized, and she remains one of those who wage "an impious warfare with the very life / Of [their] own souls" (Addendum, 67–68).

Seen thus, the story of Margaret shifts between 1797 and 1798 from subject to object lesson, from pathetic to cathartic. Margaret's fatalism, we now must realize, is not warranted, and her fate is not inevitable. And we, the readers, now that we have been tutored by Wordsworth even as is the narrator by the Pedlar, should know to rouse ourselves from all such idle dreaming as constituted Margaret's doom.

v

While the revised *Ruined Cottage* seems strongly continuous with Wordsworth's poetry of 1797 in its refined analysis of Margaret's blind and self-destructive egotism, yet in its more positive aspects, as a statement and exemplification of the Pedlar's "one life" creed, it quite obviously signals a new stage in Wordsworth's poetical and philosophical development. Not only does he now embrace a metaphysics radically different from that informing his earlier work, he also, consequently and necessarily, begins to write a different kind of poetry—different not simply in form or subject matter, but in its very assumptions about what poetry should do and be.

In 1797, as we have seen, Wordsworth and his characters tend to regard nature with an emblematizing eye. This tendency correlates with and derives from a philosophy that takes man's mind and feelings as the sole source of meaning and morality in the universe. In the poetic world governed by such an epistemology, the significances of nature's presences and forms are necessarily extrinsic, and accordingly their mode of expression— which to an important degree determines the poetry's mode as well—is necessarily analogical or allegorical. In the 1798 *Ruined Cottage*, on the other hand, meaning and morality are assumed to proceed not exclusively from man but from the one life in all things, from the sheer fact of being. In this quite different poetic world, the significances of nature's forms are intrinsic and universal, and their mode of expression is accordingly synecdochal; for the life of each thing is not only representative of but continuous with the life of the observer-poet and the one life of the whole. Such a philosophical vision tends toward and corresponds to a distinctively symbolic poetry, "founded on an intimate unity between the image that rises up before the senses and the supersensory totality that the image suggests," wherein "no disjunction of the constitutive faculties takes place, since the material perception and the symbolical imagination are continuous, as the part is continuous with the whole."[16]

This new, symbolical quality of Wordsworth's poetry, which prominently manifests itself through the Pedlar's consciousness, seems to call particular attention to its distinctiveness from the 1797 emblematic mode near the end of the poem, in the Pedlar's consolatory vision of the mist-silvered speargrass overgrowing the ruined cottage (the passage is quoted above, Chapter 1, section iv). The narrator, when he regards the cottage a moment earlier, is still seeing it emblematically, if more sensitively than he had before. He "trace[s] . . . / That secret spirit of humanity" amidst the overwhelming natural growth just as he "retrace[s] that womans story" in his mind,[17] broodingly correlating natural prospect with mental retrospect, for he has come to understand how extensively the history of this ruined cottage and garden figures and suggests the history of Margaret herself. The Pedlar, in contrast, has learned to read the "spirit of humanity" in a quite different and truly universal way, as an intrinsic element of any scene. To him not some but "all things shall speak of Man" (Addendum, l. 36), not because all things have felt man's touch, as this ruined hut, garden, and spring have felt Margaret's, but because all things are connected and related to man, as he is to them, within the one life: "All things shall live in us and we shall live / In all things that surround us" (Addendum, ll. 79-80). Thus the "image of tranquillity" he once perceives in the misted speargrass is no mere emblem of the peacefulness of the grave—though his prefatory line, "She sleeps in the calm earth and peace is here" (Addendum, l. 122), initially leads us to expect such an application and has indeed misled some readers—but a true symbol of the one life of which it is itself a part. As the Pedlar makes clear in explaining his response, the image's human significance to him is not that now after years of suffering Margaret in death, like her cottage in decay, has become "calm and still, and . . . beautiful" (Addendum, l. 128), but rather that beneath our "uneasy thoughts," beneath "what we feel of sorrow and despair / From ruin and from change," there is *always* a continuing, essential, and universal life, tranquil and beautiful, would we but see it.

The speargrass trope, then, images not death, but life. It is no emblematic sequel and response to Margaret's sufferings, but a timeless counterpoint to them, a vision of an essential tranquillity that existed just as surely during Margaret's lifetime as it does now after her death. Thus the passage becomes something of a model for the poem as a whole; for it both embodies Wordsworth's new philosophical principles and exemplifies his new, symbolic mode for creating a poetry accurately representative of his faith.

CHAPTER 2
"We See into the Life of Things":
Tintern Abbey and
the Early *Prelude*

i

WHILE THE Pedlar, wonderfully sensitive as he is to the one life of love and joy flowing through and inseparably linking all things, has attained to a remarkable serenity, "his mind in a just equipoise of love" (*PW* 5:386 app. crit.), his good fortune is all too uncommon in this imperfect world. The vast majority of men are instead like Margaret, perceiving only a world of "solitary objects, still beheld / In disconnection dead and spiritless" (Addendum, ll. 61–62). However automatic or instinctive the Pedlar's development of his refined sensibilities, then, the process would seem to be far from obvious or natural to others. And insofar as the Pedlar is gloriously, even uniquely favored in the circumstances of his growth—as the narrator summarizes, "He was a chosen son" (l. 272)—his example might well seem discouragingly remote and inimitable to men less fortunate in their situations. It provoked Mary Lamb to the wry observation, when a version of *The Ruined Cottage* finally appeared in print as book 1 of *The Excursion*, "that by your system it was doubtful whether a Liver in Towns had a Soul to be Saved."[1] How, if at all, can other men too come to know the Pedlar's vision and happiness? It thus becomes vitally important for Wordsworth to learn, not simply what the Pedlar's soul-satisfying vision is, but also how it can be disseminated and cultivated.

At first, it is true, Wordsworth does little in *The Ruined Cottage* to address this latter question. But in his long Addendum to the poem, written and appended shortly after he had first put "The End" to the Pedlar's story of Margaret, he does in fact most pointedly consider just how man may learn to

29

commune with the one life, broaching the issue both theoreti-
cally, in the Pedlar's analytical monologue, and practically, in
the Narrator's personal education into spiritual insight. And
a few months after this, in another meditative and philosophical
poem, he develops these ideas still further, reaffirming his
earlier thoughts and insights but also refining and extending
them. The poem, *Tintern Abbey*, though still, since William
Empson's attack, typically criticized as vague, ambiguous, and
philosophically inconsistent, is in fact a taut and carefully struc-
tured work, complex but remarkably astute, a thoughtful and
genuinely innovative analysis of the mind's proper dialectic with
nature.[2]

Perhaps the most obvious and familiar philosophical scheme
in *Tintern Abbey*, and one already nascent in the Pedlar's
biography, is that of the "ages of man," or the stages of man's
intellectual development. To Arthur Beatty, who first investi-
gated it, this scheme revealed Wordsworth's great debts to
Locke's sensationalistic philosophy and, particularly, Hartley's
associationism.[3] Beatty's picture of a Hartleian Wordsworth no
longer seems entirely valid, but the three stages he indicates—
childhood, the age of sensation; youth, the age of feeling; and
maturity, the age of thought—are indeed explicitly and even
pointedly distinguished here and elsewhere in Wordsworth's
work. And while the poem does not simply or exclusively
formulate a doctrine of "the three ages of man," yet it does
evince a consistently tripartite metaphysical structure, wherein
the three particular ages which Beatty notes do have special
significance.

Let us begin, then, by reviewing these three stages as they
appear in *Tintern Abbey*. First, and here only parenthetically
noted, is the age of childhood, time of "the coarser pleasures of
my boyish days, / And their glad animal movements" (ll. 73-
74). The second, the age of youth, is a time when nature "to me
was all in all," and the poet's reactions to her are essentially
emotional:

> The sounding cataract
> Haunted me like a passion: the tall rock,
> The mountain, and the deep and gloomy wood,
> Their colours and their forms, were then to me
> An appetite; a feeling and a love,

That had no need of a remoter charm,
By thought supplied, nor any interest
Unborrowed from the eye.—That time is past.
And all its aching joys are now no more,
And all its dizzy raptures.[4]

[Ll. 76-85]

At present the poet's younger sister is still flourishing in this
same age of "thoughtless youth" (l. 90), of the eye's interest
and the heart's joyance in nature:

In thy voice I catch
The language of my former heart, and read
My former pleasures in the shooting lights
Of thy wild eyes.

[Ll. 116-19]

And thirdly, in maturity the poet has attained the intellectual
plane, the age of thought:

I have learned
To look on nature, not as in the hour
Of thoughtless youth; but hearing oftentimes
The still, sad music of humanity.

[Ll. 88-91]

Now his joy in nature is not ecstatic and immediate, but sober
and thoughtful, as his tone no less than his matter declares.
Wordsworth anticipates that his sister will experience a similar
transition from her passionate youth into a maturity wherein
nature's appeal will be primarily not to the heart but to the
mind, which nature will "inform," "impress / With quietness
and beauty," and "feed / With lofty thoughts" (ll. 125-28).
Like his own, her "wild ecstasies shall be matured / Into a sober
pleasure," her "mind / Shall be a mansion for all lovely forms"
(ll. 138-40).

Such a tripartite process of development is by no means
limited in *Tintern Abbey* to the lines just cited, but significantly
informs the poem in other places and ways as well. Consider,
for example, Wordsworth's description in the second paragraph
of how his earlier visit to the Wye had since influenced him:

Though absent long,
These forms of beauty have not been to me

As is a landscape to a blind man's eye:
But oft, in lonely rooms, and 'mid the din
Of towns and cities, I have owed to them
In hours of weariness, sensations sweet,
Felt in the blood, and felt along the heart;
And passing even into my purer mind,
With tranquil restoration.

[Ll. 22-30 and app. crit.]

Here Wordsworth is discussing, not the gradual development of his intellect, but the much quicker, perhaps almost instantaneous development of a thought; yet the pattern is in both cases essentially the same. Beginning with "sensations sweet"—here an accurate memorial re-cognition and appreciation of the scene's "forms of beauty" in all their sensational particularities—he next experiences an internalizing and emotionalizing of these sensations: now they are no longer felt merely through (or, memorially, as if through) eye and ear, but are "felt in the blood, and felt along the heart."[5] Finally, he experiences them as "passing"—and the shift from past to present participle signals the advent of a discrete stage—"passing even into my purer mind."[6]

This same three-part progression also appears in the third paragraph of *Tintern Abbey*, though here the initial sensations are unpleasant: these sensations of "darkness" and "the many shapes / Of joyless daylight" come to "[hang] upon the beatings of my heart" (l. 54), presenting an imminent threat to the "spirit" (l. 55). The third paragraph thus closely parallels the opening of the second in pattern even while carefully contrasting with it in matter—a confessed "darkness" recalling the previously denied vision of the "blind man's eye," "joyless" sensations replacing "sweet," and a "fretful stir" and "fever" (ll. 52-53) pointedly inverting the earlier "tranquil restoration." That two such contrasting experiences as lines 22-30 and 50-54 describe should yet thus evolve in such similar ways strongly indicates how fundamental is this developmental pattern itself.

From the sensational, to the "heart-felt," to the mental or spiritual: this sequential pattern of the three stages of a thought anticipates and closely parallels the larger pattern of mental growth presented in the poem's fourth paragraph. Wordsworth

seems clearly here to be suggesting an analogy between the ages
of an individual's mental development and the stages of the de-
velopment of a single thought or attitude: in thought as in life,
ontogeny recapitulates phylogeny.[7]

ii

Thus far Wordsworth's philosophical musings as we have fol-
lowed them here have been quite respectably and unexception-
ably Hartleian. But remarkably, the same tripartite structure
also informs the poem's strikingly un-Hartleian, visionary appre-
ciation of the one life:

> Nor less, I trust,
> To them I may have owed another gift,
> Of aspect more sublime; that blessed mood
> In which the burthen of the mystery,
> In which the heavy and the weary weight
> Of all this unintelligible world
> Is lightened:—that serene and blessed mood,
> In which the affections gently lead us on,—
> Until, the breath of this corporeal frame
> And even the motion of our human blood
> Almost suspended, we are laid asleep
> In body, and become a living soul:
> While with an eye made quiet by the power
> Of harmony, and the deep power of joy,
> We see into the life of things.
>
> [Ll. 35–49]

Here, however, we find a crucial difference: the visionary devel-
opment of which Wordsworth is now speaking *reverses* the pat-
tern of natural development we have previously been tracing.
Beginning with the mental or spiritual ("mystery," "unintelli-
gible")—which is yet figuratively expressed as sensational, for it
is unburdened and "lightened"—this new development proceeds
through an intermediate stage imaged again by internal, organic
processes ("the breath of this corporeal frame," "the motion of
our human blood"), now strangely tranquilized, on to a final
stage of sensation.[8] But now this is a visionary sensation, figura-
tively spiritual even as the initial, spiritual stage of this sequence
was figuratively sensational; now the eye, sensor not merely of

33

the body but of the soul, sees not merely the externalities of forms but "into the life of things."

Here, where the proper, nature-fostered development of man's mind and spirit returns upon itself to nourish him with unanticipated, imaginational recompense, we confront the essential dialectical pattern of Wordsworth's metaphysics in its barest and purest form. Sensations drawn from direct contact with nature nurture the feelings, and these in turn nurture the mind; and then, ideally, from the nourished mind a reciprocating restoration proceeds back through the feelings to the very senses, now enabled to perceive in the world the presence and workings of noumenal Being itself.

I have called this passage visionary; and Wordsworth is careful to indicate the status and nature of his vison by direct comparison with his poetic father, Milton. Herbert Lindenberger has observed that "Wordsworth's verse does not become noticeably Miltonic until after the period—beginning with his residence in Grasmere in 1800—that he undertook an intensive study of the earlier poet," and in general this seems quite true. But Lindenberger's mild prefatory qualification that "there are Miltonic elements, of course, in the 1798-99 *Prelude*, as there are in all non-dramatic blank verse before the twentieth century" deserves to be taken with some seriousness. The occasional but explicit Miltonic echoes and allusions in the earliest version of *The Prelude* should alert us to Wordsworth's attentiveness to *Paradise Lost* even in 1798.[9] And in fact, I would suggest, Wordsworth in this second paragraph of *Tintern Abbey* is allusively defining his visionary claim in comparison with and opposition to Milton's invocation to light at the beginning of book 3 of *Paradise Lost.*

We may sense that Wordsworth is implying this Miltonic context even in the first paragraph, when the poet locates himself in the landscape. Where Milton, after wandering to "where the Muses haunt / Clear Spring, or Shady Grove, or Sunny Hill, / Smit with the love of sacred Song" (3.27-29), on settling compares himself to a bird singing darkling, hidden in the shadiest covert (3.38-40), Wordsworth in his own bucolic wandering analogously pauses within the shade of a dark sycamore to speak his own poem (ll. 9-10). And on one level, Wordsworth goes on to insist, the vision he celebrates here is like Milton's: in both, the inward eye is being irradiated. In the absence of this gift, all vision is merely of the darkness of outer light; "darkness, and . . . the many shapes / Of joyless daylight" are equally blank. But in its presence, "laid asleep / In body"—and with our corporeal eyes thus figuratively blinded by their sleep-closed lids—we, too, through the complementary vision of our "living soul," can "see into the life of things," see things otherwise "invisible to mortal sight" (3.55). When Wordsworth writes that "the burthen of the mystery, / . . . the heavy and the weary weight / Of all this unintelligible world / Is lightened," his metaphor is visual as well as tactile.

Nevertheless, Milton's is explicitly a blind seer's vision, while Wordsworth's vision is at once spiritual and natural. It is precisely because "these forms of beauty have *not* been to me / As is a landscape to a blind man's eye" that they have their peculiar power to nourish and restore his mind.[10] Where Milton found that his blindness brought, or at least allowed, visionary compensation—the affliction is thereby a type of the Fortunate Fall—Wordsworth's position, Platonic rather than Christian in its implications, is instead that the inner eye is irradiated through the outer and thus depends upon the good agency of an "interested" perception (see l. 82).

In the second great climax of *Tintern Abbey*, Wordsworth once again celebrates the grand tripartite progression of the visionary man's interaction with nature. Now, however, he offers a supplementary perspective on this dialectic. First quickly reasserting his communion with nature in a statement subtly suggestive, again, of his three-stage spiritual development—"I have felt / A presence" (sensational), "that disturbs me with the joy" (emotional), "of elevated thoughts" (intellectual) (ll. 93–95)—he now also more specifically identifies this envisioned "life of things" as truly one life, a "something far more deeply interfused" both "in the mind of man" and through all the natural world, "a motion and a spirit" that "rolls through all things" (ll. 96–102). And his meditative apprehension of this life seems analogously interfused and holistic, "a sense sublime" (l. 95) which is apposite simultaneously to the felt presence, the disturbing joy, and the elevated thoughts.

These philosophical implications find further allusive confirmation in the common accompaniment, figuratively musical but soundless (a "still . . . music" [l. 91], a "harmony" which "quiet[s]" the eye [11. 47-48]), which the two parallel visionary climaxes of *Tintern Abbey* share. Behind Wordsworth's imagery in these two passages is the classical tradition of the music of the spheres, a cosmic harmony audible—and the experience is a veritable hearing "into the life of things"—only to the purged and purified individual.[11] But when the worldfevered poet of *Tintern Abbey* is thus restored to his "purer mind," the great harmony that he detects in the life of things he feels also in his own mind. The attuned consciousness is itself an instrument of the harmonizing Power, even as the attuned world of beautiful forms is. The great force of being impels both "all thinking things" and "all objects of all thought" (l. 101), consciousness and nature, equally, "and rolls through all things." Earlier in the poem we may have read this last, potentially vague noun to mean "inanimate objects": "we see into the life of things." Now Wordsworth gives us to know that the term is specific and all-encompassing: to see into the life of things is also, in part, to see into oneself, and into the minds of all men.

We have already seen how the interaction of nature and mind moves reflexively from this visionary point, through specific stages, to nourish and recompense man. Now Wordsworth alludes to nature's ordering and nurturing reciprocity once again, thus repeating and confirming his earlier vision of its patterned response to man. Here at the end of the fourth paragraph once again appear these reflexive stages of the dialectical process, in the now familiar mind-heart-soul progression, as Wordsworth recognizes in the sublime interaction of himself and nature: (1) "the anchor of my purest *thoughts*" (cf. "my purer mind" [l. 29]); (2) "the nurse, / The guide, the guardian of my *heart*"; and (3) the "*soul / Of all my moral being*" (ll. 109-11; my emphases).

Wordsworth is not simply repeating his earlier insight of lines 37-49 here, but is also clarifying its significance. His language in lines 109-11, so different from that of the parallel passage in the second paragraph, makes explicit his emphasis on the moral import of this dialectical progression. Values perhaps only figuratively implicit in the vague "blessed" (ll. 37, 41)

and "soul" (l. 46) and the Bunyanesque image of this Romantic
pilgrim's unburdening now stand forth more clearly—emblemat-
ically in the anchor, but explicitly in the nurse-guide-guardian
figure, and with absolute insistence in that final, unblinkable
phrase, "soul / Of all my moral being." Once we recognize the
sequential relationship of these three stages, we can see in this
passage not only the repeated message that man's interaction
with nature teaches him morality, but also a provocative sugges-
tion as to how he learns it.

iii

"Nor perchance, / If I were not thus taught, should I the
more / Suffer my genial spirits to decay," the poet immediately
says to his sister: "For thou art with me here upon the banks /
Of this fair river" (*Tintern Abbey* ll. 111-15). In one sense the
phrase "genial spirits" is suggestive of the "sylvan Wye" itself,
the genius loci,[12] which as the poem's focal "wanderer thro' the
woods" (l. 56) in turn figures Wordsworth himself and, the
poem shall soon indicate, his dryadlike sister as well. But more
directly, "genial spirits" here denotes not simply Wordsworth's
native powers generally, but an important product and agent of
his dialectic with nature, his "affections" (l. 42). These, he be-
lieves, derive, like mental tranquillity, from man's apprehension
of nature's "forms of beauty." For to these forms he owes not
only the "sensations sweet" which restore the mind but

> feelings too
> Of unremembered pleasure: such, perhaps,
> As may have had no trivial influence
> On that best portion of a good man's life;
> His little, nameless, unremembered, acts
> Of kindness and of love.
> [Ll. 30-35 and app. crit.]

But if nature must initially prompt or create the affections,
they can continue, in ways we have already seen, with a life of
their own. Their importance to the Wordsworthian dialectic be-
comes clear with his statement that, in our meditative, ulti-
mately reflexive process toward becoming "a living soul," "the
affections gently lead us on" (l. 42). Created by physical sensa-
tion of nature, they become creative of spiritual appreciation.

Thus the boy is led on into love by nature; but the man, moved by a more spiritual love—and "hearing oftentimes / The still, sad music of humanity" (ll. 90-91)—can ultimately see into nature, and will wish to share his pleasures with, and extend his love to, at least one or a few of his fellow creatures.[13] The "genial spirits" thus indicate a turning point of the spirit, as well as of the poem.

It is nevertheless remarkable that this final movement of so grand and encompassing an affirmation of life should sound at times so somber a tone. What is the unspecified "music of humanity" Wordsworth can now hear, that, "nor harsh nor grating" (l. 92), it should yet be "sad"? Certainly it is not the cacophony of society—"the din / Of towns and cities," "the fretful stir / Unprofitable, and the fever of the world," "evil tongues, / Rash judgments, . . . the sneers of selfish men, / . . . greetings where no kindness is, . . . all / The dreary intercourse of daily life" (ll. 25-26, 52-53, 128-31)—which, in Wordsworth's careful presentation, the terms *harsh* and *grating* describe quite accurately. Rather the "chasten[ing] " ("restraining," but also "purifying") and "subdu[ing] " (l. 93) music Wordsworth now hears is a universal but still a personally felt burden: the music of mortality. Wordsworth's attitude, as the poem draws to a close, becomes proleptically self-elegiac; anticipating finally a possible time when "I should be where I no more can hear / Thy voice, nor catch from thy wild eyes these gleams / Of past existence" (ll. 147-49), he is implicitly referring to and preparing to console himself for, his own death. As the first, familiar words Wordsworth explicitly addresses to his sister—"for thou art with me"—forcefully suggest, this beautiful valley of the Wye, this "green pastoral landscape" (l. 158), is the valley of the shadow of death.[14]

Following as it does upon the dialectical musings of the first four paragraphs of *Tintern Abbey*, this closing turn to the issue of mortality seems necessary and inevitable; for the topic, quite simply, constitutes the missing piece of the larger metaphysical pattern which Wordsworth has been so concerned to trace. Already in the poem he has suggested that the process of man's mental and spiritual growth from childhood to maturity is analogous to the developmental process of a single mental or spiritual experience from sensation to thought. But he has also suggested that, in those visionary extensions of ordinary mental experience when thought is "elevated" and transformed into a "sense sublime," the spirit's progress to "living soul" is yet in a way reflexive, doubling back on a higher level through the earlier stages of its development. Thus the corresponding issue of the individual's possible growth beyond the third, intellectual stage of life inevitably arises. What is the fate of intellect, of mindfulness, after the prime of life? And can the analogy between a thought's and a mind's development extend itself to this further length?

Tintern Abbey cannot answer these questions, simply because Wordsworth has not yet lived on into those waning years of life. He can as yet say with certainty only that "nature never did betray / The heart that loved her" (ll. 122–23), not that she never will in his later years.[15] So the poem's scheme of analogously developing mind and thoughts must necessarily remain incomplete at this one point. Nevertheless, Wordsworth does imply that the analogy holds even into the all-important stage of man's prime. Just as visionary thought, for example, reflects backwards through and thus encompasses its earlier stages of feelings and sensations, so the mature mind reflectively—both memorially and vicariously—relishes its own earlier modes of joy. More fundamentally and importantly parallel still are the striking influxes of sympathetic feeling which seem to mark the bournes of both meditative vision and intellectual maturity. It is significant that when Wordsworth shifts into the visionary mode—and *only* then—he also changes his song from singular to plural, from one about himself to one about us, all men. Thus, the gift which "*I* may have owed" to nature's forms of beauty is "that serene and blessed mood, / In which the affections gently lead *us* on,— / Until . . . *we* are laid asleep / In body," and "*we* see into the life of things." Similarly, "*I* have felt / A presence . . . Whose dwelling is . . . in the mind of *man*: / A motion and a spirit, that impels / *All thinking things*" (ll. 93–101); and again, "Therefore am *I* still / A lover . . . of all that *we* behold" (ll. 102–4; my emphases). And this change from solitary to sympathetic self-consciousness in the course of a single visionary experience thematically and syntactically parallels the changed cast of mind acquired in maturity, the development of a genial spirit:

> *I* have learned
> To look on nature, not as in the hour
> Of thoughtless youth; but hearing oftentimes
> The still, sad music of *humanity.*

That which provokes Wordsworth into an awareness of humanity thus proves to be the visionary experience itself, a mood which comes to a solitary but leaves behind a man spontaneously conscious of kind. Wordsworth's meditative vision and intellectual maturity in *Tintern Abbey* thus bring "abundant recompense" (ll. 88) indeed—nothing less than the assurance that man, who had thought himself solitary and separated from nature, is after all integrated with nature and his fellow men into the world's serene and beautiful whole, himself potentially as glorious as anything he sees or hears. If human consciousness by itself can perceive only an "unintelligible world," it nevertheless can build upon sensation and emotion to evolve a blended "sense sublime," a deeper, visionary consciousness of the world's great harmony, beauty, and joy.

iv

While *Tintern Abbey* echoes *The Ruined Cottage* in hymning the one life, it nevertheless displays a new consciousness of the important differences between "all thinking things" and "all objects of all thought," between man and nature. And with his first work later in 1798 on the openly autobiographical poem ultimately to become *The Prelude*, Wordsworth pushes beyond this recognition toward a fundamental reconception of his relation to nature. Now, though even in the face of his own repeated denials, he begins to see man's intellectual distinctiveness, not nature's or life's universality, as the paramount factor in his personal development.[16] While it frequently claims to be about nature's generous disciplining of his mind and imagination, her ways of "form[ing] / A favored being" (*Prelude 1799* 1.69-70), the early *Prelude* in fact takes as its truer, though secret, theme the human mind's disguised disciplining of itself.

This subliminal revisionism begins to disturb the surfaces of Wordsworth's argument very early in *The Prelude*, from his first reference to nature's severe but nurturing ministry of fear. Though fear played little part in the Pedlar's natural education (despite the passing allusion to his youthful communication with nature as "not from terror free" [*The Ruined Cottage* 1. 78]), Wordsworth was clearly becoming most interested in the role it played in his own. But notwithstanding his repeated insistence on nature's responsibility for such "severer interventions" (*Prelude 1799* 1. 79) of fearsomeness in his boyhood, the particular fearful episodes he recalls as especially formative of his personality would seem after all to derive little of their power from their ostensible source.

Near the opening of part 1 Wordsworth recounts three episodes customarily taken as specific illustrations of nature's ministry of fear—the snare-robbing, bird-nesting, and boat-stealing episodes.[17] The conventional reading of these episodes sees them all as violations of nature, guilty actions immediately rebuked; the critical debate then centers on the ultimate attribution of these rebukes to nature, perception, or conscience. In fact, however, the experiences appear to be of markedly dissimilar kinds. Of the three, the stealing of eggs from the raven's nest would seem to be most obviously a violation of nature. But Wordsworth exhibits no sense of guilt for this act,[18] any more than he does later in the book for fishing or nutting (1.234–40) or, by implication, for hunting hares (1.158–60); instead, his mood is purely one of physical exhilaration at hanging perilously, exposed to the wind, on the rocky cliff. It is significant in this connection, I think, that very early on Wordsworth removed from *The Prelude* two closely related passages which do concern explicit violations of nature and consequent guilt, *Nutting* and "I would not strike a flower" (*Prelude 1850*, pp. 612–14, 641), "intended as part of a poem on my own life, but struck out as not being wanted there" (*PW* 2:504).[19] They were not wanted, I would suggest, because their emphases, though compatible with the mature Pedlar's respectful and loving relation to all manifestations of the one life ("I would not strike a flower" is particularly reminiscent of the *Ruined Cottage* Addendum), were inconsistent with the quite different sensibilities Wordsworth was now tracing through his own boyhood. And in

thus excising these passages, Wordsworth was effectively elimi-
nating from his early version of *The Prelude* the whole basis for
relating the ministry of fear to any violation of nature.

That there is indeed such a ministry of fear the two com-
panion episodes vividly attest. But in both cases what the boy
violates is not nature, but a human, social code of ethics. In the
woodcock-snaring passage, for instance, Wordsworth feels no
more guilt for trapping birds—quite the contrary: "in thought
and wish . . . I was a fell destroyer" (*Prelude 1799* 1.33–35)—
than he does for stealing birds' eggs. His guilt stems entirely
from his looting of someone else's traps, stealing "the bird /
Which was the captive of another's toils" (1.43–44).[20] Similarly,
what disturbs the boy in the boat-stealing episode is precisely
his theft of the boat, "an act," he acknowledges, "of stealth /
And troubled pleasure" (1.90–91). Here again, the offense is
against not nature but man. Thus in both cases nature's severe
and palpable intervention can only be what Wordsworth soon
will recognize as a "secondary" passion (2.241; cf. 1.376–77,
423), subordinate to the primary passion, his social sense of
guilt, already present in his mind.

While these vivid memories and new-formed speculations
range far afield from the musings of *Tintern Abbey* and *The
Ruined Cottage*, at the same time they come strangely and
strikingly close to the earlier thought of *The Borderers*. Their
relevance to the play appears most clearly, perhaps, in the
guilty boy's projected imaginings of a pursuing and censuring
nature-spirit—his anxious notion, after stealing a woodcock
from another's trap, that

> I heard among the solitary hills
> Low breathings coming after me, and sounds
> Of undistinguishable motion, steps
> Almost as silent as the turf they trod,
>
> [1.46–49]

and his comparable impression, as he rows from shore in the
stolen boat, that

> from behind that rocky steep, till then
> The bound of the horizon, a huge Cliff,
> As if with voluntary power instinct,
> Upreared its head: I struck, and struck again,

And, growing still in stature, the huge cliff
Rose up between me and the stars, and still
With measured motion, like a living thing,
Strode after me.

[1.107-14]

In these passages Wordsworth is unmistakably attributing to his
younger self an iconic vision reminiscent of Mortimer's and
Robert's beliefs in *The Borderers*, a sense that nature can sen-
tiently wreak the threats and punishments decreed by the
omniscient, judicial Power it veils. But Wordsworth also care-
fully presents these impressions as in fact childish delusions,
subjective externalizations of the boy's strong sense of guilt; he
recognizes them retrospectively, this is to say, as the workings
of an emblematic vision, moral texts which were actually cre-
ated by the boy himself. As Hartman summarizes, "For the
retrospective poet, . . . the power that belonged to the external
world is now seen to have belonged to the mind."[21]

Something quite similar to this also happens in the "spots of
time," clearly related to the episodes of nature's ministry just
discussed but distinguished from them by Wordsworth as some-
how different in their effect. The distinction, I would suggest,
involves something of a shift of the boy's role from protagonist
to chorus of the episodes. The spots of time center upon "acci-
dents in flood or field, . . . Distresses and disasters, tragic facts /
Of rural history" (1.280-83), but always events which occurred
to someone else; specifically, they center upon human deaths—
the man drowned in Esthwaite, the murderer gibbeted near
Penrith Beacon, the death of Wordsworth's father.[22] Apart
from this constant focus, however, and from a very few re-
curring characteristics of Wordsworth's role—his solitariness, his
straining concentration, his gradual buildup to the moment of a
confrontation of death—the various spots of time have little in
common. Their natural settings vary from "beauteous scene"
(1.277) to "visionary dreariness" (1.322), their weather from
"breathless stillness" (1.274) to "wind, and sleety rain" (1.361);
the deaths upon which they center may or may not be antici-
pated, and may or may not make an actual part of the scene.
(In the final spot of time, the waiting for the horses, the death
of Wordsworth's father actually occurs some ten days later,
while in the second spot, the gibbet, the murderer's death had

43

occurred years before.) But this disparateness of the spots, after all, is very much to the point. For what makes these experiences so memorable is not any particular quality of the scenes themselves, but a particular intensity in the mind of the viewer. The boy's sudden and stunning consciousness of death lends a vividness to each scene, rather than the reverse,[23] just as does the boy's guilt in the ministry-of-fear episodes. In every case, to apply a relevant distinction Wordsworth developed soon after this for another context, "the feeling therein developed gives importance to the action and situation, and not the action and situation to the feeling" (*Prose* 1:128).

The interaction of visionary experience and spiritual restoration characterizing the spots of time and nature's ministrations of fear thus not only differs extensively in its pattern from the process explored in *Tintern Abbey*, but in fact even constitutes a kind of inversion of that process. In *Tintern Abbey* sweet sensations ultimately nourished the mind, which then reflexively and reciprocally nourished and spiritualized the sensations. In the early *Prelude*, however, the process of furnishing "life and food / For future years" (*Tintern Abbey*, ll. 64-65) begins not with sweet sensations but with disturbing thoughts—of death, of guilt, of fear. Some such painful consciousness first heightens the sensations, making the scene particularly vivid, and then these intense sensations reflexively and reciprocally nourish the mind and imagination, exercising "a fructifying virtue" by which "our minds / (Especially the imaginative power) / Are nourished, and invisibly repaired" (*Prelude 1799* 1.292-94). Rather than a seeing, by way of the mind, into the life of things, this is a thinking, by way of sensation, into the life of one's mind. So it is that the mental vision persisting with the boy after the boat-stealing episode is not a sense of the one life or even of mysterious forces in nature, but a vision into the psyche itself:

> For many days my brain
> Worked with a dim and undetermined sense
> Of unknown modes of being: in my thoughts
> There was a darkness, call it solitude
> Or blank desertion; no familiar shapes
> Of hourly objects, images of trees,
> Of sea or sky, no colours of green fields,
> But huge and mighty forms that do not live

Like living men, moved slowly through my mind
By day, and were the trouble of my dreams.

[1.120-29]

This experience is not, as some critics have assumed, "the memory of what he had seen," though it is certainly provoked by what he had seen (hence the relation of the "huge and mighty forms that do not live / Like living men" to "the huge cliff . . . like a living thing"). His mind here is a solitude unto itself; the darkness of his thoughts is a darkness not of nature's ominous presence, but of her absence. A helpful reading comes implicitly from Harold Bloom, who suggests in passing that Wordsworth's strange sense of these "unknown modes of being" "is like the Titanism of Blake, with its Giant Forms like the Zoas wandering a world substantially our own."[24] It is indeed very like; for Blake's Zoas, we remember, are no other than the constituent mental aspects of archetypal Man himself.

By no means is Wordsworth deciding in late 1798, as he evolves his new sense of the individual mind's responsibility for its own development, to abandon his earlier belief in the one life. While that belief plays little or no role in part 1 of the two-part *Prelude*, it regains a certain prominence in part 2, written late in 1799. There Wordsworth honors Coleridge as one to whom "the unity of all has been revealed" (2.256), celebrates "this *active* universe" with its "one great mind" (2.296, 302), and even claims as his own adolescent experience the Pedlar's great, sympathetic vision, "in all things / I saw one life and felt that it was joy" (2.459-60). But now he hedges this feeling with qualifications: perhaps he was indeed seeing the one life truly, but perhaps he was only projecting his own feelings, "to unorganic natures [transferring] / My own enjoyments" (2.440-41).[25] And when near the close of part 2 he affirms, "I yet / Despair not of our nature" (2.487-88), it is not a universal essence, but our peculiarly *human* nature to which he is referring, "these human sentiments which make this earth / So dear" (2.468-69). The "great birth-right of our being" (2.316), as he sees it now, is not mere Being itself, but our "creative sensibility," "the first / Poetic spirit of our human life" (2.409, 305-6)—a gift which comes not from nature but from man,[26] and a distinction not of existence or even sentience, but of our intellectual humanness.

PART II: 1798–1804

Introduction

B‍Y LATE 1798 Wordsworth was coming to regard his belief in the one life as simply inadequate to sustain and console him in the face of inevitable human loss. His later delineation of his "high argument" in the *Prospectus* to *The Recluse*, a passage written only in 1806,[1] affords a most helpful perspective on the crisis which shook his new faith shortly after the Alfoxden months. Here Wordsworth proclaims, first, "How exquisitely the individual Mind . . . to the external World / Is fitted" (*HG*, 1006-9); and this is precisely what he had rejoiced to discover in 1798. His subsequent, revisionary meditations upon the topic, however, especially in the Lucy and Matthew poems, lead him by early 1799 to a new and devastatingly unsettling recognition—not so much that the mind is not fitted to world, but rather that is is not as well fitted as is mindlessness. Robert Frost would later drive home the same point conversely in a markedly Wordsworthian poem, "The Need of Being Versed in Country Things," where the murmur of the phoebes now happily nesting in an abandoned, fire-ruined farmstead sounds, but only to the unversed, like a grieving "from too much dwelling on what has been."[2] Wordsworth, on the other hand, already well versed in country things, is coming at this time to appreciate the more universal experience of dwelling on what has been.

Though the Lucy and Matthew poems recognize loss, they offer no remedy. But Wordsworth struggles with the question of how the bereaved can cope with or limit their loss throughout his poetry of 1799-1800. The first, defensive stage of his response takes shape most notably in such "memorializing" poems as *The Brothers*, *Michael*, and the *Poems on the Naming of Places*. Here Wordsworth works to seize and develop the lesser but attainable consolation of memorial survival, "a kind of second life," and so postpone—he can hope to do no more—the second death of oblivion.[3]

Wordsworth's eventual resolution of this crisis involves no less than a reconception of the nature of nature itself. The continuation of his *Prospectus* argument again indicates his way:

> And how exquisitely too—
> Theme this but little heard of among men—
> The external world is fitted to the mind.
>
> [*HG*, 1009-11]

Having in 1798 effectively subsumed mind under nature, Wordsworth's subsequent revisionary course culminates in his subsuming nature under mind. Just as the Pedlar's vision of the one life represented a naturalizing of Mortimer's egotistically flawed iconic version, so in such poems as *Hart-Leap Well* Wordsworth's new vision of a Being beyond nature reveals itself as an analogous naturalizing of Rivers's egotistically flawed emblematic vision. And this Being increasingly defines itself as something like a type of mind, as Wordsworth discovers in the nature beyond nature a tendency parallel to man's mental tendencies. Increasingly, in the poetry of 1802-1804, Wordsworth fastens upon a new help and stay, more secure than that of his love of nature, to preserve man from betrayal by his own mindfulness. He now begins to posit the existence of a transcendental Power beyond the immanent nature he had earlier celebrated and begins also to emphasize the potential strength and magnificence of the human mind. And in the process, God increasingly acquires definition here, as He had more anonymously and vaguely in *Hart-Leap Well*, as a great type of Mind.

CHAPTER 3
"Even of the Good Is No Memorial Left": Inscriptions, Monuments, and the Memorializing Impulse

i

AMONG THE NEW POEMS first published in the 1800 *Lyrical Ballads*, the little-noted " 'Tis said that some have died for love" speaks perhaps more directly and more darkly than any other to the hopes and assertions of Wordsworth's 1798 poetry. The poem presents an almost archetypal bucolic scene now especially familiar to us from *The Ruined Cottage*: a cottage among the trees, with one old oak in particular towering overhead, in its branches a singing thrush. Here again we see something like the beautiful, tranquil setting which the initially naïve narrator fantasizes at the beginning of *The Ruined Cottage*, or the kindred setting which, at the end of that poem, his newly educated senses reveal as actually his own. The inhabitant of this tranquil spot, moreover, is again one sensitive to the beauties around him—the murmuring of the oak's leaves, the haunting sounds of falling water from the stream nearby, the pattern of chimney-smoke rising behind the oak toward the sky. Yet he lives in misery among all this natural beauty, made wretched even by his awareness of such beauty.

The explanation of this wretchedness amidst beauty is quite simple: the man is a bereaved lover, now constantly reminded by what he has of what he has lost. The beauties of nature once habitually associated with his romantic and domestic happiness maintain their familiar places and ways oblivious of the great change that has occurred, the death of his loved one; and their continuity in the face of this discontinuity pains his sensibilities intolerably. Hence his mad plea that the elements of the scene simply *change*—that his cottage move or the oak fall so that his hearth smoke may rise skyward "in some other way" (" 'Tis said that some . . . ," l. 15); that the familiar thrush "sing another song, or choose another tree" (l. 28); that the stream, which "haunt[s] the air with sounds / That cannot be sustained," reverse its course or, if it must rush on, fall silently: "be anything, sweet Rill, but that which thou art now" (ll. 31–32, 36).

The man who raises these complaints may seem after all, despite his sensitivity to natural beauty, to have less in common with the Pedlar and narrator of *The Ruined Cottage* than with Margaret or with the yew-tree solitary. But if this be idle dreaming, yet now Wordsworth himself appears markedly more vulnerable to it, less confident of his own ability to find consolation for such grief. The poem's conclusion is strikingly personal:

> Ah gentle Love! if ever thought was thine
> To store up kindred hours for me, thy face
> Turn from me, gentle Love! nor let me walk
> Within the sound of Emma's voice, nor know
> Such happiness as I have known to-day.
> [Ll. 48-52]

The power of these lines comes from their pathos; for here Wordsworth is praying to be spared an intolerable "grievous pain" (l. 5) to which he nevertheless knows that his very happiness makes him absolutely liable. As he now emphatically visualizes a husband surviving rather than predeceasing his wife, his confidence in the "saving power" of "our intellectual soul" (*Ruined Cottage* Addendum, ll. 32, 99) visibly ebbs. The contrast of this short poem with the conclusion of *Tintern Abbey* could not easily be more pointed or striking. In 1798 he had assured his sister that in later years, when

> Thy memory [shall] be as a dwelling-place
> For all sweet sounds and harmonies, oh! then
> If solitude, or fear, or pain, or grief,
> Should be thy portion, with what healing thoughts
> Of tender joy wilt thou remember me,
> And these my exhortations!
> [*Tintern Abbey*, ll. 141-46]

By 1800, however, his great fear is that in solitude and grief such remembrance shall inevitably bring with it thoughts that do not heal, but destroy. The concluding consolation offered in *Tintern Abbey* proceeds from the faith that "Nature never did betray / The heart that loved her." We could say of Margaret and the yew-tree solitary that theirs were never truly such hearts. But can we say the same of this present lover? Any such judgment seems obviated by Wordsworth's surprising apostrophe, addressed not to Nature but to Love. Whether nature can after all betray seems no longer even to be the issue. The betrayal that Wordsworth now knows he must face, yet even in this stark poem can confront only indirectly or obliquely—"Ah gentle Love! if ever thought was thine / To store up kindred hours for me"—is betrayal by thought, betrayal by his own mind.

ii

A noted critic has argued that "the history of Wordsworth's later [after spring, 1798] philosophical poetry is one of declining belief in the One Life." Certainly a significant change appears in the poetry by the end of this year; but as "'Tis said that some have died for love" suggests, the cause would seem to be less a decline in belief than a displacement of concern. By late 1798, this is to say, Wordsworth was coming to regard his belief in the "one life" as, not wrong, but in some respects simply inadequate to sustain his spirit in the face of inevitable loss.[1]

The consequences particularly troubling Wordsworth are perhaps most familiar to us from the Lucy poems. Coleridge's guess about one of these, that "most probably, in some gloomier moment he had fancied the moment in which his sister might die" (*STCL* 1:479), while only a guess, at least shrewdly emphasizes and accounts for the new sense of immediacy so distinguishing these elegiac and epitaphic lyrics. The eschatological vision of "A slumber did my spirit seal"—

No motion has she now, no force;
  She neither hears nor sees;
Rolled round in earth's diurnal course,
  With rocks, and stones, and trees
         [Ll. 5–8]

—accords perfectly with Wordsworth's "one life" tenets: individual lives must end, but the encompassing and inclusive life of nature continues, and man's death is but a metamorphosis into a different aspect of that "one interior life / Which is in all things" (*Prelude 1850*, p. 525). But now Wordsworth is patently disturbed by such a fate, less than wholly consoled by such a vision: "But she is in her grave, and, oh, / The difference to me!" ("She dwelt among the untrodden ways," ll. 11-12).

The confrontation with mortality which the Lucy poems record unsettles Wordsworth on two particular counts. First, Lucy in death is both insensate and oblivious: "No motion has she now, no force; / She neither hears nor sees." Second, Lucy's personality made her something more than a mere "compendium" of the natural forces which shape and survive her,[2] something special and irreplaceable—gave her *individuality*, a uniquely human potentiality and characteristic—so that her death *matters*, the loss of her individuality produces a significant and permanent void in the world:

> She died, and left to me
> This health, this calm, and quiet scene;
> The memory of what has been,
> And never more will be.
> ["Three years she grew," ll. 39-42]

The first of these is of great moment to us as men who must also die; the second, similarly important to us as men who must meanwhile live. And both concerns receive additional emphasis in the several Matthew poems, written during the same brief period (October 1798-February 1799). In what was probably the earliest of these, *Address to the Scholars*, Wordsworth asserts the finality of death almost as bluntly as in "A slumber":

> He lies beneath the grass-green mound
> A prisoner of the silent ground.
> He loved the breathing air,
> He loved the sun—he does not know
> Whether the sun be up or no,
> He lies forever there.
> [*PW* 4:452]

But it is chiefly the second concern, the loss to the living, that occupies him as he writes of Matthew. The two elegies to Matthew (*PW* 4:452-54), one ("Could I the priest's consent have gained") stressing how much the speaker misses him, the other ("Remembering how thou didst beguile") how so many people for many reasons will miss him, very naturally sound this theme. More memorably, the climactic incidents of both *The Two April Mornings* and *The Fountain* turn on Matthew's own recognition that in the deaths of his children he has suffered great and irremediable loss. In the former poem, he recalls a moment of intense grieving by his young daughter's grave followed unexpectedly by the sudden appearance, like the dead child's apparition, of a beautiful, happy young girl. Matthew spontaneously responds to her natural beauty: " 'To see a child so very fair, / It was a pure delight!' " (ll. 47-48). But he does not, cannot, regard her as a potential replacement for his own daughter:

> "There came from me a sigh of pain
> Which I could ill confine;
> I looked at her, and looked again:
> And did not wish her mine!"
> [Ll. 53-56]

And in much the same way, in *The Fountain*, when the speaker, moved by Matthew's assertion that " 'many love me! but by none / Am I enough beloved,' " cries,

> "Now both himself and me he wrongs,
> The man who thus complains!
> . . . .
>
> And, Matthew, for thy children dead
> I'll be a son to thee!"

Matthew again spontaneously responds to the offer—"At this he grasped his hands"—but still knows, " 'Alas! that cannot be' " (ll. 55-64 and app. crit.).

It is noteworthy that neither of the two concerns so troubling Wordsworth in the Lucy and Matthew poems had particularly colored his optimism and tranquillity in early 1798. The Pedlar may at first lament of Margaret that "she is dead, / The worm is on her cheek," but ends with a soothing and consoling revision of her fate: "She sleeps in the calm earth and peace is here" (*The Ruined Cottage*, ll. 353-54; Addendum, l. 122). Even more strikingly, the specific relationship which Matthew insists

is unique and inimitable—that of family, of man to "the house-
hold hearts that [are] his own" (*The Fountain*, 1. 51), and
more particularly of father to child—has no such distinctiveness
in the poetry of the preceding year. The Pedlar (who, however,
is apparently unmarried and childless) says of Margaret, "I loved
her / As my own child" (*The Ruined Cottage*, ll. 345–46) (while
the narrator, for his part, comes to think of her "with a brother's
love"). And in *Anecdote for Fathers* (written April or May
1798) Wordsworth (who, though a father, had never yet even
seen his French child), while basing the poem on an incident he
actually experienced, represents himself as the father of a child,
Basil Montagu, who in real life was not his son at all but only
temporarily a ward.

iii

Thus Matthew raises several important points of disagreement
with the Pedlar across the intervening year of Wordsworth's de-
velopment. Curiously, the two men are in many respects very
like, so much so that Matthew could almost be only a later
poetic version of the Pedlar. One of the narrator's episodic
portraits of the Pedlar, for example—

> Many a time
> He made a holyday and left his pack
> Behind, and we two wandered through the hills
> A pair of random Travellers—His eye
> Flashing poetic fire he would repeat
> The songs of Burns and as we trudged along
> Together did we make the hollow grove
> Ring with our transports
> [*The Ruined Cottage*, ll. 265–70 and app. crit.]

—could easily be a picture of Matthew and the speaker of *The
Two April Mornings* and *The Fountain*, an old man and a youth
"on a spring holiday" out "to pass / A day among the hills"
(*Two April Mornings* ll. 8, 11–12), ready "with some old border-
song, or catch / That suits a summer's noon" (*The Fountain*,
ll. 11–12; and cf. ll. 59–60). Like the Pedlar, Matthew is blithe,
yet fundamentally serious, a man of wisdom as well as experi-
ence and joy:

Yet sometimes, when the secret cup
Of still and serious thought went round,
It seemed as if he drank it up—
He felt with spirit so profound.
                    [*Matthew*, ll. 25-28]

And like the Pedlar, Matthew is a child of nature, one in whom, as Wordsworth here describes the condition, Nature "hath tempered so her clay, / That every hour [his] heart runs wild, / Yet never once doth go astray" (*Matthew*, ll. 2-4).

As *The Two April Mornings* and *The Fountain* unexpectedly reveal, however, Matthew differs importantly from the Pedlar in some of his fundamental philosophical beliefs. There are differences as well in their backgrounds, of course—the Pedlar is "untaught, / In the dead lore of schools undisciplined" (*The Ruined Cottage*, ll. 270-271), solitary, and itinerant, while Matthew is a village schoolmaster, a husband and father—but these seem essentially symptomatic rather than causal. To understand the change that is taking place here in Wordsworth's thought from early 1798 to early 1799, we need to probe to the very axioms of the Pedlar's and Matthew's creeds.

The determinant axioms would seem to be these: the Pedlar sees in the world a universal *egalitarianism* of spirit—one life everywhere, and everywhere equally precious:

He felt the sentiment of being, spread
O'er all that moves, and all that seemeth still,
O'er all which, lost beyond the reach of thought,
And human knowledge, to the human eye
Invisible, yet liveth to the heart,
O'er all that leaps, and runs, and shouts, and sings,
Or beats the gladsome air, o'er all that glides
Beneath the wave, yea, in the wave itself,
And mighty depth of waters. . . .
                              . . . in all things
He saw one life, and felt that it was joy.[3]
              [*The Ruined Cottage*, ll. 242-52]

Matthew, in contrast, recognizes in the world *hierarchies* of spirit and spiritual values. While truly loving the beauties of nature—the "sweet season" of spring (*Two April Mornings*, l. 30) and the "delightful day[s]" of summer (*Fountain*, l. 25),

57

the sun and the "breathing air" (*PW* 4:452), a blowing hawthorn (*PW* 4:452-53), a merrily running fountain (*Fountain*, l. 22)—he quite obviously loves and values his fellow men more dearly than these. Thus he finds fulfillment in a social role as a "shepherd," not "on the lonely mountain tops" so inspirational to the young Pedlar (*The Ruined Cottage*, l. 142), but in a village, tending a flock of schoolchildren (cf. *PW* 4:452); and thus also he serves as something of a center of village life. But he loves his own family, his "household hearts," more dearly still. His values are reminiscent of those which, proceeding especially from Herbert, largely inform the society of *The Borderers*, where the greatest bond of love is a bond of blood. As Mortimer with building emphasis summarizes Herbert's ties to Matilda,

> Thou loved'st the infant that had fed thee[,]
> Thy daughter—she that was the light of thy path [,]
> The very blood that moved in thee.
> [*The Borderers*, ll. 1823-56 app. crit.]

In such a society, Margaret's sorest reproach to her husband for his cowardly abandonment of the dying old man who "was muttering something about his Child—his Daughter" (ll. 1942-43) is the heartsick "Robert, you are a father" (l. 1945), and the greatest recompense for charity Herbert can make is the wish, "May the God of Heaven bless your old age with such a daughter" (l. 827 app. crit.).

As a consequence of these fundamental axioms of faith, the Pedlar and Matthew must necessarily feel the effects of memory and intelligence very differently. To the Pedlar, from whose philosophical perspective life is spiritually as well as physically a continuum, eternally maintaining and repeating itself, memory and anticipation are simply sensation back and forth across time rather than across space. Thus his practical wisdom, about man as about nature, derives straightforwardly from extended observation:

> He had observ'd the progress and decay
> Of many minds, of minds and bodies too
> The history of many families,
> And how they prosper'd, how they lived in peace

And happiness, and how they were o'erthrown
By passion or mischance.
[PW 5:387 app. crit.]

In a very real sense, then, Margaret leaves to the Pedlar "this heath, this calm and quiet scene; / The memory of what has been, / And *ever* more will be"—world without end, amen. For Matthew, however, as for the Lucy poet, the pressure of "the difference to *me*" inevitably darkens this larger, impersonal view of life's continuity with a personal apprehension of something like spiritual entropy. And this pressure is specifically due to memory and anticipation, which for him vary importantly in their effects from simple sensation. For Matthew, like the Lucy poet and the grieving man of "'Tis said that some have died for love" (and in this they differ significantly from Margaret of *The Ruined Cottage*), can still appreciate sensationally, immediately, that nature, far from betraying man, continues an eternal source of "overseeing power / To kindle or restrain" ("Three years she grew," ll. 11–12). But memory imposes upon him the continual consciousness of greater spiritual treasures now lost, "kindred laid in earth" (*The Fountain*, l. 50), while foresight promises that he too must decay into insensateness. Nature herself teaches that nature is not to blame; thought itself teaches that thought is. "[T]he wiser mind / Mourns less for what age takes away / Than what it leaves behind" (*The Fountain*, ll. 34–36); and what it leaves behind is that selfsame "wiser mind," the intellectual awareness, memorial and prospective, that age takes things away. The true children of nature which Matthew goes on enviously to note—

"The blackbird in the summer trees,
The lark upon the hill,
Let loose their carols when they please,
Are quiet when they will.

"With Nature never do *they* wage
A foolish strife; they see
A happy youth, and their old age
Is beautiful and free"
[The Fountain, ll. 37–44 and app. crit.]

—are content precisely because of their mindlessness. The condition which the Pedlar defines and celebrates as the apotheosis of

59

thought, then, Matthew recognizes to be simply the absence of thought; not, after all, a sublime heightening of "our intellectual soul," but rather an elimination of its intellectual characteristics. And such a course is impossibly impracticable because these very characteristics are what define us as human rather than animal, because we are inescapably endued, as the Pedlar himself readily admits, "with apprehension, reason, will and thought" (*The Ruined Cottage*, Addendum, l. 75).

It is interesting to watch Wordsworth soon after this, in the summer of 1799, beginning to dismiss the Pedlar's philosophy more directly. Towards the end of the early, two-part *Prelude* he incorporates into his own autobiography the central description from *The Ruined Cottage* of the Pedlar's visionary experience of the one life: "I felt the sentiment of being spread / O'er all that moves, and all that seemeth still. . . . In all things / I saw one life, and felt that it was joy" (*Prelude 1799* 2.446-64; cf. *The Ruined Cottage*, ll. 238-56). And now he expatiates upon this immediately with a passage explicitly rejecting all forms of thought as antagonistic to such fulfillment:

> By such communion I was early taught
> That what we see of forms and images
> Which float along our minds and what we feel
> Of active, or recognizable thought
> Prospectiveness, intelligence or will
> Not only is not worthy to be deemed
> Our being, to be prized as what we are
> But is the very littleness of life
> Such consciousnesses seemed but accidents
> Relapses from the one interior life
> Which is in all things, from that unity
> In which all beings live with God, are lost
> In god and nature, in one mighty whole
> As undistinguishable as the cloudless east
> At noon is from the cloudless west when all
> The hemisphere is one cerulean blue.[4]
>
> [*Prelude 1850*, p. 525]

Yet even as he voices such opinions, he hastens to undercut them: perhaps "this be error, and another faith / Find easier access to the pious mind" (*Prelude 1799* 2.465-6). As he goes directly on to speak favorably of "my lofty speculations" (*Pre-*

lude 1799 2.493), moreover, his self-contradictions (for can "lofty speculations" be free of "active, or recognizable thought"?) become blatant. Surely the recognition that to reject thought is to reject one's humanness is forcing Wordsworth's evasiveness here. Consequently, when he revises the 1799 *Prelude* shortly afterwards (between 26 November and 17 December 1799 [*CMY*, p. 630 n]) he eliminates the anti-intellectual passage quoted above. Now the reservation "if this be error" refers instead to the belief that "in all things / I saw one life," while the discouraging suggestion that thought per se "is the very littleness of life" entirely disappears.

iv

In the Lucy and Matthew poems Wordsworth explicitly acknowledges the inadequacy of his belief in the "one life" fully to sustain and console him in the face of human loss. But these poems offer no remedy: Matthew simply accepts his situation, and the grieving poet of both sets of poems himself can do no more. The dead are insensate, oblivious, and forceless, "silent as a standing pool" (*Matthew*, l. 18); their deaths represent the loss of unique and valuable human personalities; and, given the intellectual awareness characterizing and defining our human condition, these two great facts must seriously matter to us. But what can man do about them?

To the first of these facts, the obliviousness of the dead, there would seem to be no remedial response possible short of conversion to an idealistic faith. Of more immediate concern to Wordsworth in 1799 is the second great fact of death, its impact upon those it spares, and the question of how the bereaved can cope with or limit their loss. Wordsworth's struggle with this question dominates his poetry and thought through most of 1799 and 1800, and not surprisingly his evolving response to death provokes changes in his attitudes toward life as well. In the poetry of these two years Wordsworth gradually develops philosophical concepts of nature and godhead markedly different from those he had formed earlier. That the change from his position of 1798 is evolutionary rather than revolutionary, gradual rather than abrupt, has tended to obscure the shift to his new attitudes, but should not blind us to their ultimate distinctiveness.[5]

There are already traces of a newly revised hope in two Goslar lyrics, *Lucy Gray* and *The Danish Boy*. In many respects these poems are evocative of the Lucy poems: Lucy Gray is another child of nature, and both she and the Danish Boy imitate Lucy's dying into nature. But the speaker of these poems is much more readily consoled than was Lucy's lover by the thought of the dead person's continuity in nature. His consolations, however, rest on wishful, fanciful impressions:

> —Yet some maintain that to this day
> She is a living child;
> That you may see sweet Lucy Gray
> Upon the lonesome wild.
>
> [*Lucy Gray*, ll. 57-60]

> In this dell you see
> A thing no storm can e'er destroy,
> The shadow of a Danish Boy.
>
> [*The Danish Boy*, ll. 9-11]

As Spencer Hall observes, "Like Lucy Gray, . . . the Danish Boy retains his aura of an individual human identity; he sings, he plays his harp, he observes the changes in nature."[6] Such superstitious optimism is hardly the faith of one who had been close enough to the dead to feel now "the difference to me!": to the poet the Danish Boy is only a figure of legend, and Lucy Gray someone he had once "chanced to see" (*Lucy Gray*, l. 3). In their impersonality these lyrics make no pretense of responding to the deep sense of personal loss expressed in the Lucy and Matthew poems. But their suggestions of how particular human characteristics may after death survive perceptibly in nature— Lucy's spirit "sings a solitary song / That whistles in the wind" (ll. 63-64) and the Danish Boy, "a Spirit of noon-day" (l. 23), similarly sings so that "often, when no cause appears, / The mountain-ponies prick their ears, / —They hear the Danish Boy" (ll. 40-42)—do go somewhat beyond "Three years she grew" in hinting at ways of preserving some aspects of personal identity from death.

A more pointed suggestion of Wordsworth's newly evolving attitudes appears in a passage added to *The Ruined Cottage* in

1799.[7] In this expansion of his first speech to the narrator, the Pedlar elaborates, in terms somewhat uncharacteristic of his 1798 "one life" philosophy, on man's response to bereavement:

"The Poets, in their elegies and songs
Lamenting the departed, call the groves,
They call upon the hills and streams to mourn,
And senseless rocks—nor idly, for they speak
In these their invocations with a voice
Obedient to the strong creative power
Of human passion. Sympathies there are
More tranquil, yet perhaps of kindred birth,
That steal upon the meditative mind
And grow with thought. Beside yon spring I stood,
And eyed its waters till we seemed to feel
One sadness, they and I. For them a bond
Of brotherhood is broken."

[Ll. 331–33 and app. crit.]

The Pedlar's new remarks here expand upon his original opening observation that

"I see around me here
Things which you cannot see. We die, my Friend,
Nor we alone, but that which each man loved
And prized in his peculiar nook of earth
Dies with him or is changed, and very soon
Even of the good is no memorial left."

[Ll. 325–30]

And this context helps clarify the yoked impulses informing the added lines. There is, first of all, the desire that some memorial of the deceased should after all be left in nature. Hence the poets call upon nature to mourn, and hence the Pedlar meditates until he can imagine the waters of Margaret's spring feeling sadness for her death. As the Pedlar well knows, there is no basis for such hopes, and no actual response to them: the features of nature remain "senseless," the spring's waters can only "seem" to feel (in 1798 Wordsworth wrote simply, "The waters of that spring if they could feel / Might mourn" [ll. 331–32]), and all of each man's imprint upon the earth "dies with him, or is changed." Yet paradoxically, the hopeless gesture rewards hope; the poets call upon nature, if ineffectually, yet not idly, for in their act "the strong creative power / Of human passion" is at work, while kindred sympathies similarly infuse the meditating Pedlar. This second impulse is, in effect, to react as if the natural scene *had* responded by somehow memorializing its former inhabitant.

This second desire to which the Pedlar alludes is, indeed, simply the desire to remember, the will that, as Leonard says in *The Brothers*, men shall "in each other's thoughts / Possess a kind of second life" (ll. 184-85). But Wordsworth, following Locke, emphatically believes that memory, by itself but a bodiless, malleable, and naturally ephemeral creature of the mind, draws substance from the relatively more enduring forms and features of actual things. Thus the hills among which Michael lives

> had impressed
> So many incidents upon his mind
> Of hardship, skill or courage, joy or fear;
> [They,] like a book, preserved the memory
> Of the dumb animals, whom he had saved,
> Had fed or sheltered. . . ;
> [They] were his living Being, even more
> Than his own blood.
>
> [*Michael*, ll. 67-74 and app. crit.]

And in his letter of January 1801 to Charles James Fox accompanying a presentation copy of the 1800 *Lyrical Ballads* Wordsworth drives home the same point: for men like Michael fortunate enough to possess "small estates, which have descended to them from their ancestors," he writes,

> Their little tract of land serves as a kind of permanent rallying point for their domestic feelings, as a tablet upon which they are written which makes them objects of memory in a thousand instances when they would otherwise be forgotten. [*LEY*, p. 261]

All of his familiar parish dale is such a tablet to the Priest of *The Brothers*. His allusion to "God who made the great book of the world" (l. 266) may seem a facile cliché, but the cliché comes curiously to life when to Leonard's query, "No doubt / You, Sir, could help me to the history / Of half these graves?" he responds,

> For eight-score winters past,
> With what I've witnessed, and with what I've heard,
> Perhaps I might; and, on a winter's evening,
> If you were seated at my chimney's nook,
> By turning o'er these hillocks one by one,
> We two could travel, Sir, through a strange round;
> Yet all in the broad highway of the world.
>
> [Ll. 185–93 and app. crit.]

He can speak so of "turning o'er these hillocks" like the pages of a book read by the fireside because, by virtue of his long and continuous familiarity with the dale, this local chapter of "the great book of the world" has become for him not only, in its changeless mountains, a testament of God (cf. ll. 180–83), but also, in its accumulation of incidental associations stretching back far before his own time (back "eight-score winters"), a chronicle of human life.

If the Priest feels no need for tombstones and epitaphs in his churchyard, however, Leonard nonetheless does. He needs them not simply because he has been ignorant of the dale's life for the past twenty years, but as well because he has been so long absent from its once familiar scenes which, like a book, tended to keep his memories of its history and his own childhood fresh and true. And he has not only lived apart from these scenes, he has long lived in the virtual absence of all scenes—on the featureless expanse of the sea, where

> the regular wind
> Between the tropics filled the steady sail,
> And blew with the same breath through days and weeks,
> Lengthening invisibly its weary line
> Along the cloudless Main.
>
> [Ll. 49–53]

His recollections of his native scenes at this time, while superficially similar to the process of memorial restoration described in *Tintern Abbey*, are explicitly the hallucinations of illness, produced by the "feverish passion" (l. 59) of a calenture; and the illness suggests the potential unreliability of his unrefreshed memory.[8] On his return home Leonard soon has this unreliability confirmed, as the dale seems different from what he had remembered:

> He had lost his path,
> As up the dale he came that afternoon
> Through fields which once had been well known to him:
> . . . .
>
> . . . he lifted up his eyes,
> And, looking round, he thought that he perceiv'd
> Strange alteration wrought on every side
> Among the woods and fields, and that the rocks,
> And the eternal hills themselves were changed.
>
> [Ll. 91–99 and app. crit.]

Certain changes have occurred, of course, as the Priest readily confirms; but to some extent Leonard's memory is simply playing tricks on him:

> *Leonard:*   . . . That dark cleft!
> To me it does not seem to wear the face
> Which then it had!
> *Priest:*   That rock for aught I know
> Is much the same.
>
> [Ll. 134–37 and app. crit.]

By itself this may seem rather trivial, but its implications are serious. For if his memory of the everlasting hills is untrustworthy, what then of his memory of his brother? Having been so long absent from natural memorials, Leonard indeed has need of artificial ones now.

Absence, of course, is a mutual relationship, and we must not disregard its other side. The Priest, ever prompted by familiar scenes, can remember the Leonard of twenty and more years ago very well; but he never recognizes Leonard in the stranger before him, the intervening changes have apparently been so great. Michael can with absolute confidence promise Luke to "bear thy memory with me to the grave" (l. 417), but cannot be so sure what will become of Luke, or what Luke will become. He has his son lay the cornerstone of a sheepfold in a solemn ceremony designed to fix the more firmly in Luke's memory not this one stone but the entire way of life that the placing of it emblematizes:

> "Lay now the corner-stone,
> As I requested; and hereafter, Luke,

When thou art gone away, should evil men
Be thy companions, let this sheep-fold be
Thy anchor and thy shield; amid all fear
And all temptation, let it be to thee
An emblem of the life thy Fathers lived,
Who, being innocent, did for that cause
Bestir them in good deeds."
                    [Ll. 403-12 and app. crit.]

Luke's subsequent "slacken[ing] in his duty" (l. 443) thus implies a slackening in his memory. But Michael, for his own part, needing memorials no more than does the Priest of Ennerdale, is here raising something the very opposite, a testament not to the past but to the future:

"When thou return'st, thou in this place wilt see
A work which is not here: a covenant
'Twill be between us."
                    [Ll. 413-15]

He intends the sheepfold's rise to parallel his son's, and its completion to signify Luke's success in his new endeavor and in his redemption of their land. Thus as long as "a good report did from their Kinsman come, / Of Luke and his well-doing" (ll. 431-32), Michael continues to work at the sheepfold; and when Luke sinks to "ignominy and shame" (l. 445) and at last "seek[s] a hiding-place beyond the seas" (l. 447), Michael correspondingly falters and then fails in his own task:

'Tis believed by all
That many and many a day he thither went,
And never lifted up a single stone.
                    [Ll. 464-66]

The sheepfold must remain unfinished (l. 481), because the covenant it represents remains unfulfilled.

V

Just as the man most needful of artificial memorials is the one who, like Leonard, has been absent (hence the epitaph, for example, typically addresses the stranger or traveler: *Siste viator*), the man most likely to erect them is the one who will soon be

absent. A passage in one of the early manuscripts of *Michael*
interestingly illuminates this point. Michael and Luke, searching
among the mountains for a stray sheep,

> pass'd
> Those small flat stones which, rang'd by Travellers' hands
> In cyphers on Helvellyn's highest ridge,
> Lie loose on the bare turf, some half o'ergrown
> By the grey moss, but not a single stone
> Unsettled by a wanton blow from foot
> Of Shepherd, man or Boy. They have respect
> For strangers who have travell'd far perhaps
> For men who in such places feeling there
> The grandeur of the earth have left inscrib'd
> Their epitaph which rain and snow
> And the strong wind have reverenced.
>
> *[PW* 2:484]

It is significant and characteristic that these inscriptions, these
initials and names, should be the ciphers of travelers and not
natives, the "epitaphs" of transient strangers whose presence
here would not otherwise be remembered. The tableau, as might
be guessed from Michael's and Luke's curious "respect" for the
inscribed initials of strange tourists, reflects a certain tension in
Wordsworth's own situation: while in a sense he was now finally,
like Michael, "permanently fixed in my native country" (*LEY*,
p. 269), he was also very much a newcomer to Grasmere. If his
neighbors and local acquaintances were many of them men like
Michael, "the Statesmen, so they are called, of this country,"
"men of respectable education who daily labour on their own
little properties" (*LEY*, pp. 266, 261), his family and friends
were much like the self-memorializing strangers whose ciphers
Michael finds on Helvellyn. Sara Hutchinson "carved her cypher
upon one of [the] bars" of a gate which "commands a beautiful
prospect" (*LEY*, p. 275); Mary Hutchinson carved hers on a
stone at the foot of Grasmere lake (*DWJ*, p. 82; cf. *LEY*, p.
275); even Dorothy Wordsworth, visiting a friend at Eusemere,
carved her own name on a tree at Dunmallet, where she herself
was the transient stranger (*DWJ*, p. 108). And Coleridge set the
example for a general carving of initials on the Rock of Names,
halfway between Grasmere and Kewsick, the point where he

and the Wordsworths customarily parted from each other after their visits (*DWJ*, p. 120; *PW* 2:499-501).

Inscribed ciphers are memorials of oneself addressed to one's successors in space, even as epitaphs similarly address one's successors in time, and like epitaphs represent one more small way of staving off the second death of oblivion. Yet Wordsworth, while obviously sympathetic to such gestures, seems anxious to give and gain "a kind of second life" somewhat more lasting and widespread than any afforded by a stranger's carved initials. With his *Poems on the Naming of Places* he takes this name-carving urge a step further, seeking to bring the transient's vestigial presence into the living store of the community's memory.

Years later, in his first *Essay upon Epitaphs*, Wordsworth would insist that epitaphs are fostered by man's innate sense of his immortality, and that without this sense we could never "have any wish to be remembered after we had passed away from a world in which each man had moved about like a shadow" (*Prose* 2:52). But in 1800 his epitaphlike *Poems on the Naming of Places* everywhere declare their contrary origin as a defensive reaction to his sense of man's mortality. Thus in the first naming poem, "It was an April morning," Wordsworth prefaces the act of naming with a strangely defensive remark: " 'Our thoughts at least are ours; and this wild nook, / My Emma, I will dedicate to thee' " (ll. 38-39). What provokes the initial exclamation? Apparently Wordsworth wishes to dedicate this particular dell to his sister not simply because it is delightful, but because it speaks to him of *eternal* delight:

> a song,
> Which, while I listened, seemed like the wild growth
> Or like some natural produce of the air,
> That could not cease to be.
> [Ll. 27-30]

Wordsworth knows that such immortality is not for Emma or him—before this poem ends he will foresee the time "years after we are gone and in our graves" (ll. 45)—but at least he cannot be stopped, he consoles himself, from imagining it for her.[9] Alternatively and more practically, he moves to secure a more lasting remembrance of her by telling the local shepherds of his name for the spot, so that in future years they, "when they have cause to speak of this wild place, / May call it by the name of Emma's Dell" (ll. 46-47).

In by far the most remarkable of the naming poems, the sadly neglected *To Joanna*, Wordsworth dramatically explores the memorializing potential of such namings on a variety of levels. As before, the chosen spot seems to have value first of all as an emblem of permanence. This time it is an impressive cliff of the enduring and "native rock" (l. 30), part of Grasmere's "brotherhood / Of ancient mountains" (ll. 69-70), which Wordsworth here delights in imagining and personifying as a living assemblage: thus the cliff echoes Joanna's laughter "like something starting from a sleep" (l. 54), and in their turn the other mountains take up the sound in "loud uproar" (l. 73). And here again the first hope of Wordsworth's naming impulse is to associate his mortal friend with this enduring life—now by actually chiseling Joanna's name "upon the living stone" (l. 83 and app. crit.).[10]

Even as Wordsworth makes this memorializing gesture, however, he as much as admits its futility. For these "rude characters" (l. 82) in which he chisels out Joanna's name "upon the native rock" (l. 30) essentially differ not at all from the several local "Inscriptions, upon the native rock," traces of an earlier age, to which Wordsworth alludes in an endnote he always published with the poem. Those inscriptions, he notes, "from the wasting of time, and the rudeness of the workmanship, have been mistaken for Runic. They are, without doubt, Roman" (*PW* 2:114). But such a controversy, no less than Wordsworth's description of the markings as rude and wasted, reminds us that these inscriptions have with time become illegible. As memorials they are now failures, ciphers which cannot be deciphered. Thus even to chisel a name into the living rock offers no surety that that name will live.

But Wordsworth, in thus inscribing Joanna's name, is serving his own purposes more shrewdly than we are at first likely to realize. Consider the Vicar's greeting to Wordsworth:

> When he had asked,
> "How fares Joanna, that wild-hearted Maid!
> And when will she return to us?" he paused;
> And, after short exchange of village news,

He with grave looks demanded, for what cause,
Reviving obsolete idolatry,
I, like a Runic Priest, in characters
Of formidable size had chiselled out
Some uncouth name upon the native rock,
Above the Rotha, by the forest-side.
[Ll. 22-31]

Implicit here in this confrontation between "Runic Priest" and Christian Vicar is something of the debate also implicit in Leonard's dialogue with the Priest in *The Brothers*, a debate between a pagan desire for continued identity on earth after death and the Christian concern instead for eternal life in heaven. But more significant than this is the Vicar's unwitting testimony to the success of Wordsworth's ploy. For why does he so suddenly inquire after Joanna? His questions seem a gratuitous pleasantry, and so, I think, they are usually taken. But surely they are not gratuitous. Joanna, after all, has been absent two years (l. 13), and the tenor of the Vicar's questions suggests he has not kept up with her fortunes since he last saw her; why then should he without provocation think of her now? The answer, of course, is that he has had provocation. He seeks out Wordsworth for this meeting (ll. 18-22) and immediately mentions Joanna because—though he doesn't acknowledge this—he has just read *and recognized* her name carved into the rock. Thus in the short run the inscription *has* served its intended purpose: it has revived someone's waning memory of Joanna.

Yet Wordsworth does not stop here; instead he carries his memorializing campaign to a higher level of intensity. "I begin to relate the story" behind the inscription, he explicates in a contemporary manuscript note, "meaning in a certain degree to divert or partly play upon the Vicar" (*PW* 2:487). As he proceeds with his narration, he deliberately pretends to be, or lets himself be, carried away by the extravagances of his recollecting imagination as a means of captivating the Vicar's own. "[M]y mind partly forgets its purpose, being softened by the images of beauty in the description of the rock, and the delicious morning" (*PW* 2:487; see ll. 45-50). But it was precisely his ravishment (l. 53) by the real, original scene of this beauty, his own mere description of which now so moves him at second hand, which had provoked Joanna's somewhat unsympathetic laughter

71

in the first place—laughter which the echoing hills immediately retorted against her. And now Wordsworth's narrative self-forgetfulness and extravagance prompt in the Vicar a perplexed amusement closely akin to Joanna's ("in the hey-day of astonishment / [He] [s]miled in my face" [ll. 67-68])—amusement which again redounds against the laughter, as Wordsworth abruptly changes the tone of his story, now "mingling allusions suffused with humour, partly to the trance in which I have been, and partly to the trick I have been playing on the Vicar" (*PW* 2:487). The very structure of the episode, this is to say, suggests that Wordsworth, once instructed by nature how to turn a laugh against the laugher, deliberately repeats the experiment himself with the Vicar in place of Joanna as his subject.

But what purpose does this wild experiment serve? An answer comes forth, I think, from the interconnected opening and closing passages of the poem. Joanna, who has long since learned devotedly "to love / The living Beings by your own fireside" (ll. 3-4), yet

Is slow towards the sympathies of them
Who look upon the hills with tenderness,
And make dear friendships with the streams and groves.
[Ll. 6-8 and app. crit.]

And there is more than a bare suggestion here that in the very narrowness of her sympathies she is perhaps slow to love those who do not dwell with her by her own fireside, those whom she doesn't frequently see. The Wordsworths ("I, and all who dwell by my fireside" [l. 84]), in contrast, have in their retirement learned how to keep their love for others alive even at a distance and despite absence: still Wordsworth nourishes his "memory of affections old and true" (ll. 81), and still he and his family "talk / Familiarly of you and of old times" (ll. 16-17). And nature herself furnishes the stimuli of these memories: it is his return to the scene of Joanna's laughter that revives them in Wordsworth, and in turn his memorializing of the scene that gives rise to the Wordsworths' familiar name for it, "Joanna's Rock" (ll. 85). Further, by astonishing the Vicar with his wild recollections even as the mountains had astonished Joanna with their wild echoes, he gives her that much more substance and life in another's memory.

Finally, as we must never forget, the naming poem *To Joanna* is itself a type of the very inscriptive and naming act it describes and celebrates.[11] Joanna does not, as does Wordsworth, have the beautiful cliff nearby to serve as a constant reminder of this episode. As a transient visitor now long gone from Grasmere, she lacks this "permanent rallying point for [her] domestic feelings, . . . which makes them objects of memory . . . when they would otherwise be forgotten." But she does now, at least, have a surrogate rallying point, Wordsworth's poem to her. And by referring to this even as Wordsworth refers to the rock itself, she can perhaps learn, as he has learned, to love and remember at a distance, throughout an absence.

More than this a memorializing poet cannot do. And even this is admittedly but a kind of rearguard action against inexorably devouring time, a more or less brief postponement of oblivion. Even in a ruined cottage, a straggling heap of stones, a rude and wasted inscription, a careful observer may read fragments of individual histories long after the men and women they memorialize have passed away, and Wordsworth rejoices in such salvage as small victories against mortality itself. As he wrote in a fragment probably once intended for *Michael*, if, when in some desolate spot,

> I have perchance perceived
> Some vestiges of human hands, some stir
> Of human passion, they to me are sweet
> As lightest sunbreak, or the sudden sound
> Of music to a blind man's ear who sits
> Alone and silent in the summer shade.
> They are as a creation in my heart;
> I look into past times as prophets look
> Into futurity, a —— of life runs back
> Into dead years, the —— of thought
> The —— spirit of philosophy
> Leads me through moods of sadness to delight.
> [*PW* 2:480]

But eventually the blind man's ears will prove as mortal as his eyes; and eventually, as the Pedlar knows, "Even of the good is no memorial left." The stones for Michael's sheepfold, which,

73

in the words of another draft fragment, "seem to keep them-
selves alive / In the last dotage of a dying form" (*PW* 2:482),
warn all too clearly that despite all memorials the past will
become "dead years" at last.

CHAPTER 4
"Sympathy Divine":
The Being beyond Nature

i

AMONG THE frequently somber speculations on physical death and memorial survival characterizing Wordsworth's poetry of 1799 and 1800, *Hart-Leap Well* stands out as a careful, if tentative, extension of his thoughts and beliefs toward new sources of consolation. Here the issue Wordsworth has been pursuing, how to cope with our mortality, he both transposes onto a different plane—the animal rather than the human world—and pushes to the verge of a transcendent hope—the possible existence of a "sympathy divine" (l. 164). As a result, this remarkable variation on and departure from the "poems on the naming of places" subgenre becomes an important bridge in Wordsworth's poetry between the eschatological somberness of 1799 and the increased hopefulness of 1802 and beyond.

Some of the most important effects of *Hart-Leap Well* relate it pointedly to the anthropomorphic apologue or fable; both the "humanness" of the hart and the poem's didactic close, for example, indicate such an association. In these respects it is reminiscent of two other fabulous poems from this same period, *The Waterfall and the Eglantine* and *The Oak and the Broom*, both, like *Hart-Leap Well*, written in 1800. All three poems, significantly, concern a "natal spot" (*The Waterfall*, l. 23 and app. crit.); the Broom even affects something like Michael's tone on the subject:

"For me, why should I wish to roam?
This spot is my paternal home,

75

It is my pleasant heritage;
My father many a happy year
Spread here his careless blossoms, here
Attained a good old age.[1]

[Ll. 65-70]

But *Hart-Leap Well* goes beyond these in identifying Nature
herself as the true parent of these natural creatures. If the hart,
the oak and broom, and the waterfall and eglantine are manlike
in their thoughts and passions, so here does nature appear like a
human survivor, a chronicler, a poet—an inscriber of epitaphs
Leonard notes in *The Brothers* of the village's unmarked church
yard,

Here's neither head nor foot-stone, plate of brass,
Cross-bones nor skull,—type of our earthly state
Nor emblem of our hopes: the dead man's home
Is but a fellow to that pasture-field.

[Ll. 170-73]

But at Hart-Leap Well the wild field has become conversely a
fellow to the more typical "dead man's home," a place of
epitaphic "monuments" (l. 176). Hence we are encouraged to
interpret the poem as genuinely fabulous in its method, actually
a moral lesson of and for men though superficially only a tale of
man, beast, and nature. Seen this way, Nature in the poem acts
like Wordsworth recalling Matthew or naming places near Gras-
mere, memorializing a loved one as a way of countering to some
degree the inexorable fact of his or her mortality and tran-
sience.

But of course *Hart-Leap Well* is not merely a fable. Its narra-
tive is not only allegorical, but factual, as Wordsworth insists in
his headnote to the poem: the chase actually occurred, and "the
monuments spoken of in the second Part of the . . . Poem . . . do
now exist as I have there described them" (*PW* 2:249). More
importantly, but much more subtly, certain aspects of the stag's
behavior, while seemingly manlike, in fact also point up how
very different is his condition from man's—most different there
where superficially appearing most similar, in the instinct to go
home to die:

"In my simple mind we cannot tell
What cause the Hart might have to love this place,

And come and make his death-bed near the well,"
> [*Hart-Leap Well*, ll. 146-48]

the Shepherd muses, but ultimately conjectures,

> "This water was perhaps the first he drank
> When he had wandered from his mother's side.
>
> . . . .
>
> And he, perhaps, for aught we know, was born
> Not half a furlong from that self-same spring."
> [Ll. 151-56]

And we learn somewhat similarly of Sir Walter, who "died in course of time," that "his bones lie in his paternal vale" (ll. 93–94). But what defines a spot as one's paternal home? To what is one returning in these extremities? The questions would seem to evoke very different answers for beast and man.

Wordsworth never saw or heard of Hart-Leap Well until December, 1799; but a few years before this he had already presented a death scene very like that which Sir Walter beholds and the Shepherd imagines. "A peasant whom we met near the spot told us the story so far as concerned the name of the well, and the hart, and pointed out the stones," Wordsworth later told Isabella Fenwick (*PW* 2:514); most of the other details of the scene, then, are surely the poet's embellishments. And some of these are strikingly evocative, surprisingly enough, of *The Borderers*. A single quatrain presents the hart "lying dead" (*Hart-Leap Well*, l. 32) by the well whose "water was perhaps the first he drank":

> Upon his side the Hart was lying stretched:
> His nose half-touched a spring beneath a hill,
> And with the last deep groan his breath had fetched
> The waters of the spring were trembling still.
> [Ll. 41-44 and app. crit.]

But our last impression of Herbert's death scene anticipates this one:

> Near the brink
> Of a small pool of water he was laid,
> His face close to the water. As it seemed
> He had stooped down to drink and had remained

Without the strength to rise.
[*The Borderers*, ll. 2032–35 and app. crit.]

And the relevance of this passage to the later *Hart-Leap Well* is emphatically driven home by Mortimer's anguished and distracted outburst shortly afterwards:

I remember
'Twas the first riddle that employed my fancy
To hunt some reason why the wisest thing
That the earth owns shall never choose to die,
But some one must be near to count his groans.
The wounded deer retires to solitude,
And dies in solitude: all things but man,
All die in solitude.[2]
[*The Borderers*, ll. 2115–24 and app. crit.]

The dark riddle which so exercises Mortimer springs from deep roots—nothing less than the questions of how and why man differs from the beasts. Herbert and the stag of *Hart-Leap Well* die very similar deaths; but while the stag's choice of a "death-bed" seems entirely proper, that Herbert should die thus alone is clearly wrong. Conscientious Margaret fully and emphatically recognizes how enormously her husband has offended in abandoning the dying Herbert:

Oh, Robert, you will die alone. You will have nobody to close your eyes—no hand to grasp your dying hand—I shall be in my grave. A curse will attend us all. [Ll. 1954–56]

Much the same horror informs *The Complaint of a Forsaken Indian Woman*, which Wordsworth himself characterized in 1800 as the "last struggles of a human being at the approach of death, cleaving in solitude to life and society" (*Prose* 1:126). And we would do well to remember here how nearly tautological, for man if not for beasts, "life" and "society" are.

As in *The Fountain*, so here in these strangely paired death scenes, it is chiefly the existence of man's intellectuality and memory that distinguishes him from the lower animals and makes a simple acceptance of his oneness with nature difficult or impossible. The stricken hart's retreat to a natural solitude is truly a homing instinct, whatever his actual birthplace, for he is wholly a "creature" (*Hart-Leap Well*, l. 168) of parental nature, to whose inner shrine he is hereby returning. And nature's seeming aloofness and impersonality are but the correlatives of the animal's mindlessness and lack of memory. For man, however, nature by itself is not and cannot be a true home; "home" for him, "intellectual soul" that he is, is a creation of family, of personal relationships, and is something apart from or at least additional to nature. Not nature, but human society established within nature, affords the proper correlative to man's self-consciousness and memory.[3]

Thus *Hart-Leap Well* functions simultaneously on two mutually reinforcing levels: implicitly as a fable, an allegory, wherein the relation between nature and hart figures that human, elegiac one between a bereaved, memorializing survivor and a deceased loved one (appropriately, the poem is written in elegiac stanzas); and explicitly as a factual narrative, a story of hart, nature, and men, which surface narrative yet contains, paradoxically, the philosophically deeper stratum of meaning. In the wholeness of his vision Wordsworth recognizes the fabulous potential of the spot's story, but then in his faithfulness to reality he goes beyond this reading to assert a fuller truth. In diverging finally from the Shepherd's creed he also diverges from the fabulous reading, regarding the decaying and doleful scene not as nature's epitaphic memorial to the hart but instead as a naturalistic, admonitory sign to men: "'She leaves these objects to a slow decay,'" he says, not that the hart may be remembered after its death, but "'that what we are, and have been, may be known'" (ll. 173–74). The lesson of this spot as he reads it centers not on the anthropomorphized hart, however noble, but on Sir Walter and more generally on man himself.

Wordsworth's incorporation within *Hart-Leap Well* of a mode of vision which he sets up only to supersede is reminiscent of his method in *The Borderers* and *The Ruined Cottage*, and suggests a similar thematic concern with moral and imaginative development. Indeed, Geoffrey Hartman has cogently proposed reading the poem as

> a little progress of the imagination, which leads from one type of animism to another: from the martial type of the knight, to the pastoral type of the shepherd, and finally to that of the poet. . . . [a] progress from primitive to sophisticated kinds of visionariness.[4]

And while I hesitate to adopt the specific labels *martial* and *pastoral*, I would propose further that this "little progress of the imagination" Hartman recognizes is also a progress through certain discrete attitudes toward nature which have hitherto informed Wordsworth's own poetry.

Thus Sir Walter's vision of Hart-Leap Well is decidedly egotistic and emblematic. Rejoicing in his triumph over the hart, he sees the death scene as a "darling place" (l. 48 and app. crit.), and literally makes over the spot into a physical emblem of his pleasure" and his pride (see l. 179). He erects there "a house of pleasure" (l. 84), "a small arbour, made for rural joy" (l. 58), and "a cup of stone" to receive—and perpetually fix—"the living well" (l. 82), all of them intended to endure "'till the foundations of the mountain fail'" (l. 73), proclaiming and memorializing not merely the hart, obviously, but more pointedly the hunter. And this egotistically emblematizing turn of Sir Walter's mind strongly evokes that of earlier figures in Wordsworth's work—preeminently Rivers, but also the yew-tree solitary and even Margaret of *The Ruined Cottage*.

The Shepherd's vision of Hart-Leap Well, by contrast—and this very juxtaposition is itself a feature already familiar to us from *The Borderers*—is what I have previously termed iconic. Superstitiously believing that the spot is eternally cursed because nature here perpetually sympathizes with and mourns the murdered hart, he thereby reveals his mental kinship to Robert and Mortimer no less than to the villagers of *The Thorn* and the narrator of *The Danish Boy*.[5] And in its implicit comparison of these two visions *Hart-Leap Well* reaffirms what *The Borderers* so vividly indicates, that while subjectively emblematic vision (Sir Walter; Rivers) and iconic vision (the Shepherd; Mortimer, Robert) may seem poles apart morally, they are yet quite closely related imaginatively. Where the former in effect more or less consciously imposes value upon nature, the latter in effect unconsciously personifies it; but both modes of vision are ultimately egotistical and self-reflective, and as such both—even the ostensibly "symbolic" vison of the Shepherd—are compatible with the fabulous, allegorical mode of the poem. Sir Walter's intent to build a lodge which will endure "till the foundations of the mountains fail" and the Shepherd's parallel faith that nature will memorialize the hart "till trees, and stones, and fountain, all are gone" (l. 160) spring from similar impulses, and bespeak a common, underlying concern for their own enduring memorializations.

But Wordsworth's own vision of nature at Hart-Leap Well differs radically from these. In simple terms, we may distinguish him from the Shepherd as seeing in the scene only what is there, not also what is subjectively interjected—the blight, but not the curse—and from Sir Walter as seeing all of what is there, not himself only—"the Being" that is everywhere (ll. 165-66), not merely the self reflected back to Sir Walter from everything. Yet this great Being, while it still seems very much a "sentiment of being, spread / O'er all that moves, and all that seemeth still," differs importantly from the "one life" the Pedlar once thought he saw, and felt was joy. No longer for Wordsworth are life and joy necessarily equivalent, and no longer is existence a universally constant value regardless of mode. The Being he detects now in *Hart-Leap Well* is a spirit transcendent of as well as immanent in nature, a spirit which bodies forth aspects of itself in nature.[6] Thus just as the Pedlar's vision of the "one life" represented a naturalizing of Mortimer's egotistically flawed iconic vision, here Wordsworth's new vision of a Being beyond nature reveals itself as an analogous naturalizing of Rivers' egotistically flawed emblematic vision.

Hartman judges that in *Hart-Leap Well* "Wordsworth's animism, his consciousness of a consciousness in nature, is the last noble superstition of a demythologized mind," and goes on immediately to note that "all nature-spirits are dissolved by him except the spirit of Nature."[7] But at the same time, interestingly, this godlike nature beyond nature is becoming, as it now emerges, increasingly humanized. It loves, suffers loss, and mourns; and its essence thereby defines itself as something other than mere being or thoughtless life—something like a type of mind. The potential consolation, if any, available from this new view of nature remains obscure: Wordsworth is quite vague about "the coming of the milder day" (l. 175) and its value, though his optimistic association of that day's advent with the disappearance of the hart's and Sir Walter's monuments (ll. 175-76), so contrary to his usual lament for the decay of such memorials, signals a striking change in his attitude. But his discovery here in a nature beyond nature of a tendency parallel to man's mental tendencies, and specifically to those memorializing tendencies whereby man struggles against his mortality, suggests whole new worlds of hope.

ii

Increasingly now Wordsworth was finding need for these new hopes, for increasingly his former defenses against what he would soon call "the fear that kills" were failing him. He had by 1802 retreated some distance from the hope of *Tintern Abbey* that man's remembering mind, as "a mansion for all lovely forms," could counter solitude, fear, pain, or grief with soothing memories from its rich store, "healing thoughts / Of tender joy." At least since the Matthew poems he had recognized that grief is itself memory, and suspected the truth of the inverse proposition, that joy thrives only in the absence of memory—as with children and animals, and in the adult's periods of forgetfulness. Even in the ostentatiously cheerful "My heart leaps up" (written 26 March 1802), with its familiar affirmation, "The Child is Father of the Man," "what is sustained from day to day," as Alan Grob notes,

> is not the poet's reenactment of moments of childhood intensity . . . but rather a faith in life's unity abstracted from such moments that enables him to carry on his usual activities with "natural piety." Thus . . . the basis of this confidence is, paradoxically, the irregular both in nature and his own being, the fluctuating emotions that respond to the brief and spasmodic appearances of the rainbow with an intensity remote from his customary feelings.[8]

And Wordsworth's change of mood by the next day, when he began the *Intimations* ode, is famous: able still to see and savor the loveliness of "the earth and every common sight," able still to sympathize with the joyful "heart of May" infusing children, animals, and the earth itself, he nonetheless knows and acknowledges that for him "there hath past away a glory from the earth." Immediately beneath this awareness, of course, a darker knowledge broods—that he himself has passed away from the glory of the earth. The same insight, with the same undertone, penetrates even one of this spring's happiest poems, *A Farewell* (written in late May and early June, 1802), with gnomic pithiness—"'Joy will be gone in its mortality'"—and provokes, like the single tree and single field of the ode which "speak of something that is gone," a memorializing, epitaphic resolve: "Something must stay to tell us of the rest" (ll. 51-52 and app. crit.).

Wordsworth's new realization of what it means, and requires, to be a favorite child of nature finds its barest and most poignant expression in his poem *To H. C.*[9] "H. C." is Hartley Coleridge, here regarded archetypally as a "happy child! / . . . so exquisitely wild" (ll. 11-12) even as he is in the *Intimations* ode. Meditating on the child's future in this subtle revision of Lucy's doom in "Three years she grew," he is moved especially by "many fears / For what may be thy lot in future years" (ll. 13-14), fears all too relevant to Wordsworth's own lot:

> I thought of times when Pain might be thy guest,
> Lord of thy house and hospitality;
> And Grief, uneasy lover! never rest
> But when she sate within the touch of thee.
> O too industrious folly!
> O vain and causeless melancholy!
> Nature will either end thee quite;
> Or, lengthening out thy season of delight,
> Preserve for thee, by individual right,
> A young lamb's heart among the full-grown flocks.
> What hast thou to do with sorrow,
> Or the injuries of tomorrow?
> Thou art a dew-drop, which the morn brings forth,
> Not doom'd to jostle with unkindly shocks,
> Or to be trailed along the soiling earth;
> A gem that glitters while it lives,
> And no forewarning gives;
> But, at the touch of wrong, without a strife
> Slips in a moment out of life.
> [Ll. 15-33 and app. crit.]

Despite his ostensible rejection of "vain and causeless melancholy," Wordsworth's mood here is very darkly melancholy indeed. He allays his initial fears for Hartley's future pains and griefs with the far more frightening conceit that Hartley is innately too rarely innocent a soul ever to be able to tolerate or withstand the tribulations of life.[10] Thus he foresees but two possible fates for the child, prolonged childhood or early death: either nature will shelter him unnaturally from reality, making it possible for him to remain an innocent child at heart even as he grows into adulthood, or impinging reality will destroy him. Yet what possibility is there of the former alternative? Even the Pedlar and Matthew, chosen sons of nature though they were, did not escape pain and grief; and Wordsworth would seem to be dismissing this unreal hope for Hartley with his exclusive closing emphasis rather on the child's fatal vulnerableness, like that of the dewdrop which not only cannot bear touching but, regardless, cannot even long outlive the dawn.[11]

Wordsworth does in fact present at about this time one verse portrait of an adult preserving "a young lamb's heart among the full-grown flocks," but in context the vision offers little encouragement or consolation. I refer to the picture of Hartley's father in Wordsworth's *Stanzas Written in My Pocket-Copy of Thomson's "Castle of Indolence,"* composed 9-11 May 1802:

> Noisy he was, and gamesome as a boy;
> His limbs would toss about him with delight,
> Like branches when strong winds the trees annoy.
> He lacked not implement, device, or toy
> To cheat away the hours that silent were;
>
> . . . .
>
> Instruments had he, playthings for the ear:
> Long blades of grass, plucked round him as he lay,
> These served to catch the wind as it came near,
> Glasses he had with many colours gay
> Others that did all little things display.
>
> [Ll. 47-59 and app. crit.]

But this portrait of Coleridge is deliberately superficial, knowingly misleading. Less than three weeks before, Coleridge had read to Wordsworth the *Letter to Asra*, a first version of his autobiographical *Dejection*, confessing the failure of his "genial spirits" and the painful joylessness of his soul. Wordsworth when he wrote his *Stanzas* therefore knew full well that Coleridge was far from being "as happy a liver as was ever seen" (l. 69 and app. crit.). The poem actually portrays not Coleridge, but a man who is in fact the "great boy in feelings" (*PW* 2:470) that Coleridge only seemed to be, who bears in fact what Coleridge only seemed to bear, "a face divine of heaven-born idiotcy"

(l. 43 app. crit.). As this description strongly suggests, the only way nature might prolong Hartley's childhood would be to give him a mind like Johnny Foy's and a long-lived parent like Betty Foy to protect him.

iii

Precisely the same fear that worried Wordsworth for Hartley Coleridge's sake in *To H. C.* haunts him more openly for his own in *Resolution and Independence* (written 3 May–4 July 1802). He himself has tried to retain "a young lamb's heart among the full-grown flocks," with, naturally enough, only partial success: he can still at times give his heart over fully to "the pleasant season" (l. 19), "as happy as a boy" (l. 18), but in his more thoughtful moods he is troubled, as a thoughtful man must be, by memories and foresight—"old remembrances" (l. 20) that undercut present joy, and the realization that

> there may come another day to me—
> Solitude, pain of heart, distress, and poverty.
>
> [Ll. 34–35]

Hartley's dilemma has become, belatedly, his own:

> My whole life I have lived in pleasant thought,
> As if life's business were a summer mood;
> And they who lived in genial faith found nought
> That grew more willingly than genial good;
> But how can He expect that others should
> Build for him, sow for him, and at his call
> Love him, who for himself will take no heed at all?
>
> [Ll. 36–42 and app. crit.]

Wordsworth's question, in other words, is simply, How can I remain "a happy Child of earth" (l. 31)? And here again he suggests the same two possible answers he had offered in his poem to Hartley. First, the world may somehow, against all practices and indications, provide. Wordsworth had devoted only three lines to this remote possibility in *To H. C.*, and now in *Resolution and Independence* he broaches it even more tentatively—indeed, only implicitly. But while not explicit, the notion would seem present nonetheless in the allusion of stanza 6 (quoted in full just above) to Matthew 6:25–26:

> Therefore I say unto you, Take no thought for your life, what ye
> shall eat, or what ye shall drink; nor yet for your body, what ye shall
> put on. Is not the life more than meat, and the body than raiment?
> Behold the fowls of the air: for they sow not, neither do they
> reap, nor gather into barns; yet your heavenly Father feedeth them.
> Are ye not much better than they?[12]

Alternatively, the world will not provide, winter will succeed
summer, and the "happy Child of earth" who lives as if "life's
business [is] a summer mood" will simply die. This was the main
burden of Wordsworth's fears for Hartley—"Nature will . . .
end thee quite"—as it is of his personal anxiety here. His ques-
tion, "How can He expect that others should / Build for him,
sow for him, . . . / . . . who for himself will take no care at all?"
is, after all, rhetorical: clearly he cannot expect it. And counter-
ing in this spirit the stanza's allusion to Matthew 6 is its even
more direct allusion to Aesop's fable of the grasshopper and the
ants—of the happy, singing poet figure who, instead of laying up
food for winter as the ants were doing, spent his summer in
song and play, "as if life's business were a summer mood," and
so perished of hunger when the winter came.

The cautionary examples of Chatterton and Burns, who as
predecessor poet-naïfs had themselves already undergone Words-
worth's present crisis, convincingly refute the forlorn hope that
nature will forever foster, and instead press home Aesop's moral.
So Wordsworth already knows the answer to his question even
before he asks it: How can he survive beyond youth's term as a
"happy Child of earth"? He can't. And with this realization he
first becomes aware of another traveler near him on the moor, a
remarkably old and decrepit man. In effect, as Alan Grob notes,
this obviously poor, sick, and lonely man

> stands before the narrator like one summoned to authenticate these
> forebodings about the destructive powers of the processes of nature
> and its necessary consequences for the destiny of man. . . . the Leech-
> gatherer seems almost a kind of döppelganger . . . a future apparition
> of the self. . . . a revelation of the poet's own fate.[13]

Yet the truth about him differs from this first impression in in-
teresting and, to Wordsworth, suggestive ways.

To begin with, although the old man, like Wordsworth, lives
apart from "all the ways of men, so vain and melancholy" (l. 21),

still he *does* take heed for himself. He is a self-employed leech-gatherer, "and in this way he gained an honest maintenance" (l. 105). The point of his working for a living is deliberate; for the real-life prototype of this old man had been defeated by the very forces against which the Leech-gatherer of Wordsworth's poem so inspirationally perseveres, his own decrepitude and the increasing scarcity of leeches—"His trade," Dorothy recorded him as saying, "was to gather leeches, but now leeches are scarce, and he had not strength for it" and now "lived by begging" (*DWJ*, p. 42).[14] Anxious to present a man able at once to resist and yet to cope with "all the ways of men," Wordsworth needed to credit his old Leech-gatherer with economic as well as spiritual self-sufficiency, and so swerved from fact to portray him "carrying with him his own fortitude, and the necessities which an unjust state of society has entailed upon him" (*LEY*, pp. 366–67).

Even more importantly, while the old man, again superficially like Wordsworth, spends his life in the eye of nature,[15] yet he is in no way the nature-lover or the "happy Child of earth" that Wordsworth himself pretends and desires to be. The Leech-gatherer is out of doors, not because he feels joyful or playful, but because he has work to do. Wordsworth looks happily on the playful hare, the glistening dew on the grass, the beautiful morning sky, listens happily to the songs of the birds, the roaring of the woods and distant waters. The old man, in pointed contrast, is oblivious to all these. Bent over both "as if [by] some dire constraint of pain, or rage / Of sickness" (ll. 68–69) and by the requirements of his task, he only stands by a pool fixedly staring into its muddy waters for leeches, seeing nothing else and apparently in his concentration hearing nothing at all, not even Wordsworth's approach. Clearly he is no "favorite child" of nature like Matthew, no "chosen son" in the mold of the Pedlar, but rather confirms all the more emphatically, as had the remembered examples of Chatterton and Burns, that the hope of such election is vain and delusive.

Yet perplexingly, provocatively, this feeble man proves after all to be one of the elect. His words, humble as they are, reveal him to be a chosen son, not of nature, but of God; speaking like those "grave Livers . . . , / Religious men, who give to God and man their dues" (ll. 97–98), he tells of his "housing, with God's good help, by choice or chance" (l. 104). He places his filial trust in neither nature nor man, but God only; and while the ways of nature and men take their toll of his body, in this faith his spirit remains triumphantly hale and firm.[16] He makes real the deeper promise of Matthew 6, which, after all, offers no ease from "all fleshly ills" to the body—"Sufficient unto the day is the evil thereof" (Matthew 6:34) bodes quite the opposite—but hope to the spirit. His spiritual kinship reaches back atavistically through Wordsworth's poetry beyond the natural pieties of the Pedlar and the *Lyrical Ballads* to the Baron Herbert of *The Borderers*, even as the teachings of Matthew 6 reflect back typologically to the Elijah sustained by birds in the wilderness who is Herbert's biblical parallel and model. Herbert precisely anticipates the Leech-gatherer's faith:

> Remembering Him who feeds
> The pelican and ostrich of the desert,
> From my own threshold I looked up to Heaven
> And did not want glimmerings of quiet hope.
> [Ll. 1352-55]

With his own adoption now, in the poem's closing lines, of this faith in a transcendent power able to sustain the spirit through "all fleshly ills," Wordsworth at last, and rather abruptly, seizes upon a new help and stay, more secure than that of his love of nature, to preserve man from betrayal by his own mind.

Wordsworth's repeated, seemingly inattentive questioning of the old Leech-gatherer in *Resolution and Independence* has been frequently parodied, most memorably, perhaps, by Lewis Carroll in *Through the Looking-Glass*. The poem is apparently—only apparently—so vulnerable to such treatment, I would suggest, because it is itself something of a Wordsworthian self-parody, directed at his earlier and genuinely vulnerable presentation of a similar confrontation in *We Are Seven*.[17] Like the old man, the little cottage girl is a marvel of mental resoluteness, in effect preaching a doctrine of the "one life" quite as firmly as does the old man his doctrine of faith in a transcendent God. But she speaks as she does out of ignorance, unable to appreciate any notion foreign to what Wordsworth later termed her own "[feeling] of animal vivacity" (*PW* 4: 463):

A simple child, . . .
That lightly draws its breath,
And feels its life in every limb,
What should it know of death?[18]

[Ll. 1–4]

By 1802 Wordsworth has already found such feelings an inadequate defense against the unkindly shocks of life. The Leech-gatherer, in contrast, standing at the other extreme of life's pilgrimage, demonstrates a "human strength" (l. 112) able to sustain itself against all the sorrows and injuries the girl has yet to feel, a resolution able to maintain the independence she has not yet been required to attempt.

iv

Wordsworth did not suddenly in 1802 become a convert to orthodox Anglican Protestant Christianity, of course; and he was still able in 1803 to disturb Coleridge with his irreverent mockery of the Divine Wisdom as interpreted in the mechanistic systems of the eighteenth-century Deists.[19] But with *Resolution and Independence* a new philosophical tone unmistakably enters his work. While not claiming to know God (though references to God do from this time on appear in his writings with increasing frequency), he now begins to posit the existence of a transcendent Power beyond the immanent natural force he had earlier been concerned to celebrate. And he begins also to emphasize the potential strength and magnificence of the human mind, and even to toy with the conceit of its potential immortality.

We gain a hint of Wordsworth's changing attitude toward the grave itself in a well-known anecdote recorded in Dorothy's journal. In 1798 the Pedlar's consoling vision of Margaret dead is simply, "She sleeps in the calm earth and peace is here." But in her entry for 29 April 1802 Dorothy writes the following of her brother:

We then went to John's Grove, sate a while at first. Afterwards William lay, and I lay in the trench under the fence—he with his eyes shut and listening to the waterfalls and the Birds. There was no one waterfall above another—it was a sound of waters in the air—the voice of the air. William heard me breathing and rustling now and then, but we both lay still, and unseen by one another. He thought that it would be as sweet thus to lie so in the grave, to hear the *peaceful* sounds of the earth and just to know that our dear friends were near. [*DWJ*, p. 117]

Now Wordsworth is tentatively, hopefully visualizing death as a kind of pleasant trance wherein we rest still conscious and thoughtful, still possessing our human identities. His notion here is occasional and private, of course, and as such by itself warrants no great emphasis. But soon after this he gives it poetic and public expression in "Methought I saw the footsteps of a throne," where he passes through the mists shrouding the throne of Death to discover there, not a grim specter, but

> one
> Sleeping alone within a mossy cave,
> With her face up to heaven; that seemed to have
> Pleasing remembrance of a thought foregone;
> A lovely Beauty in a summer grave!
>
> [Ll. 10-14]

And his subsequent poetry continues to confirm that Dorothy's journal entry does indeed mark a new tendency of his thought.

The episode at John's Grove occurred only four days before Wordsworth began writing *Resolution and Independence*. Dorothy records an even more uncharacteristic anecdote about her brother on 13 June, apparently only shortly before he renewed work on the poem:

> The full moon (not quite full) was among a company of steady island clouds, and the sky bluer above it than the natural sky blue. William observed that the full moon above a dark fir grove is a fine image of the descent of a superior being. [*DWJ*, p. 135]

Significantly, Wordsworth repeats and elaborates upon this figurative allusion in a new context late in 1802:[20]

> It is no Spirit who from heaven hath flown,
> And is descending on his embassy;
> Nor Traveller gone from earth the heavens to espy!
> 'Tis Hesperus—there he stands with glittering crown,
> First admonition that the sun is down!
>
> ["It is no Spirit," ll. 1-5]

And this time he dares to make explicit the transcendental hope which his imagery but thinly veils, a hope to become himself that heavenly traveler and immortal spirit:

> O most ambitious star! an inquest wrought
> Within me when I recognized thy light;
> My mind was startled at the unusual sight:
> And, while I gazed, there came to me a thought
> That I might step beyond my natural race
> As thou seem'st now to do; might one day trace
> Some ground not mine; and, strong her strength above,
> My Soul, an Apparition in the place,
> Tread there with steps that no one shall reprove!
> [Ll. 9-17 and app. crit.]

These transcendental thoughts remain but momentary flights above Wordsworth's customarily more earthbound concerns in 1802-3, although certainly his preservation in verse of one such moment in "It is no Spirit" constitutes an important preface to the *Intimations* ode of early 1804. As *Resolution and Independence* makes clear, his new hopes for the grace of a supplementary, transcendental strength instead seek more immediately a "help and stay" for man's earthly life. And as a further expression of this search, the *Ode to Duty* (early 1804) is forthrightly a natural sequel to the more genuinely crucial poem of 1802. Carefully in the *Ode to Duty* Wordsworth recapitulates the anxieties provoking *Resolution and Independence.* Those innocents

> who, in love and truth,
> Without misgiving do rely
> Upon the genial sense of youth
> [Ll. 10-12 and app. crit.]

are happy and blessed, but nevertheless, in their blissful ignorance, vulnerable to failure; so "even these may live to know / That they have hopes to seek, strength which elsewhere must grow" (ll. 23-24 and app. crit.). This specifically "human strength" which yet comes from without is precisely that which Wordsworth finds and receives in *Resolution and Independence*, and which he here, "made lowly wise" (l. 61; see *Paradise Lost* 8.173-74), characterizes as "the spirit of self-sacrifice" joined to "the confidence of reason" (ll. 62-63). He commends himself now, at the conclusion of the *Ode to Duty*, to God's "Stern Lawgiver" that "dost wear / The Godhead's most benignant grace" (ll. 49-50)—the grace, clearly, of Miltonic "right reason" itself—just as he had commended himself to God at the conclusion of the earlier poem. These parallels are pointed; Wordsworth is now confirming his dedication, ceremonially and as it were publicly reaffirming his private vow. In the process, he formally recognizes mankind's radical distinctness from the natural world—the distinctness, in effect, of "Thy will be mine" from "Thy will be done." Nature definitionally obeys, in its very being manifests, God's will; the most famous lines of the poem, "Thou dost preserve the stars from wrong; / And the most ancient heavens, through Thee, are fresh and strong" (ll. 55-56), make this quite clear. But man instead in his wisdom *chooses* God's will—

> I supplicate for thy control;
>
> . . . .
>
> Yet not the less would I throughout
> Still act according to the voice
> Of my own wish; and feel past doubt
> That my submissiveness was choice:
>
> . . . .
>
> Denial and restraint I prize
> No farther than they breed a second Will more wise
> [Ll. 35-48]

—or in his foolish willfulness rejects it (l. 8/9 app. crit.). Man alone, this suggests, is created mentally in God's image, possessing will and reason—which is also to say that God acquires definition, as he had more anonymously and vaguely in *Hart-Leap Well*, as a great type of Mind.

PART III: 1804–1805

Introduction

THE NEW METAPHYSICS of man, nature, and God which Wordsworth had been meditating and evolving since 1800 at last matures into its finest and fullest expression in 1804, first in the *Intimations* ode and then, most grandly, in *The Prelude*. The chief impetus to this philosophical development, as we have seen, was his increasing and increasingly conscious valuation of that which is uniquely human in life, of reasoning man as something special in the world. As he pursued the ramifications of this new tenet, Wordsworth came to revise his earlier beliefs in two significant and closely related respects. First, he gradually shifted from a monistic to a dualistic view of the universe. By 1804, he recognizes not one but two fundamental forces in the world: nature and the human mind. Second, he gradually reconceived the ultimate Presence of the natural world—be it called the Nature-behind-nature, Power, or God—as not simply a life-force, but a mental force.

As a result of these fundamental philosophical reconceptions, Wordsworth in 1804 develops a new way of seeing and understanding the natural world and man's relation to it. He now sees nature's essence and power as being analogous to the human mind's. This is not, be it noted, equivalent to making a claim for the human mind's divinity or immortality, to apotheosizing it as a demiurge of the created and perceived world. Notwithstanding Geoffrey Hartman's contention that the Snowdon episode provides "a culminating evidence that imagination and the light of nature are one," precisely the opposite would seem to be true. Analogy is not identity; and Wordsworth is quite careful in *The Prelude* never to claim that these two autonomous imaginations, these two lights, are one—on the contrary, he takes particular care to distinguish them.[1]

Wordsworth's belief in nature's autonomous, objective significance (as opposed to the purely subjective significance he had allowed it in *The*

Borderers) lends new importance to his emblematic reading of her forms. Now, as James Heffernan has observed in a more general context, "abstract meaning is not imposed upon an object; it is elicited *from* the object. . . . the imagination *extracts* from the object its *internal* significance, and it [the object] becomes an emblem or a part of a complex emblem. It becomes the incarnation of a timeless, invisible truth."[2] At the same time, Wordsworth's sense of the great, essential analogy between nature and mind inevitably nurtures, thrives upon, and vastly enriches his imagination's emblematizing tendency, his bent toward allegorically apprehending the world's truths. And both the *Intimations* ode and *The Prelude* demonstrate how subtle and complex his handling of this mode in his poetry could be. In these poems more than anywhere else in his work, Wordsworth's allegorizing impulse blends effectively with his more celebrated attentiveness to "the vulgar forms of present things / And actual world of our familiar days" (*Prelude 1805* 12.361-62). We shall do well, as we read them, to remember that what Wordsworth saw "in life's every-day appearances" was not simply those appearances, but

> a new world, a world, too, that was fit
> To be transmitted and made visible
> To other eyes.
>
> [12.369, 371-73]

Thus if his vision was natural in its orientation, it was yet allegorical in its mode: beholding "the letter of the outward promise," he aspired to "read the invisible soul" (12.254-55).

CHAPTER 5
"The Eternal Mind":
The *Intimations* Ode and the
Early Books of *The Prelude*

i

VERY EARLY IN 1804, with Coleridge on the point of leaving the Lake District forever, Wordsworth resumed work on his "poem to Coleridge," *The Prelude*. Five years had lapsed since the winter at Goslar when he had begun writing an autobiographical poem, and at least four since he had completed (save for an introduction) and set aside the two-part *Prelude* of 1798–99. In the following few years he tinkered with the poem occasionally, probably completing the 54-line "preamble" in January 1800 (*CMY*, p. 629) and the opening 167 lines of book 3 (36 important lines of which he had originally written in 1798 and 1799 for *The Ruined Cottage* and now transferred from it) by the end of 1801 (*CMY*, p. 633), but did nothing to alter its philosophical stance. As we have seen, however, Wordsworth's metaphysical attitudes had by 1804 altered significantly. Now, returning "after a long sleep" (*LEY*, p. 432) to his autobiographical narrative and meditations, he was prepared and increasingly inclined to interpret his intellectual growth in a new light.

In the first few months of 1804 Wordsworth reviewed and lightly revised what he had already written of *The Prelude*, and probably also now filled out book 1 with lines 55–271 (*CMY*, pp. 12, 634). Beyond this, going on regularly and rapidly in a prolonged fit of poetic effort (see *LEY*, pp. 432, 440, 451, 456, 477), he composed the bulk of book 3, all of books 4 and 5, and the opening sections of book 13 in about ten weeks, by 18 March. And sometime before 6 March he also returned to and completed the *Intimations* ode, begun and then shelved almost two years before. Written at such a time and surveying as it does the period of childhood already treated years before in the first two books of *The Prelude*, the ode affords not only a strong, summary sense of the new philosophical stance Wordsworth was assuming at this time and its differences from his earlier beliefs, but also a particularly interesting perspective on Wordsworth's linking of those two early books with the subsequent ones of 1804–1805.

In a very real, if perverse, sense, the *Intimations* ode provides the rhetorical glue which binds the 1798–99 and the 1804–1805 books of *The Prelude* together. Whether or not Wordsworth consciously intended the effect, he very definitely evokes in the ode certain specific recollections from books 1 and 2 in guises nicely tailored to the philosophy of the books which follow. He thereby obscures, within the broader sweep of the complete *Prelude*, an important truth to which Geoffrey Hartman has recently sensitized Wordsworth's readers within the much narrower compass of a single episode in book 6—that "reflection, in Wordsworth, becomes reflexive," that, in a poem which is also an autobiography, interpretation can be revised in the reviewing or retelling, that *The Prelude* kinetically represents as well as statically records "the growth of a poet's mind."[1]

Wordsworth's obscuration in 1804 of his own earlier beliefs has in truth proved notably effective. All too often, for example, we see the "intimations" of the *Intimations* ode identified with the "obscure feelings representative / Of joys that were forgotten" (*Prelude 1805* 1.634–35) and similarly linked to "those fleeting moods / Of shadowy exultation" wherein

> the soul,
> Remembering how she felt, but what she felt
> Remembering not, retains an obscure sense
> Of possible sublimity.[2]

[2.331–32, 334–37]

This practice, moreover, is entirely understandable. For Wordsworth himself all too obviously provokes precisely this critical association and identification with his talk in the ode of birth as a "forgetting" which Nature does all she can to foster and his thanksgiving that, nonetheless, the child experiences and the man vestigially remembers intimations of his soul's source in

> Blank misgivings of a Creature
> Moving about in worlds not realized,
> High instincts before which our mortal Nature
> Did tremble like a guilty Thing surprised:
> . . . those first affections,
> Those shadowy recollections. . . .
>
> [Ll. 145-50]

Yet if we restore these isolated passages to their proper contexts in the two poems, we must see at once how essentially disparate the ode and the early *Prelude* actually are. For the intimations of immortality which the ode celebrates are quite definitely not natural but supernatural in origin, not from "inland" experience but from "that immortal sea" (ll. 163-64), not from our nurse and foster-mother, Nature (ll. 82-83), but from "God, who is our home" (l. 65). But those "obscure feelings representative / Of joys that were forgotten," by contrast, are in context patently naturalistic experiences. Wordsworth's immediate reference here is to "the vulgar joy [which] by its own weight / Wearied itself out of memory,"

> those fits of vulgar joy
> Which, through all seasons, on a child's pursuits
> Are prompt attendants, . . . that giddy bliss
> Which, like a tempest, works along the blood
> And is forgotten,

times when "the earth / And common face of Nature spoke to me / Rememberable things" (*Prelude 1805* 1.609-16, 625-26). And much the same thing is true of the book 2 passage, where again the stimulus of "those fleeting moods / Of shadowy exultation" is clearly naturalistic; for Wordsworth here specifically attributes this "sublimer joy" (2.321) to his increasing openness to "Nature's finer influxes" (2.298), his new, watchful sensitivity to the "transitory qualities" (2.309) and "minuter properties / Of objects which already are belov'd" (2.301-2).[3]

These early *Prelude* passages are not, of course, incompatible with the ode. On the contrary, they accord perfectly with the scheme of growth propounded in the poem's fifth section:

Shades of the prison-house begin to close
   Upon the growing Boy,
But he beholds the light, and whence it flows,
   He sees it in his joy;
The Youth, who daily farther from the east
Must travel, still is Nature's Priest,
   And by the vision splendid
   Is on his way attended.
                                    [Ll. 67-75 and app. crit.]

But Wordsworth's interpretations of these childhood experiences differ significantly in the two poems. Seen from the ode's 1804 perspective, the book 1 passage appears to be an example of the growing boy's joy in the visionary gleams of whose supernatural quality he (and Wordsworth still in 1799) is nevertheless ignorant, and the book 2 passage, an example of the youth's (and the 1799 Wordsworth's) increasingly mistaken service as Nature's priest. Indeed, in the larger context of this latter passage Wordsworth explicitly presents his behavior as a kind of priestly service—an "intimate communion" (*Prelude 1805* 2.300), a "spirit of religious love in which / I walked with Nature" (2.376-77), a time of "obeisance" and "devotion" (2.394). Even the claim, "Thence did I drink the visionary power" (2.330), strikes the hierophantic tone of one initiated into the sacred mysteries. And the book ends with a direct address to Coleridge as

                                    one,
The most intense of Nature's worshippers
In many things my Brother, chiefly here
In this my deep devotion.
                                    [2.476-79]

   In summary, it seems clear, first, that in 1799 Wordsworth was not thinking of birth as a forgetting and of godhead as something to be obscurely sensed only outside of and despite the sensations fostered by nature; and second, that when he came in 1804 to finish the *Intimations* ode, Wordsworth was careful to integrate into its fabric not just the experiences of his youth, but also the tone and almost the very language of his own earlier (but not youthful), 1799 meditations upon those experiences.
   To these conclusions we may perhaps add a third, that in

the ode Wordsworth was actually revising the biography of his earlier years in more than one sense—not just "reviewing" or "reseeing" it, but even tampering with its constituent facts, changing or adding to its historical episodes. For the language of the ode does indeed, however misleadingly, associate the two early *Prelude* passages we have been examining with the ode's explications of our natal forgetting of heaven and our youthful "blank misgivings of a Creature / Moving about in worlds not realized." The effect is as if Wordsworth were attempting retroactively to credit his earlier poem with the recognition and presentation of feelings about which it (and for that matter all of Wordsworth's poetry before 1804) in truth remained silent—or, alternatively and even more disturbingly, as if he were attributing to his earlier life feelings which in truth he had not then experienced.

Wordsworth was in later life quite explicit about the nature and quality of these feelings, which he ascribed to his youthful "indisposition to bend to the law of death, as applying to our own particular case" (*LMY* 2:619). In the famous Fenwick note to the ode, speaking of those "particular feelings or *experiences* of my own mind on which the structure of the poem partly rests," he elaborates,

Nothing was more difficult for me in childhood than to admit the notion of death as a state applicable to my own being. I have said elsewhere—

"A simple child,
That lightly draws its breath,
And feels its life in every limb,
What should it know of death!"—

But it was not so much from feelings of animal vivacity that *my* difficulty came as from a sense of the indomitableness of the Spirit within me. I used to brood over the stories of Enoch and Elijah, and almost to persuade myself that, whatever might become of others, I should be translated, in something of the same way, to heaven. With a feeling congenial to this, I was often unable to think of external things as having external existence, and I communed with all I saw as something not apart from, but inherent in, my own immaterial nature. Many times while going to school have I grasped at a wall or tree to recall myself from this abyss of idealism to the reality. At that time I was afraid of such processes. In later periods of life I have deplored, as we have all reason to do, a subjugation of an opposite character, and have rejoiced over the remembrances, as is expressed in the lines—

> "Obstinate questionings
> Of sense and outward things,
> Fallings from us, vanishings;" etc.[4]
>
> [*PW* 4:463]

The oft-quoted anecdotes of R. P. Graves and Bonamy Price very aptly reinforce the Fenwick note:

> I remember Mr. Wordsworth saying that, at a particular stage of his mental progress, he used to be frequently so rapt into an unreal transcendental world of ideas that the external world seemed no longer to exist in relation to him, and he had to reconvince himself of its existence *by clasping a tree*, or something that happened to be near him. [*PW* 4:467]

> The venerable old man [Wordsworth] . . . clenched the top bar [of a gate] firmly with his right hand, pushed strongly against it, and then uttered these ever-memorable words: "There was a time in my life when I had to push against something that resisted, to be sure that there was anything outside me. I was sure of my own mind; everything else fell away, and vanished into thought." [*PW* 4:467]

And Wordsworth himself reaffirms in his first *Essay upon Epitaphs* his belief and personal experience that "the consciousness of a principle of immortality in the human soul," the "intimation or assurance within us, that some part of our nature is imperishable," dates from the very dawn of life:

> If we look back upon the days of childhood, we shall find that the time is not in remembrance when, with respect to our own individual Being, the mind was without this assurance. [*Prose* 1:50]

In the face of all this testimony, however, there remains the striking fact that not once before 1804 does Wordsworth allude to such a remembrance or such a childhood experience. The letter to Catherine Clarkson dates from December 1814; the Fenwick note, from 1843; the Graves and Price anecdotes, from the poet's old age; and the *Essay upon Epitaphs*, from December 1809 or early 1810. There are only, I think, two instances in

Wordsworth's writings before 1804 which attest to the child's sense of immortality. The better known of these, often cited as an anticipation of the *Intimations* ode and associated with it in the Fenwick note by Wordsworth himself, is *We Are Seven.*[5] Less familiar—indeed, only a manuscript revision which Wordsworth never published—are a few lines, dating from 1794, added to his *An Evening Walk* of 1793:

> What tribes of happy youth have gambolled here [in the Grasmere
> churchyard],
> Nor in their wild mirth ever thought how near
> Their sensible warm motion was allied
> To the dull earth that crumbled at their side.
> Even now of that gay train who there pursue
> Their noisy sports with rapture ever new
> There are to whom the buoyant heart proclaims
> Death has no power oer their particular frames
> As the light spirit the perpetual glee
> The spring of body once proclaimed to me.[6]
> [*PW* 1:7 app. crit.]

But as we have seen, Wordsworth himself in the Fenwick note to the ode explicitly attributes the girl's attitude in *We Are Seven* to "feelings of animal vivacity" quite distinct from the transcendental intimations which are the ode's true subject; and the *Evening Walk* lines similarly are quite explicitly about and specifically limited to that same sense of animal vivacity. By 1810, to be sure, Wordsworth was outspokenly anxious to refute such a derivation of the child's sense of immortality:

> Forlorn, and cut off from communication with the best part of his
> nature, must that Man be, who should derive the sense of immor-
> tality, as it exists in the mind of a child, from the same unthinking
> gaiety or liveliness of animal Spirits with which the Lamb in the
> meadow, or any other irrational Creature, is endowed; who should
> ascribe it, in short, to blank ignorance in the Child; to an inability
> arising from the imperfect state of his faculties to come, in any point
> of his being, into contact with a notion of death; or to an unreflect-
> ing acquiescence in what had been instilled in him! [*Prose* 1:50-51]

Before 1804, however, there is not the slightest evidence that he himself had ever derived it any other way.[7]

I am not trying to argue that Wordsworth never as a child

experienced those feelings of the immateriality of the external world which he later so frequently recollected, though I think it salutary to see that the issue is genuinely moot. More important is that we recognize the philosophical discontinuousness of the 1799 and 1804 autobiographies, a discontinuousness which Wordsworth's language in 1804 is calculated to obscure. The ode does not represent an absolute break with Wordsworth's past thought, of course, but far less is it simply a reorganized presentation of familiar ideas. In order properly to appreciate Wordsworth's special philosophical stance in this poem, we must take particular care not to confuse his ideas here anachronistically with notions prelevant in his work of a few years before or after.

ii

What is the "immortality" of which the great *Intimations* ode treats? Critics separate into two basic schools of thought on this all-important question. The great majority, regarding the poem as an essentially humanist document, interpret its "immortality" figuratively in one way or another—a view all the more dominant for being shared by readers whose interpretations of Wordsworth otherwise so widely diverge. A few brief quotations can quickly indicate the general character of this position: Beatty holds that "the 'immortality' in this poem is not the theological term which signifies endlessness of life, but the infiniteness of the human consciousness"; G. Wilson Knight, that the poem is "a vision of essential, all-conquering, life"; Hirsch, that "immortality is continuous cyclicity" of life (cf. Knight); Bloom, that immortality is the reverse of "separateness," is precisely that "'primal sympathy' of one human with another" which is fostered by "the imaginative power"; and Hartman, that man's intimations of immortality are "intimations of his unself-conscious powers of relationship" (cf. Bloom).[8]

Against this view a distinct minority of critics persist in taking "immortality" personally and literally and so reading the poem as a genuinely transcendental statement. Thus Thomas M. Raysor contends that Wordsworth is declaring a "faith in the permanence of self-conscious individual identity," his "philosophic mind" being "that of the Christian philosopher who perceives through reflection what the child perceived intuitively, that is, the immortality of the soul"; Florence Marsh rather reluctantly concludes that in the ode Wordsworth turns "from divine immanence to divine transcendence," from "the kingdom of heaven within us" to "a kingdom of heaven after death"; and Grob, following Raysor in accepting at face value the poem's "Christian dualism of heaven and earth, soul and body, immortality and mortality," sees the poet here finally acquiring "the knowledge of a fixed and changeless order beyond nature and of the indestructibility of his own spiritual being."[9]

While my critical sympathies here incline somewhat toward the latter group of readers insofar as they are willing to confront the unmistakably transcendental implications of what Wordsworth writes, I cannot concur with either of these two basic readings of the poem. Clearly, when Wordsworth dictated the Fenwick note on the ode, and even when he wrote his first *Essay upon Epitaphs*, he believed, along philosophical lines at least close to those of orthodox Christianity, in the immortality of the individual soul. But when he wrote the ode in early 1804, I would suggest, he did not quite or exactly believe this; and the ode carefully records the tentativeness and the skepticism of his faith and speculations.

The major interpretative crux of the ode is not, despite the straw-man arguments of various critics, the image of the child, which has perplexed few if any readers since Coleridge and did not, I think, so entirely baffle him as is usually assumed. The real crux, and still a crux today despite so many assaults upon it, centers upon Wordsworth's multiple tropes for the individual soul. A great deal depends, for example, upon how we conceive of "our life's Star" (l. 59). Is its light innate or borrowed? Transient or eternal? Wordsworth's at once daring and tentative—and potentially confusing—answer to these questions is, ambivalently, "Both." In order properly to follow his speculations here, however, we must first clearly understand the poetic cosmography through which he presents them.

Wordsworth's cosmological model images all of life in terms of two hemispheres of sky: the hemisphere over our heads, which we see throughout our lives, and the hemisphere of our antipodes, the sky over the opposite side of the earth, which of course we cannot see. He presents the former as the mortal, naturalistic world, the latter as the heavenly, transcendent world; the boundary between them, the horizon of man's mortal sight, demarcates the events of birth and death and the bournes of human understanding, the limits of man's mortal experience and the extremes of knowledge. And just as this mortal world is illuminated by the sun, "the light of common day" (l. 77), so is the heavenly world illuminated by God, the source of supernatural light and glory.[10]

Using this cosmography as a poetic framework, Wordsworth is able to pick up the transcendental notion implicit in his earlier mention of the "celestial light" which once seemed to "apparel" all the earth (l. 4) and elaborate it into a quasi-Platonic (or, as we perhaps more accurately should say, quasi-Vergilian) myth of origins, the first side of his ambivalent larger trope. He begins by postulating God, the source of heavenly light, as our true father (in contrast to our foster mother, Nature). Man, as he passes the boundary of birth separating the heavenly world from this earthly one, simultaneously leaves God's realm of light, just as a planet or star rising above the horizon into our view simultaneously is setting from the antipodal hemisphere. But in infancy man is still very close to God's realm, and its now indirect light remains present to him like a twilight; thus "heaven lies about us in our infancy" (l. 66) even though we are then no longer in heaven. For a while the "visionary gleam" (l. 56) of this indirect celestial light clothes all that man sees in nature.[11] Gradually, however, as he ages, this special, celestial gleam fades from his vision, just as the stars and planets of the nighttime sky "fade into the light of common day" (l. 77), the sunlight which outshines and overwhelms them.

In the terms of this complex trope, immortality and divinity inhere in the celestial light, which is of God; for Wordsworth here as for Milton in *Paradise Lost*, "God is Light" and the celestial light is "bright effluence of bright essence increate" (*Paradise Lost* 3.3, 6). And this celestial light, properly a feature of the transcendent, heavenly world, enters this mortal world with the newborn man as a kind of afterglow, an evanescent nimbus of glory. It matters not whether we regard the soul-star of Wordsworth's trope as a planet reflecting the celestial light or a true star actually radiating a portion of that light, so long as we recognize that this light ultimately originates not in the star but in God.[12]

But to understand Wordsworth's figure of celestial light here is also to understand, finally, what he means in the ode by "immortality." The Immortality which broods on the child is not his personal immortality, but the glorious aura of God, his source and home, which yet for a while surrounds him. Wordsworth's 1804 phrasing, "O Thou on whom thy Immortality / Broods like the Day" (ll. 119-20 and app. crit.), points up a significant parallel construction obscured by later revision: the Immortality broods on the child just as the great truths of life rest on him (l. 116). Both the immortality and the truths are extrinsic to him; and inevitably he will lose the one just as he will lose the other (as we all do, who "are toiling all our lives to find" those truths again [l. 117]), and just as he will lose the celestial light. And when Wordsworth shifts his figure in stanza 9 he is careful nonetheless to reaffirm this fundamental distinction between the child and the Immortality:

> Hence in a season of calm weather
> Though inland far we be,
> Our Souls have sight of that immortal sea
> Which brought us hither,
> Can in a moment travel thither,
> And see the Children sport upon the shore,
> And hear the mighty waters rolling evermore.
>
> [Ll. 162-68]

Here the sea is immortal; the Children, however, are not. To repeat: the immortality of which Wordsworth speaks in the ode is not the immortality of the particular individual but rather the immortality of his transcendent source.[13]

Balancing his figuration of man's soul as shining with immortal but extrinsic light, Wordsworth also develops in the ode a figure very much the reverse, comprising the other side of his ambivalent larger trope. This, as stanza 9 finally makes explicit—"O joy! that in our embers / Is something that doth live" (ll. 130-31)—is the traditional image of man's life as a fire burning with intrinsic but mortal radiance. Even while the growing man is being gradually divested of the transcendent raiment which clothed him at birth, he is simultaneously putting on the sadly contrasting burdens of mortality—"the inevitable yoke" (l. 125), the "earthly freight" (l. 127), the weight of custom, "heavy as frost, and deep almost as life!" (ll. 128-29). Wordsworth's trope in this aspect figures mortality even as in its other aspect it figures immortality. And the consolations available to mortal man's "philosophic mind" are but finite; "the faith that looks through death" (l. 126), though often taken too readily as a distinctively Christian affirmation, seems in context to be after all more genuinely humanistic and even stoic, a reliance on "the human heart by which we live" (l. 201) and "the soothing thoughts that spring / Out of human suffering" (ll. 184-85).[14]

Thus while Wordsworth in the ode certainly recognizes a transcendent and immortal life-force in the world, he carefully stops short of ceding transcendence and immortality to the individual, self-conscious identity. He does not, we must note, claim in the great affirmation of stanza 9 to know that his individual soul possesses this immortality. As Kenneth Johnston cogently observes in his admirably sensitive and sensible essay on the ode,

> [Wordsworth's] "shadowy recollections" (49) are not of his childhood; they are the recollections he *had* in his childhood of the immortal state of the soul which, metaphorically speaking, preceded childhood. Now, in the present tense of the poem, the "visionary gleam" (56) has fled, because Wordsworth cannot recall his immortal condition, not even in a shadowy fashion. But he can recall that he could once recall his immortal state, and this memory of a memory is the source of consolation and ground of faith articulated in the concluding sections of the Ode.[15]

But this consolation, by its very nature, can be only tentative and partial, for certainty lies irrecoverably lost behind the veil of forgetfulness. And Wordsworth remains true throughout the poem to this tentativeness. We see it clearly, for example, in his final allusion to the light:

> The Clouds that gather round the setting sun
> Do take a sober colouring from an eye
> That hath kept watch o'er man's mortality.
> [Ll. 197-99]

In truth, we must remember, such sunset clouds are gloriously colored and irradiated, even as are the eastern clouds of dawn and this natural fact accords perfectly with Wordsworth's transcendent, cosmological trope, according to which our death should be but an awakening and a remembering, and the setting of our life's star a rising into the transcendent world, a return to the celestial light which is our source and home. That this image affords Wordsworth less than a personal or a complete consolation, however, appears starkly in his envisioning of it here, as the sober coloring lent these clouds by his mortality-conscious eye simply overwhelms the bright coloring lent them by the sun. What may be clouds of glory are still but too certainly also the mists of death.

But if Wordsworth does not in the ode grant immortality to the human mind, yet he again does, as he has so often since *Hart-Leap Well*, grant Mind to the Immortality. And now, significantly, he makes this attribution explicit: the Child, he says, the "best Philosopher, who yet dost keep / [His] heritage," is "haunted for ever by the eternal mind" (ll. 111–14). Increasingly now in 1804 Wordsworth found himself haunted by the intimations of this haunting. Ultimately, his meditations on this theme become the true counterplot of *The Prelude*, pervasively underlying the explicit plot, his account of and musings on the growth of his mind, and together with that plot climaxing in the great passage on the ascent of Snowdon.

iii

The striking tropes of the *Intimations* ode are perhaps unexampled in Wordsworth's poetry, but the new metaphysical tenets and attitudes which enter his work with this poem also significantly inform the contemporary books of *The Prelude*. Even the notion of our preexistence reappears there, as when he speaks of childhood as an

> isthmus which we cross
> In progress from our native continent
> To earth and human life,
>   [*Prelude 1805* 5.560-62]

or when he exclaims,

> O Heavens! how awful is the might of Souls,
> And what they do within themselves, while yet

The yoke of earth is new to them, the world
Nothing but a wild field where they were sown.[16]
[3.178-81]

We should remember also the striking and little-noted passage in book 4 wherein Wordsworth, newly home on summer vacation from his freshman year at Cambridge, takes stock of himself during his first walk of the year around his familiar Lake Esthwaite:

> I had hopes and peace
> And swellings of the spirits, was rapt and soothed,
> Convers'd with promises, had glimmering views
> How Life pervades the undecaying mind,
> How the immortal Soul with God-like power
> Informs, creates, and thaws the deepest sleep
> That time can lay upon her; how on earth,
> Man, if he do but live within the light
> Of high endeavours, daily spreads abroad
> His being with a strength that cannot fail.
> Nor was there want of milder thoughts, of love,
> And more than pastoral quiet, in the heart
> Of amplest projects; and a peaceful end
> At last, or glorious, by endurance won.
> [4.152-66]

The explicit division of Wordsworth's thoughts here interestingly continues the dualistic pattern of the ode. His musings on mind and soul are outspokenly idealistic intimations of immortality; but his accompanying "milder thoughts," culminating as they do in the calm anticipation of a peaceful or glorious death, clearly bespeak a contrasting watch over man's mortality. Here again, as in the ode, Wordsworth sustains himself with a balance of idealistic and naturalistic consolations.[17] And as in the ode, his idealistic speculations remain tentative—"glimmering views" at best. "Our simple childhood sits upon a throne / That hath more power than all the elements," he claims, but he claims no more: "I guess not what this tells of Being past, / Nor what it augurs of the life to come" (5.532-35).

Perhaps the most succinct indication of *The Prelude*'s new direction appears not in an addition, however, but in a revision. The passage in point, following immediately upon the boat-stealing episode, is Wordsworth's thankful apostrophe to the

power or powers which shaped his growing soul by the discipline
of fear. In 1799, Wordsworth addresses

> ye Beings of the hills!
> And ye that walk the woods and open heaths
> By moon or star-light.
> [*Prelude 1799* 1.130-32]

But in 1804 his sense of this power has changed radically:

> Wisdom and Spirit of the Universe!
> Thou Soul that art Eternity of Thought!
> That giv'st to forms and images a breath
> And everlasting motion!
> [*Prelude 1805* 1.428-31]

What had once seemed to him to be spirits of nature he now
conceives as a power beyond nature—and this power not merely
a great life-force, but no less than "the eternal mind"; not
merely a sensibility, but an intelligence, a presence of true
Wisdom and Thought.[18]

CHAPTER 6
"The Perfect Image of a Mighty Mind":
Snowdon and Its Analogues

i

EVEN AS EARLY AS the first months of 1804, while still thinking of his "Poem to Coleridge" as a work in five books now nearing completion, Wordsworth intended to open the final book with the account of his ascent of Snowdon. When in the course of writing this concluding book he suddenly and drastically, on about 10 March 1804, changed his conception of the poem and reoriented his efforts toward realizing its longer, thirteen-book form, he still reserved the Snowdon episode for the opening of the final book. Now, moreover, he emphatically presented it, in splendid isolation, as the culminating and concluding vision of *The Prelude*.[1]

While Wordsworth utilizes his Snowdon vision as a perfectly summarizing image of his theme, however, he in fact wrote the episode before composing the great bulk of books 5-13. Indeed, he seems to have been explicating the Snowdon vision at the very time he decided to recast the poem and expand it with those books; and very possibly, I would suggest, its explication actually provoked that revision and expansion.[2] Quite simply, Wordsworth's meditations upon Snowdon represent an important development, even a breakthrough, in his thought. Despite the episode's belatedness in the finished poem, it stands chronologically as a precursor and prototype of the visionary insights in the preceding seven books, and both guides and organizes Wordsworth's argument throughout the entire *Prelude*. Here in the poem, as before Wordsworth in the Snowdon scene itself, lies the breathing place wherein lodges "the Soul, the Imagination of the Whole" (*Prelude 1805* 13.65).

As the climactic passage of *The Prelude*, the Snowdon episode has of course attracted considerable and intense critical scrutiny. Nevertheless, some of its more explicit and fundamental effects continue to go generally unappreciated. I think we may approach these essential features by way of one simple, even obvious question: exactly why does Wordsworth regard and single out this particular scene, this one view among all those he has beheld, as "the perfect image of a mighty Mind" (13.69)? For the notion of such a correspondence of mind and nature is frequently close to the surface of *The Prelude*. Thus Wordsworth speaks of his intention at college

> To apprehend all passions and all moods
> Which time, and place, and season do impress
> Upon the visible universe.
> [3:85-87]

Similarly in a MS. Y passage, omitted from the completed poem, he recounts how the growing youth, in the "season of his second birth,"

> feels that, be his mind however great
> In aspiration, the universe in which
> He lives is equal to his mind, that each
> Is worthy of the other. . . .
>
> . . . .
>
> Whatever dignity there be ——
> Within himself, from which he gathers hope,
> There doth he feel its counterpart the same
> In kind before him outwardly express'd,
> With difference that makes the likeness clear.
> [*Prelude 1850*, pp. 575-76]

More specifically still, he alludes to the chaotically opposed and mingled aspects of the Gondo Ravine as "workings of one mind, the features / Of the same face" (*Prelude 1805* 6.568-69). Never, though, does Wordsworth so insist upon and develop the notion as here in the Snowdon episode. Precisely what makes the Snowdon mind image so "perfect"?

What makes this scene particularly remarkable and unusual,

at any rate, is its structural reflexivity or *dédoublement*, its repetition of itself:

> On the shore
> I found myself of a huge sea of mist,
> Which, meek and silent, rested at my feet:
> A hundred hills their dusky backs upheaved
> All over this still Ocean, and beyond,
> Far, far beyond, the vapours shot themselves,
> In headlands, tongues, and promontory shapes,
> Into the Sea, the real Sea, that seem'd
> To dwindle, and give up its majesty,
> Usurp'd upon as far as sight could reach.
>
> [13.42-51]

The scene is so powerfully suggestive to Wordsworth, so uniquely able to stop and stun him with the force of sudden revelation, by virtue of the unusual layering and doubling of its features, with their consequent imagistic implication of presence beneath presence, power beyond power. The agent of this suggestive doubling is the thick mist, which comes finally to play a provocative and wonderfully ambivalent role. In relation to the land on which Wordsworth is standing, the mist appears as a sea—"on the *shore* / I found myself of a huge *sea* of mist," "this still *Ocean*"—above which the nearby peaks of Snowdonia rise like so many islands. In relation to "the real Sea," however—the Irish Sea, in good weather visible in the distance from Snowdon and still at this moment visible near the horizon beyond the expanse of mist, the cloud cover overhanging Wales—the mist appears as land: "the vapours shot themselves, / In *headlands, tongues,* and *promontory shapes,* / Into the Sea, the real Sea." Thus the panorama comprises a strange duplicating of itself, and the mist a covering veil which, paradoxically, shadows forth the very scene it hides—in Wordsworth's term, "usurps" that scene.

As Wordsworth goes on to develop and explicate "this analogy betwixt / The mind of man and nature" (*Prelude 1850,* p. 623; MS. W), moreover, he interpretatively redoubles his already doubled imagery, pursuing it by turns from two distinct, if complementary, perspectives. From one viewpoint he seeks to understand the essences of his twin subjects, to know what mind and nature are; from the other, he seeks to understand their powers, to know what they can do. Thus Wordsworth's meditation upon this complex analogy epitomizes the entire philosophical inquiry of *The Prelude*; and not only does it accordingly constitute a singularly appropriate climax to the poem, but it also, as we shall see, pervasively influences many of the poem's other great meditative passages in books 5 through 12—passages which, we must remember, though preceding and indeed building up to the ascent of Snowdon in the finished poem, yet followed it in the order of their composition.

ii: Essence and Substantiation

Wordsworth's image for the essence of both nature and mind, then, is the entire scene before him, with its reflexive layers of surface and depth:

> It appeared to me
> The perfect image of a mighty Mind,
> Of one that feeds upon infinity,
> That is exalted by an underpresence,
> The sense of God, or whatsoe'er is dim
> Or vast in its own being.
> [*Prelude 1805* 13.68-73]

Ordinary nature, the visible face of outward things, he sees metonymically imaged here by the counterfeiting mist, an apparition of sea and shoreline and land. But beneath this masking face, he knows, is a deeper, truer nature, an "underpresence" of real sea and shoreline and land; and in his meditation he takes this known but hidden underpresence, this now literally "invisible world" (13.105), as a figure of the ever-invisible spiritual or ideal world, the infinite realm of spirit and power underlying, informing, and exalting nature. And just as this hidden, spiritual world will sometimes intimate its existence, so here on Snowdon an intimation of the hidden undernature, powerful and infinite, rises up through the superficial mist:

> At distance not the third part of a mile
> Was a blue chasm; a fracture in the vapour,
> A deep and gloomy breathing-place thro' which
> Mounted the roar of waters, torrents, streams
> Innumerable, roaring with one voice.

. . . .

. . . In that breach
Through which the homeless voice of waters rose,
That dark deep thoroughfare had Nature lodg'd
The Soul, the Imagination of the whole.

[13.55-65]

In the same way, Wordsworth simultaneously apprehends this
scene as emblematic of man's mind—superficially familiar, but
with hidden spiritual depths of "infinity" and "the sense of
God" whence come its true exaltation and strength, depths of
whose existence he yet receives occasional intimations.[3]

Wordsworth's use of the Snowdon scene to image man's
mind is thus metaleptic:[4] he reads the natural, visible scene as a
figure of nature's greater whole, the invisible as well as the visi-
ble world, and then in turn takes this figure metaphorically as a
type of the mind. The precise motivation and effect of his
practice here does not yet, I think, have a received name, nor
does Wordsworth himself offer one. I shall term it simply *sub-
stantiation*, both for the meaning of the word and for its highly
relevant and appropriate connotation of a sustaining under-
presence. Nature and mind, in their respective and analogous
ways, are liminally but appearances, perceptions; by substantia-
tion Wordsworth poetically recognizes a meaning and meaning-
fulness, an essence, originating and supporting these superficies.[5]
Substantiation is thus Wordsworth's defense against the exist-
ential anxiety: underpresence valorizes presence, depth con-
stitutes the significance of surface.

The initial stimulus of Wordsworth's meditation upon man's
mind in book 13 is, as we have seen, a sudden and transient
spectacle in nature. In book 7, the "Residence in London"
book, however, he ultimately attains to a parallel and closely
related moment of visionary insight under the equally sudden
and more direct stimulus of a human rather than a natural
image. The parallels are in fact quite extensive; to a significant
degree the insight of book 7 mirrors—both substantively repeats
and formally reverses—that of book 13. But in book 7 Words-
worth unconsciously approaches visionariness by stages, seem-
ingly requiring a gradual familiarization with the world of men—

as indeed he had required with the world of nature—before he can begin to read it emblematically.

Wordsworth's initial presentation of London life is a catalogue of superficial impressions—a "motley imagery" (7.150),

> the quick dance
> Of colours, lights and forms, the Babel din
> The endless stream of men, and moving things.
>
> [7.156-58]

His description of the city as a variegated spectacle continues, with occasional interruptions and digressions, for hundreds of lines, almost the full extent of the book. And we come to realize that his account is thus shallow because his experience of the city had then been so; in London, he admits, his "imaginative Power" had

> slept, even in the season of my youth:
> For though I was most passionately moved
> And yielded to the changes of the scene
> With most obsequious feeling, yet all this
> Pass'd not beyond the suburbs of the mind.[6]
>
> [7.499, 503-7]

There are stories behind all these appearances, and occasionally a story attempts to tell itself—the story of a sailor, for example, now crippled and reduced to beggary:

> In Sailor's garb
> Another lies at length beside a range
> Of written characters, with chalk inscrib'd
> Upon the smooth flat stone.
>
> [7.220-23]

The chalked inscription surely tells how the sailor came to be wounded in the service of his country; but Wordsworth is not yet the man to pause and read.[7]

Yet even as the Wordsworth of 1791 amuses himself in London with man's superficialities, he is being prepared by his experiences to sense man's depths. Seen as a part of this process, the interjected account of a Sadler's Wells entertainment reveals itself as a masterful stroke of thematic plotting. "Nor was it mean delight," Wordsworth tells us, explaining his fondness for lowbrow theater,

117

To watch crude nature work in untaught minds,
To note the laws and progress of belief;
Though obstinate on this way, yet on that
How willingly we travel, and how far!

[7.297-301]

His attitude here, the attitude of the 1791 Wordsworth ("at that time / Intolerant" [7.289-90]), is one of condescending superiority. But the performance to which he is about to condescend does in its figurative way for its rude audience what Wordsworth has been unable in London to do for himself—it passes beyond the visible to reveal the invisible world:

To have, for instance, brought upon the scene
The Champion Jack the Giant-killer, Lo!
He dons his Coat of Darkness; on the Stage
Walks, and atchieves his wonders from the eye
Of living mortal safe as is the moon
"Hid in her vacant interlunar cave."
Delusion bold! and faith must needs be coy;
How is it wrought? His garb is black, the word
INVISIBLE flames forth upon his chest.

[7.302-10]

If the stage effect of Jack's invisibility is too boldly and unrealistically artificial a device to suit Wordsworth's own naturalistic style, it yet points up a sensitivity to the depths of the human spirit (and what is Jack but a type of essential Man?) which he must learn to cultivate in his own experience and to convey in his own art. Indeed, this figure of what we may term "the labeled man," the visible sign locating but hiding the invisible significance, seems by way of becoming the dominant motif of book 7. And finally both motif and book climax in a stunning moment of revelation and insight on a London street, as Wordsworth's unappreciated views of the labeled sailor-cripple and the labeled Giant-killer, now only latent in his memory, suddenly coalesce and revive in a new incarnation.

Wordsworth has already quietly prepared us, much as he himself was prepared, for this new development. For after admitting how in London his imagination slept while his theatergoing experiences moved him "not beyond the suburbs of my mind," he goes on to hint of certain exceptions to this languor in his personal life:

If aught there were of real grandeur here
'Twas only then when gross realities,
The incarnation of the Spirits that mov'd
Amid the Poet's beauteous world, call'd forth,
With that distinctness which a contrast gives
Or opposition, made me recognize
As by a glimpse, the things which I had shaped
And yet not shaped, had seen, and scarcely seen,
Had felt, and thought of in my solitude.

[7.508-16]

Having said this much, he breaks off without further explanation. But his meaning finally becomes clear some hundred lines later, as he begins at last to be troubled by the superficiality of his London experience:

How often in the overflowing streets,
Have I gone forward with the Crowd, and said
Unto myself, the face of every one
That passes by me is a mystery.

[7.595-98]

And once, he says, as he walked through the city musing on this oppressive truth, oblivious to his surroundings,

               'twas my chance
Abruptly to be smitten with the view
Of a blind Beggar, who, with upright face,
Stood propp'd against a Wall, upon his Chest
Wearing a written paper, to explain
The story of the Man, and who he was.
My mind did at this spectacle turn round
As with the might of waters, and it seemed
To me that in this Label was a type,
Or emblem, of the utmost that we know,
Both of ourselves and of the universe;
And, on the shape of the unmoving man,
His fixed face and sightless eyes, I look'd
As if admonished from another world.

[7.610-23]

Here again is the philosophical insight and the substantiating vision of the Snowdon episode, now stimulated not by the countenance of nature but by the countenance of man. Again Wordsworth confronts a layering and doubling of imagery—on one level of appearances, the beggar himself; on another level, the descriptive label—precisely analogous to the layered and doubled imagery of Snowdon. This time "the outward face of things," the superficial identity and history of the man—"the utmost that we know"—is metonymically imaged by the label, the "written paper." But behind this label stands the real man himself; and so Wordsworth can take this real man as a type of that which we do not know, the essential, spiritual being, and so figuratively an apparition "from another world," that is, from the invisible world. Wordsworth's "mind did at this spectacle turn round / As with the might of waters" because it has just been smitten by "the homeless voice of waters" it would soon hear on Snowdon,[8] the intimating voice rising up to man from the underlying depths of the mind, bespeaking its hidden and infinite source.

As he had with the Snowdon scene, so here again Wordsworth extends his emblem metaleptically, though this time he does not immediately elaborate upon the extension. Where in book 13 he had taken an emblem of nature as an emblem of the mind, however, here in book 7 he does the reverse, reading his initial emblem of "ourselves" as also an emblem of "the universe." This bare suggestion comes belatedly to life in the final paragraph of the book, when Wordsworth offers the bustling chaos of Bartholomew Fair as a parallel emblem of London itself—

> Oh, blank confusion! and a type not false
> Of what the mighty City is itself
> To all except a Straggler here and there[9]
>
> [7.696-98]

—yet repeats anew the consolations his insights have won for him:

> But though the picture weary out the eye,
> By nature an unmanageable sight,
> It is not wholly so to him who looks
> In steadiness, who hath among least things
> An under-sense of greatest; sees the parts
> As parts, but with a feeling of the whole.
>
> [7.708-13]

And now he likens and attributes this undersense of greatness beneath the surface of man's triviality to the similar under-sense conveyed to him by natural scenes, so that even in the midst of Bartholomew Fair he can say,

> The Spirit of Nature was upon me here;
> The Soul of Beauty and enduring life
> Was present as a habit.
>
> [7.736-38]

The emblematically reflexive figure of "the labeled man," or more broadly of the layered man, which Wordsworth develops in book 7 becomes in the succeeding books his habitual trope for man's essential nature. Thus near the opening of book 8, and picking up directly from the conclusion of book 7, he proclaims,

> With deep devotion, Nature, did I feel
> In that great City what I owed to thee,
>
> . . . .
>
>   . . . a watchful eye
> Which with the outside of our human life
> Not satisfied, must read the inner mind.
>
> [8.62-68]

And this contrast of those who read the outer surfaces of man's life with those who read its deeper truths comes eventually to revive the "labeled man" image which originally compelled his insight:

>   Call ye these appearances
> Which I beheld of Shepherds in my youth,
> This sanctity of nature given to man
> A shadow, a delusion, ye who are fed
> By the dead letter, not the spirit of things,
> Whose truth is not a motion or a shape
> Instinct with vital functions, but a Block
> Or waxen Image which yourselves have made,
> And ye adore.
>
> [8.428-36]

Himself refusing to be "fed / By the dead letter" of the label, Wordsworth learns rather to see "into the depth of human souls, / Souls that appear to have no depth at all / To vulgar eyes" (12.166-68), and so ultimately becomes instead one of "those / Who to the letter of the outward promise / Do read the invisible soul" (12.253–55), in his spiritual literacy setting an example for us all. We should note finally of Wordsworth's parallel and reflexive emblematic readings of man and nature in books 7 and 13 that they explain, simply and elegantly, what Wordsworth badly belabors and overdetermines to the point of near unintelligibility in book 8 when he tries too hard to make himself perfectly clear: how his love of nature led him to a love of man. Jonathan Wordsworth has sharply criticized Wordsworth's argument here, contending that book 8's famous pictures of shepherds "hardly bear out the claim they were intended to illustrate," that

> I already had been taught to love
> My Fellow-beings, to such habits train'd
> Among the woods and mountains.[10]
> [8.69–71]

And certainly there is some provocation for this objection, for Wordsworth is slow to make clear that he is speaking of "an *unconscious* love and reverence / Of human nature" (8.413–14; my emphasis). Still, the process Wordsworth describes now, as he analytically reexamines his childhood, is both intelligible in itself and consistent with the ideas of books 13 and 7. To begin with, as he now understands it, nature taught him to read *herself* emblematically, seeing her parts "as parts, but with a feeling of the whole," intuiting among her "least things / An undersense of greatest." This, as he says, is "of all acquisitions first" (7.714); and while he himself owes it to nature, he readily allows that it can be inculcated by many other, "sundry and most widely different modes / Of education" (7.715–16), not nature's only. As a direct result of this training, secondly, Wordsworth learned not merely to read *nature* emblematically, but, more essentially, simply to *read* emblematically. Thus it becomes "second nature" for him later to read *man* emblematically, especially "where appear," with man as with the more elemental scenes of nature, "most obviously simplicity and power" (7.720–21), as is the case with the shepherd apparitions of book 8. These shepherds, we need to understand, are pure emblems to the young Wordsworth. He comes to love, not these men themselves, but the "under-sense of greatest," of man's spiritual greatness, that he intuits through them. The men themselves are mere avatars of their own, and his own, deeper significance. Thus when Wordsworth seemingly qualifies his stated love of man at that time by saying that then man, in contrast to the "immediate joy" of nature, remained to him

> distant, but a grace
> Occasional, an accidental thought,
> His hour being not yet come,
> [8.488-90]

we yet absolutely must recognize, as I fear has not been recognized, the huge and compelling significance of his allusion here to mankind as a Christ—"'Mine hour is not yet come'"—Whose hour, when it does come, marks the ultimate proof of His essence.[11] Just as to value man superficially is idolatrously to value him only as "a Block / Or waxen image," an appearance unsubstantiated by any underpresence, so to exist superficially, without "th' authentic sight of reason" (4.296), is to be only such a "senseless Idol" (4.304). Wordsworth would call us away from this "old idolatry" (13.425) to a truer religion, revealing to us "that religious dignity of mind / That is the very faculty of truth" (4.297-98), bringing us the message that the mind of man, potentially and naturally "exalted by an underpresence," is thereby more than its mere perceptions and appearances—is "of substance and of fabric more divine" (13.445).

iii: Power and Defamiliarization

As I noted earlier, Wordsworth takes the Snowdon scene as a doubly significant topos, imaging not only what mind and nature are, but also what they can do—imaging not only their essences, but also their powers. He insists upon this double significance from the very beginning of his meditation, first taking the spectacle as "the perfect image of a mighty Mind," a passive image of essence, but also finding that "above all / One *function* of such mind had Nature there / Exhibited" (*Prelude 1805* 13.73-75; my emphasis), an active image of power. But Wordsworth is not, despite the initial impression of ambivalence his argument may give here, reading the same emblem in two different ways. Rather—and the distinction is genuine and important—he is reading the same scene as two different emblems. As he proceeds to suggest how Snowdon images the functions of mind and nature, he not only reinterprets but fundamentally reconceives the terms of his emblem, the mist and landscape which together comprise the scenic image.

As we have already seen, in his interpretation of the Snowdon scene as an image of nature and of mind Wordsworth reads the covering mist as an image of the outwardly apparent world or individual, and the underlying landscape and seascape as an image of the invisible, spiritual underpresences. When he comes to interpret the scene as also emblematic of natural and mental activities, however, he revises and to a great degree even reverses these paired readings. This radical change soon becomes quite explicit in the terms of his explanation:

> Above all
> One function of such mind had Nature there
> Exhibited by putting forth, and that
> With circumstance most awful and sublime,
> That domination which she oftentimes
> Exerts upon the outward face of things,
> So moulds them, and endues, abstracts, combines,
> Or by abrupt and unhabitual influence
> Doth make one object so impress itself
> Upon all others, and pervade them so
> That even the grossest minds must see and hear
> And cannot chuse but feel.
>   [13.73-84]

Now, very clearly, Wordsworth is taking, not the mist, but the actual underlying landscape to represent "the outward face of things" (thus the landscape now images superficial nature through simple synecdoche), and taking the mist instead to represent the dominating, shaping Power over her own appearances which nature sometimes exerts. And next, metaleptically extending his emblem of nature's power even as he had his cognate emblem of nature's essence, he correspondingly regards the mist as an emblem of the human mind's informing and transforming power:

> [The Power] which Nature thus
> Thrusts forth upon the senses, is the express
> Resemblance, in the fulness of its strength

Made visible, a genuine Counterpart
And Brother of the glorious faculty
Which higher minds bear with them as their own.
This is the very spirit in which they deal
With all the objects of the universe;
They from their native selves can send abroad
Like transformations, for themselves create
A like existence, and, whene'er it is
Created for them, catch it by instinct.
[13.85-96]

As Hartman observes, the import of this extension, "daring if taken literally, is that there exists an imagination in nature analogous to that in man."[12]

As we have already noted, Wordsworth's motivation and effect in reading the Snowdon episode as an image of nature's and the mind's essence is what I have termed *substantiation*, a recognition of and insistence on a sustaining underpresence informing and valorizing outward appearances. In reading the scene instead as an image of nature's and the mind's power, he realizes a complementary motivation and effect, the renovating "transformation" of "the outward face of things," which again he does not name but which is most aptly today called *defamiliarization*. The term may require clarification to distinguish it from the *ostranenie* ("defamiliarization, making strange") of twentieth-century formalist critics, for Wordsworth values these quickening transformations far differently than do the formalists. Thus Shklovsky insists that

> an image is not a permanent referent for those mutable complexities of life which are revealed through it; its purpose is not to make us perceive meaning, but to create a special perception of the object—*it creates a "vision" of the object instead of serving as a means for knowing it.*

For Shklovsky, in other words, defamiliarization is a virtue and an end in itself. But Wordsworth emphatically contradicts such an assumption, as indeed do the Romantics generally. For Wordsworth, quite explicitly, such defamiliarizing is ultimately valuable not as an end but as a means: what really matters, he says, is that the men who are thus "quicken'd" and "rouz'd" are "made thereby more fit / To hold communion with the invisible world" (13.104-5), the underpresence sustaining "the external universe" (13.116).[13]

Wordsworthian defamiliarization, then—and it is thus that I shall be using the term—maintains not only a complementary but even a symbiotic relationship with substantiation. Without the experience of defamiliarization, the mind is gradually depressed and dulled by "custom," "trivial occupations, and the round / Of ordinary intercourse" (11.245, 263-64), victimized by that "tendency . . . / Of habit to enslave the mind," to

> Oppress it by the laws of vulgar sense,
> And substitute a universe of death,
> The falsest of all worlds, in place of that
> Which is divine and true.
>
> [13.135-40]

Without the sense of substantiation, on the other hand, the experience of exquisitely sensitive perception is but "a transport of the outward sense, / Not of the mind, vivid but not profound" (11.188-89). Substantiation, the effect of nature's "influence habitual" (7.722), gradually and subliminally impresses with "an under-sense" of greatness and unity, "the Soul of Beauty and enduring life" (7.712, 737-38); defamiliarization, the pointedly complementary work of "abrupt and unhabitual influence" (13.80), suddenly and overtly reminds us of this undersense. Every defamiliarization in *The Prelude* is fundamentally an abrupt sensitizing to substantiation.

Just as Wordsworth repeats his Snowdon-inspired insight into man's essence in the structurally parallel episode of the blind Beggar in book 7, he quite similarly repeats his complementary and accompanying insight into the mind's power in an analogously parallel episode, the famous celebration of the imagination interrupting the Simplon Pass narrative of book 6. Once again the images, patterns, and terms of the Snowdon revelation infuse the later-written apotheosis:

> Imagination! lifting up itself
> Before the eye and progress of my Song
> Like an unfather'd vapour; here that Power,
> In all the might of its endowments, came
> Athwart me; I was lost as in a cloud,

Halted without a struggle to break through.
And now recovering, to my Soul I say
I recognize thy glory; in such strength
Of usurpation, in such visitings
Of awful promise, when the light of sense
Goes out in flashes that have shewn to us
The invisible world, doth Greatness make abode,
There harbours whether we be young or old.
Our destiny, our nature, and our home
Is with infinitude, and only there;
With hope it is, hope that can never die,
Effort, and expectation, and desire,
And something evermore about to be.[14]

[6.525-42]

Wordsworth's allusion here to the Snowdon experience is all the more striking in that the Simplon scene reproduces only the mental sensations, and not the actual imagery, of that experience. Now imagination comes like a mist, yet also like a flash of revelatory light, upon one who, previously seeing only by the light of sense, had thereby been sadly, unknowingly beclouded. That which obscures becomes suddenly a type of that which illuminates; and Wordsworth's imagery makes clear his renewed emphasis here on the reflexive doubling prompting the visionary experience. Here cloud usurps cloud, light usurps light, as imagination usurps the senses. And the original figure of this "usurpation" is, as we have noted, the Snowdon scene, where, beneath the sealike mist,

the Sea, the real Sea, . . seem'd
To dwindle, and give up its majesty,
Usurp'd upon as far as sight could reach.

The deliberateness and preciseness of Wordsworth's reference in 6.533 to the imagination's "usurpation" of the senses, already indicated by his parallel use of the term in 13.51, receives further confirmation from his elaboration of the basic image in these and other contexts in *The Prelude*. Not to be the senses' usurper and master is to be their subject and slave; and Wordsworth several times states these alternatives thus starkly. Higher minds which exert upon the senses their powers of imagination, for example, are consequently, he says, "by sensible impressions not enthrall'd" (13.103); and he himself, one of those higher minds, when he gazes upon the beautiful scenery of the Swiss lakes explicitly eludes such thralldom:

> Not prostrate, overborn, as if the mind
> Itself were nothing, a mean pensioner
> On outward forms, did we in presence stand
> Of that magnificent region.
>
> [6.666-69]

Rather than acknowledge or endure such pensioning to the senses, Wordsworth instead celebrates his

> deepest feeling that the mind
> Is lord and master, and that outward sense
> Is but the obedient servant of her will.
>
> [11.271-73]

And certainly the passage immediately following the Simplon paean to imagination, the account of his journey through the Ravine of Gondo, serves to illustrate the imagination's usurpation of the senses. For imaginative minds, Wordsworth claims, live "in a world of life"; not enthralled by sensible impressions, they are instead "quicken'd, rouz'd, and made thereby more fit / To hold communion with the invisible world," and so are able to intuit their great, divine source "through every image, and through every thought, / And all impressions" (13.102-5, 110-11). And just this is clearly happening in the Ravine of Gondo. For here, confronted by the chaotic and incoherent elements of the scene, Wordsworth is able, despite their seeming irreconcilability (they comprise both "tumult and peace," both "the darkness and the light" [6.567]), to escape the sensational thralldom they threaten and, instead, imaginatively to perceive in them a deeper unity and life, seeing them as

> all like workings of one mind, the features
> Of the same face, blossoms upon one tree,
> Characters of the great Apocalypse,
> The types and symbols of eternity,
> Of first, and last, and midst, and without end.
>
> [6.568-72]

On the other hand, one closely preceding and two closely following episodes illustrate the contrasting state of bondage to the senses, thereby serving most pointedly as foils to Wordsworth's Simplon and Gondo insights. In the first instance, Wordsworth's first view of Mont Blanc, his fancifully extravagant preconception of Europe's highest mountain is disappointed, and consequently his mind is entirely subdued, by the actual appearance of the reality, so that this time the senses usurp upon the imagination: he

> griev'd
> To have a soulless image on the eye
> Which had usurp'd upon a living thought
> That never more could be.
>
> [6.453-56]

And in the latter two episodes, those of the night succeeding Wordsworth's Simplon passage, spent in an Alpine inn (6.573-80), and the second night after this, spent beyond the town of Gravedona (6.621-54), a quite different set of experiences produces a fundamentally similar result. "Deafen'd and stunn'd / By noise of waters" (6.578-79), "bewilder'd among woods immense" (6.631), surrounded by allusively hellish mountains only "by darkness visible" (6.645; cf. *Paradise Lost* 1.63), and mocked by the "unintelligible voice" of the unfamiliar Italian clocks (6.648), Wordsworth on these two occasions is effectively rendered senseless by his senses, "as if the mind / Itself were nothing, a mean pensioner / On outward forms" indeed.

iv: Snowdon as a Spot of Thought: *The Prelude* and Wordsworth's Emblematization of the Mind

The Snowdon scene, then, serves Wordsworth so perfectly as an image of the mind because with unexampled aptness it simultaneously emblematizes both of the mind's significant characteristics: essential depth and transfiguring power. Nor is its service transient. Wordsworth no sooner comes to appreciate this complex emblem than he begins to take it into his poetry in subtle and various ways. His meditation upon the vision in truth becomes what we might, by analogy, call a spot of thought, informing Wordsworth's subsequent work on *The Prelude* much as the spots of time informed his life, retaining "a vivifying Virtue" (*Prelude 1805* 11.260) to which he often repairs for the nourishment of his poetry. Wordsworth had of course already begun to conceive of the mind in terms of such complementary depths and emanations as early as 1798, with his "sense sublime / Of something far more deeply interfused" in both the mind of man and the natural world which man's senses "half create." And late in that year he even epitomized the more specific complementarity of substantiation and defamiliarization in a scene curiously proleptic of Snowdon's, the sketch of the Boy of Winander trying to provoke the silent owls into song by his own mimic hootings:

> And when it chanced
> That pauses of deep silence mock'd his skill,
> Then sometimes, in that silence, while he hung
> Listening, a gentle shock of mild surprize
> Has carried far into his heart the voice
> Of mountain torrents; or the visible scene
> Would enter unawares into his mind
> With all its solemn imagery, its rocks,
> Its woods, and that uncertain Heaven, receiv'd
> Into the bosom of the steady Lake.
> [5.404-13]

Here the sound of the torrents, of which the boy becomes unexpectedly and vividly conscious while he strains to detect a quite different sound (the hootings of owls), quickens and rouses him with its defamiliarized effect, while the visible scene, which he is all the while thoughtlessly absorbing into his mind, quietly nurtures his substantiating underpresence. Wordsworth does not, as it happens, develop the implications of this particular formulation of the mind, any more than he develops this particular version of himself (the Boy, originally Wordsworth himself [*Prelude 1850*, pp. 639-40], now is allowed instead to die in childhood [*Prelude 1805* 5:414-15]); but in Snowdon he finds a fitter vehicle for his insight, and one which he applies repeatedly throughout the later books of *The Prelude*.

The ground of this great, controlling emblem is necessarily always a surface, the surface of appearances—usually the visible face of nature or man, but sometimes, by analogy, a superficial

narrative or label or garment. Beneath this surface lie the sub-
stantiating depths of the mind, whether in man or in nature;
and Wordsworth's emblem for these depths is water, and more
particularly the voice of waters. Literally present on Snowdon,
these waters and their voice also significantly intimate their
presence figuratively on several other occasions when Words-
worth approaches these depths—most strikingly in his vision of
the blind Beggar, when "my mind did at this spectacle turn
round / As with the might of waters," but also, for example, in
his musings upon the "stream" of Imagination, traced from
"the very place of birth / In its blind cavern, whence is faintly
heard / The sound of waters" (13.166-68). Above this surface
of appearances, on the other hand, play the transfiguring powers
of the mind, whose emblem is mist. Thus the literal mist of
Snowdon also works its defamiliarizing magic upon the rude
shepherds of Helvellyn as they suddenly appear, "girt round
with mists" (8.96) or "stalking through the fog" (8.401), to the
young Wordsworth, while the figurative mist of the imagination
usurpingly rises up "before the eye and progress of my Song"
even as he writes of his passage through Simplon.

Wordsworth's use of this mist and water imagery on such
occasions is hardly inevitable (witness the somewhat different
figuration of the Boy of Winander passage), but it does seem to
be consistent in the later books of *The Prelude*. Thus within this
context, at least, the poetry invites a clarification or correction
of the common tenet that Wordsworth indiscriminately refers
to the imagination "sometimes . . . as a mist or vapor, sometimes
as a stream, sometimes as nothing more than the sound made by
an unseen stream."[15] The more accurate observation, I have
been suggesting, is that by mist and stream Wordsworth is in
fact referring to two different aspects of the imagination, its
power and its essence, aspects as interrelated and as distin-
guishable as are mist and water themselves.

I have dared to call Wordsworth's Snowdon meditation a
spot of thought because Wordsworth himself, when he comes to
reintroduce the spots of time into book 11 of *The Prelude*,
seems carefully to associate them with that culminating vision.
Snowdon, we may surmise, helps Wordsworth retrospectively
understand or reinterpret what was so distinctive and powerful
about those rare passages. Most of the memorable episodes in

Wordsworth's childhood were in truth defamiliarizations founded simply upon sensational illusion—the optical illusion of a mountain's striding after him like a living thing, the aural illusion of "low breathings coming after me" (which Wordsworth in 1798 unmistakably anticipates and implicates with his preceding reference to "how my heart / *Panted* . . . / . . . how my bosom beat / With expectation! [*Prelude 1799* 1.39-42]), the disorienting dizziness making the landscape appear to be "wheel-[ing] by me, even as if the earth had roll'd / With visible motion her diurnal round" (1.485-86). These are strong, vehement sensations, what Wordsworth terms "extraordinary calls" (*Prelude 1805* 13.101; cf. *Prelude 1850*, p. 574), and tend to obscure and distract from the personal substantiation to which they are contributing; for the child feels dependent on nature or on physiological disequilibrium for these defamiliarizings, even in those instances where we (and Wordsworth retrospectively) may well suspect that his own sense of guilt plays a major part.

The two episodes that Wordsworth still in 1804, calls spots of time, on the other hand, obviously, even in the child's eyes, derive their unusual vividness not from the extraordinariness of the scene but from some defamiliarizing faculty of the mind itself. "It was, in truth, / An ordinary sight" (*Prelude 1805* 11.308-9), he acknowledges of the first episode; its "visionary dreariness," then, can only be his own visionary contribution: "From thyself it is that thou must give, / Else never canst receive" (11.334-35). What Wordsworth now explicitly values in the spots of time—he appends this analysis for the first time in 1804—is that therein he has "had deepest feeling that the mind / Is lord and master, and that outward sense / Is but the obedient servant of her will" (11.271-73). Gentle and unmistakably self-created defamiliarizings, the spots of time thus also intimate to the boy his own underpresence.[16] And it is this simultaneous evocation of the mind's essence and its power, a rarity in Wordsworth's experience, which both gives the spots of time such "distinct pre-eminence" and leads Wordsworth to associate them with his vision on Snowdon.

This association, as Wordsworth now develops it in 1804, is remarkably subtle, an allusive evocation of Snowdon's spirit which yet makes no explicit mention of Snowdon's features:

Oh! mystery of Man, from what a depth
Proceed thy honours! I am lost, but see
In simple childhood something of the base
On which thy greatness stands, but this I feel,
That from thyself it is that thou must give,
Else never canst receive. The days gone by
Come back upon me from the dawn almost
Of life: the hiding-places of my power
Seem open; I approach, and then they close;
I see by glimpses now; when age comes on,
May scarcely see at all.

[11.329–39]

All seems impressionistic and indeterminate here, but nonetheless a mental landscape is taking shape. For that which intermittently opens a vista only to close it, that which allows vision only by glimpses, is thereby a type of Snowdon's mist, the mist of the defamiliarizing imagination which provokes the not quite paradoxical cry, "I am lost, but see." Pointedly, Wordsworth has exclaimed this before, in his meditation on Simplon, and his repetition here thus evokes that earlier cry and its context: "I was lost as in a cloud." And again beneath this figurative mist the substantiating underpresence of the mind intimates itself like the might of Snowdon's hidden waters, not only in such words as "mystery" and "depth" but even in the elegiac skewing of the Snowdon "breathing-place" for the waters into what he is now coming to think of as "the hiding-places of my power."[17]

Wordsworth originally intended his last, fifth book of the poem to Coleridge to open with the ascent of Snowdon and conclude with the spots of time. His subsequent separation of these two passages in the thirteen-book *Prelude*, dictated by his revised conception of and ambition for the poem, has obscured their close relationship; but their pairing, if now more subtle, continues to color and shape the entire poem. The Snowdon vision emblematizes the spots of time; the spots of time reify the Snowdon vision. And Snowdon alone, I would suggest finally, holds—and merits—the place of emphasis and honor in the finished poem precisely because Snowdon is the poem's (not the poet's) chief "spot," continually nurturing and vivifying the poem just as the spots of time nurtured and vivified

Wordsworth's mind, and so should present in the poem just that "distinct pre-eminence" which the spots of time themselves retained in Wordsworth's life.

v

The philosophical argument informing *The Prelude* which I have been tracing here is not my concept, but Wordsworth's; I have tried, in my analysis, to be faithful to his ideas, his emphases, and his terms. His concept is not obscure, not vague, not incomplete, though it has often been slandered by these complaints. It has seemed difficult chiefly, I think, because it lies so intrinsically bound up in his poetry that only by the most careful attention to his poetic strategies can we begin fairly to comprehend his philosophic ones. Schematically and summarily restated, the central philosophical argument of *The Prelude* offers and develops the following ideas.

The Two Essences and Powers. First, there are on earth two great essences and powers—not one, as Wordsworth had believed in early 1798. These two powers are "Nature, and the power of human minds" (*Prelude 1805* 12.224). Nature, like man, abounds "with passion and with life" (11.147; and cf. 12.280-93); there are innately "excellence, pure spirit, and best power / Both in the object seen, and eye that sees (12.378-79). In book 13 Wordsworth speaks of these two powers specifically as, on the one hand, the power of the Nature informing nature, "that domination which she oftentimes / Exerts upon the outward face of things," "the Power . . . / . . . which Nature thus / Thrusts forth upon the senses," and on the other, the power of the Imagination potentially informing man, "the glorious faculty / Which higher minds bear with them as their own": "Such minds are truly from the Deity, / For they are Powers" (13.106-7).[18]

Their Derivation from God. Second, as the lines just quoted indicate, ultimate Power is—by definition, as it were—from God. Wordsworth continues,

> And hence the highest bliss
> That can be known is theirs, the consciousness
> Of whom they are . . .

. . . .

. . . hence religion, faith,
And endless occupation for the soul.
                                                    [13.107-12]

And he very definitely means *whom* here—"consciousness / Of whom they are," of whence such higher minds come. The same "highest bliss," now called "highest joy" (8.834), appears in Wordsworth's almost identical intuition in book 8 of the spiritual unity of man—

For there,
There chiefly, hath she [the soul] feeling whence she is,
And, passing through all Nature rests with God
                                                    [8.834-36]

—and appears yet again, this time as an "overflowing" and inundating joy (6.543-48), with the famous recognition in book 6 that "our destiny, our nature, and our home / Is with infinitude, and only there" (6.538-39). This definitional assumption that ultimate Power proceeds from God is of course as true of nature's power as it is of the mind's. So Wordsworth similarly speaks of "Nature's self," here explicitly a hallowed power, as "the breath of God" (5.222), and again of "the laws of things," "the life of nature," as "by the God of love / Inspired, celestial presence ever pure" (11.97-100).

Their Analogousness. Third, these two great presences and powers, of nature and of mind, are as extensively analogous as they are essentially cognate, so that the imaginative power of the mind is "the express / Resemblance," "a genuine Counterpart / And Brother" of nature's power. This analogousness constitutes the most fundamental theme of *The Prelude.* On one level, it underlies Wordsworth's dual rhetorical practice of personifying nature and naturalizing persons, a practice so pervasive in *The Prelude* that we sometimes forget its significance—his tendency to speak of Helvellyn's "unshrouded head" (8.15) or "the changeful language of [the hills'] countenances" (7.728), for example, and alternatively of "the great tide of human life" (7.631; cf. 7.206) or the "gulph" he hoped would part the man to come from the man who had been (11.59-60).

Similarly this analogousness brings to life Wordsworth's leit-motif of the "corresponding . . . breeze" (1.43) and the grove which "now tossing its dark boughs in sun and wind / Spreads through me a commotion like its own" (7.50-52).[19] And it assumes a curious symmetry, to cite a final example, in Words-worth's account of how Dorothy and Nature together came to redeem him from despair—she working on him like a natural influence,

                          now speaking in a voice
Of sudden admonition, like a brook
That does but cross a lonely road, and now
Seen, heard and felt, and caught at every turn,
Companion never lost through many a league,
Maintain[ing] for me a saving intercourse
With my true self,

                                    [10.909-15]

Nature contrastingly helping him like a human agent, "through the weary labyrinth / Conduct[ing] me again to open day" like another Ariadne (10.922-23).

On a deeper level, this same analogousness justifies Words-worth's central emphasis on nature's potential to effect "the discipline / And consummation of the Poet's mind" (13.263-64). For nature, seen in her pure and basic forms, can nurture, orient, and guide man's soul precisely because she herself es-sentially typifies that soul. Thus the healing of Wordsworth's imagination by nature described in books 10-12 in truth simply repeats the process of its original shaping by nature in books 1-4, and for that matter repeats the process of its shaping by London in books 7-8. Always the underpresence without, if but man can and will attend to it, molds after its own image the underpresence within. Thus in nature,

By influence habitual[,] to the mind
The mountain's outline and its steady form
Give a pure grandeur, and its presence shapes
The measure and the prospect of the soul
To majesty.

                                    [7.722-26]

And similarly in London,

> all objects, being
> Themselves capacious, also found in me
> Capaciousness and amplitude of mind;
>
> . . . .
>
> The Human nature unto which I felt
> That I belong'd, and which I lov'd and reverenced,
> Was not a punctual Presence, but a Spirit
> Living in time and space, and far diffus'd.
>
> . . . .
>
> . . The external universe,
> By striking upon what is found within,
> Had given me this conception.
>
> [8.757-68]

Thus while Wordsworth in *The Prelude* is the poet not of nature but of the imagination, yet he finds that nature has such power both to exemplify and to nurture the imagination that he concludes his poem by aspiring with Coleridge to the role of "prophets of Nature" (13.435), even though his prophecies paradoxically are not of nature but of "the mind of man" (13.439).

Power and Reason. Fourth and finally, these two powers are thus analogous as well as cognate because both are types of Reason. Wordsworth suggests this repeatedly in *The Prelude*, and frequently states his meaning quite forthrightly. Thus "imagination," he says,

> in truth
> Is but another name for absolute strength
> And clearest insight, amplitude of mind,
> And reason in her most exalted mood.
>
> [13.160-63]

And this power is indeed "the express / Resemblance" of nature's, for Wordsworth is speaking of his love of nature when he says,

> Not in vain
> I had been taught to reverence a Power
> That is the very quality and shape
> And image of right reason.
>
> [12.23-26]

It is this inchoate recognition of Reason as the nature of nature's power which informs his revised, abrupt apostrophe to Nature in book 1, "Wisdom and Spirit of the universe! / Thou Soul that art the Eternity of Thought!" and which similarly leads him in book 6 to take his sense "of permanent and universal sway / And paramount endowment in the mind," derived from his meditations upon the abstractions of geometry and their relevance to actual nature, as

> An image not unworthy of the one
> Surpassing Life, which out of space and time,
> Not touched by welterings of passion, is
> And hath the name of God.

                                                    [6.152-57]

We have seen Wordsworth approaching this recognition ever since the writing of *Hart-Leap Well*. Now, in *The Prelude*, it stands forth as an explicit tenet of his philosophy.

The great unity that Wordsworth now deeply perceives in the world,

> the life
> Of all things and the mighty unity
> In all which we behold, and feel, and are,

                                                    [13.246-48]

is thus a concept refined and qualitatively different from the "one life" which he had perceived in 1798. The earlier vision celebrated nature's existence itself as the ultimate power and infinitude to which all creatures and things belong and of which all are more or less transient features. But in 1804 Wordsworth comes to sense the more fundamental infinitude of mind, of reason, and thus to characterize the ultimate power as not simply existential, but intellectual. Now, accordingly, Godhead, still an extrapolation of faith, is not a prototype of Being, but a prototype of Mind. Thus it is finally from the progress of Imagination, the development of reason, and not from his earlier awareness of "the one Presence, and the Life / Of the great whole" (3.130-31), that Wordsworth in *The Prelude* draws "the feeling of life endless, the great thought / By which we live, Infinity and God" (13.176-77). And I would emphasize here that "the great thought," far from being a vague rewording of that "feeling," instead definitionally describes and specifies it.

Wordsworth is indeed saying what he appears to say, what his syntax insists on saying—that "from [the Imagination's] progress have we drawn / . . . Infinity and God."

The poetry of 1800, as we have seen, suggests that Wordsworth eventually found his "one life" philosophy of 1798 inadequate because it did not attribute particular value to man above the rest of nature. *The Prelude*, in contrast, makes much of man's preeminence, even to the point of exalting it in the very last lines of the poem, Wordsworth's promise that he and Coleridge will

> Instruct [men] how the mind of man becomes
> A thousand times more beautiful than the earth
> On which he dwells, above this frame of things
> . . . .
> In beauty exalted, as it is itself
> Of substance and of fabric more divine.
> [13.439-45]

Wordsworth can now celebrate man's unique superiority by virtue of just that characteristic which similarly elevates man above nature in Christian theology, man's dual nature: "sensuous and intellectual as he is, / A twofold Frame of body and of mind" (11.169-70). As a merely sensuous creature, man indeed has no exceptional value. In those individuals where "th' authentic sight of reason," "that religious dignity of mind, / That is the very faculty of truth," is lacking,

> either, from the very first,
> A function never lighted up, or else
> Extinguish'd, Man . . .
> Seems but a pageant plaything with wild claws.
> [4.296-302]

It is his intellectual capacity that elevates man above the rest of nature and associates him with divinity. Always Wordsworth takes care to emphasize man's *reason* as his divine aspect: thus his cry:

> Great God!
> Who send'st thyself into this breathing world
> Through Nature and through every kind of life,

And mak'st Man what he is, Creature divine,
In single or in social eminence
Above all these raised infinite ascents
When reason, which enables him to be,
Is not sequester'd.

[10.385-92]

And thus, again, his estimation:

Then rose
Man, inwardly contemplated, and present
In my own being, to a loftier height,
As of all visible natures crown; and first
In capability of feeling what
Was to be felt; in being rapt away
By the divine effect of power and love,
As, more than anything we know instinct
With Godhead, and by reason and by will
Acknowledging dependency sublime.

[8.631-40]

When God is conceived of as the great type, not of simple
Being, but of Mind, then it is not as life, but as mind, that
man is made in God's image.

CHAPTER 7
"The Mystery of Words":
Poetic Power and
the Poet's Ambition

i

WHILE WORDSWORTH makes very clear in *The Prelude* his belief that nature gave him a good education, he never claims that hers is the only possible one. Rather, "that through which I pass'd" is, as he specifically notes, but one of "sundry and most widely different modes / Of education" (*Prelude 1805* 7.715–17). Another possible mode, and indeed one which Wordsworth himself—"a wild, unworldly-minded Youth, given up / To Nature and to Books" (4.281–82)—experienced to a great if still secondary degree, is education by books and tales. Thus when he tells us, in a passage we have recently noted, that in London

> the external universe,
> By striking upon what is found within
> Had given me this conception

that human nature is a living and pervasive spirit, he adds to this attribution another: "with the help / Of Books, and what they picture and record" (8.766-69). In fact this educational power of charming narrative, whether fictitious or historical, particularly impresses and works upon Wordsworth in London:

> A sense
> Of what had been here done, and suffer'd here
> Through ages, and was doing, suffering, still
> Weigh'd with me, could support the test of thought,
> Was like the enduring majesty and power
> Of independent nature; and not seldom

141

Even individual remembrances,
By working on the Shapes before my eyes,
Became like vital functions of the soul;
And out of what had been, what was, the place
Was throng'd with impregnations, like those wilds
In which my early feelings had been nurs'd.

[8.781-92]

And his magisterial advice to the young De Quincey in 1804 is
evenhandedly double:

Love Nature and Books; seek these and you will be happy; for
virtuous friendship, and love, and knowledge of mankind, must in-
evitably accompany these, all things thus ripening in their due sea-
son.[1] [*LEY*, p. 454]

Wordsworth's recognition of this power of narrative thus to
supplement and intensify the teachings of the external universe
surely prompts his own narrative interjections into his auto-
biography: the story of Mary of Buttermere in book 7, the
Matron's Tale of book 8 (an example of the tales that impreg-
nated his native haunts for him—"tales / . . . which in my walks /
I carried with me among crags and woods / And mountains"
[8.216-20]—just as more famous historical events impregnated
for him the scenes of London), the tale of Vaudracour and Julia
in book 9. But only in book 5 does he pause to analyse this
power; and here again, as in so many crucial passages of *The
Prelude*, we find him working through emblematic modes of
vision to new but structurally familiar conceptions of deeper
truth.

ii

Wordsworth opens book 5 of *The Prelude* with a lament for the
impermanence of man's glorious intellectual and artistic achieve-
ments, "the consecrated works of Bard and Sage" (5.41). His
sorrow, however, seems curiously impersonal and abstract:

Thou also, Man, hast wrought,
For commerce of thy nature with itself,
Things worthy of unconquerable life;
And yet we feel, we cannot chuse but feel
That these must perish. Tremblings of the heart

It gives, to think that the immortal being
No more shall need such garments; and yet Man,
As long as he shall be the Child of Earth,
Might almost "weep to have" what he may lose,
Nor be himself extinguish'd; but survive
Abject, depress'd, forlorn, disconsolate.

[5.17–27]

The quoted phrase in line 25, from Shakespeare's Sonnet 64, rings strangely false in its new context. For Shakespeare's sorrow, sung in the recognition that "nothing 'gainst Time's scythe can make defense" (Sonnet 12), is the very personal and immediate one

That Time will come and take my love away.
This thought is as a death, which cannot choose
But weep to have that which it fears to lose.

[Sonnet 64]

Wordsworth, in contrast, raises not a personal but a racial lament: the "Man" of his song here is not an individual, but collective mankind, and the potential loss he may survive, the destruction of the books which preserve "all the meditations of mankind" (5.37).[2] In effect Wordsworth is extending Shakespeare's anxiety to a further remove. Shakespeare had extolled his verse as *monumentum aere perennius* (see Sonnets 55, 65) and a means of preserving after death the memory and glory of his loved one for "the eyes of all posterity" (Sonnet 55):

Where, alack,
Shall Time's best jewel from Time's chest lie hid?[3]
Or what strong hand can hold his swift foot back?
Or who his spoil of beauty can forbid?
O, none, unless this miracle have might,
That in black ink my love may still shine bright.

[Sonnet 65]

But Wordsworth fears that even "black ink" may in time perish, and the figuratively characterized "adamantine holds of truth" (5.38) prove too veritably but a paper fortress.

Wordsworth's mention of these forebodings one day to a friend provokes the responsive anecdote of a strange dream, the concentrated imaging-forth of the friend's own "kindred hauntings" (5.55) which once came to him when he fell asleep while reading *Don Quixote* by the seaside. The main features of this dream—the Arab-Quixote figure; the stone which is also "Euclid's Elements," the book of "geometric Truth," and the "Shell / Of a surpassing brightness" that is also a book, Poetry; the mission "to bury those two Books" to preserve them from the coming deluge, prophesied by the Shell and even now pursuing the Arab across the wasteland—all correspond to features of Wordsworth's own anxiety (indeed, in the 1850 version of *The Prelude* he claims the dream as his own). While Wordsworth himself is immediately aware of this, however, he proves, in his self-interpretation, to be a somewhat evasive and misleading exegete. We need, I think, to examine some elements of this dream afresh.

We may begin by asking why the dream's two books appear as a stone and a shell. Of the two emblems, the shell is surely the more immediately expressive of its significance. Most obviously, of course, it is in its rhythmical, seemingly sculptured form a natural type of a work of art. Again like a work of art, it is created by a living being and is able to survive its creator. It is at once organic in its genesis and inorganically enduring in its final, mature form, exempt from organic degeneration or decay; thus it almost perfectly illustrates, in ways no plant or animal can, the Romantic concept of the organic nature of great art.

The stone which is "Euclid's Elements" may seem an emblem relatively inexpressive of its significance. Wordsworth gives not the slightest encouragement, for example, to the facile expectation that this stone representing "geometric Truth" will prove to be a regular crystal, a symmetrical polyhedron.[4] It is simply, and only, a stone. Compared to the shell, it suggests inorganic rather than organic, natural rather than human, "intellectual" rather than "sensuous" truth (5.42). At a deeper level of significance, however, the stone figuratively parallels the shell as the created, excrescent body of a living force. For where the human spirit sets forth its truths in works of art just as the conch creates its shell-body, so does the world's "sovereign Intellect" set forth its own truths in its own works (including the stone), which are effectively its body—"the speaking face of earth and heaven" (5.12), its "bodily Image" (5.15). The implications of this deeper analogy lend the enrichment of a powerful ambiguity to Wordsworth's summational cry,

> Oh! why hath not the mind
> Some element to stamp her image on
> In nature somewhat nearer to her own?
>
> [5.44-46]

Suddenly, "element" bears its technical meaning, one of the fundamental, constituent materials of the world, and "nature" demands the upper case. The world's "sovereign Intellect" stamps its "bodily Image" on the permanent elements in Nature, shrines which will survive all cataclysms:

> Should earth by inward throes be wrench'd throughout,
> Or fire be sent from far to wither all
> Her pleasant habitations, and dry up
> Old Ocean in his bed left sing'd and bare,
> Yet would the living Presence still subsist
> Victorious; and composure would ensue,
> And kindlings like the morning; presage sure,
> Though slow, perhaps, of a returning day.
>
> [5.29-36]

The human mind, by contrast—whether we read the lines to mean that the mind can stamp her image on no element of a nature (character) nearer to her own nature, or on no element in Nature nearer her own (spiritual) element, or on no elemental (essential, irreducible) thing at all—can only preserve its creations in the frail, perishable shrines of books and artifacts.[5]

The Arab of the dream commands Wordsworth's friend to hold the shell to his ear. When he does so, he hears

> in an unknown Tongue
> Which yet I understood, articulate sounds,
> A loud prophetic blast of harmony,
> An Ode, in passion utter'd, which foretold
> Destruction to the Children of the Earth,
> By deluge now at hand.
>
> [5.94-99]

It is curious and noteworthy, I would suggest, that the stone is not somehow the source of this prophecy. For the prediction of approaching natural catastrophe is traditionally the business of the Sage rather than the Bard—of the astrologer or astronomer, the meteorologist, the geologist. It becomes the business of the Bard only when the cataclysm represents not simply a random natural disaster but a moral punishment or purgation, a divine visitation upon man; but in the dream we are not warned that such is the case. Why, then, should the shell usurp a prophetic role properly belonging to the stone?

The answer to this question—actually a double answer—lies deeper in the emblematic significance of the shell and its ode. The dreamer hears this ode when he holds the shell to his ear; but what is it he hears? We know this from having shared the experience ourselves: he hears the sea. And the sea is, of course, precisely the matter of the shell's song—"deluge now at hand," "the waters of the deep" (5.130) which soon, as predicted, appear.

The shell, then, rather than the stone speaks this prophecy because it speaks of its own source. And its message foretelling "destruction to the Children of the Earth, / By deluge now at hand" is thus, paradoxically, "A joy, a consolation, and a hope" (5.109). For the shell promises that it shall be reclaimed from the desert wasteland by its native element; and the sea, the shell's source and home, is, in the language of the dream, the source and home of the human spirit. Here again we find the major threat and consolation informing Wordsworth's thought since 1798, the promise of a final merging in death with the great living spirit which infuses the entire world.

The coming of the sea, a type of the cataclysm Wordsworth had been brooding upon at the beginning of book 5, brings death to individual men, but not to all mankind. That the Arab, like Wordsworth, is concerned with a situation wherein mankind would not entirely be extinguished is apparent from his very attempt to bury the stone and shell: he is trying to preserve them for the flood's survivors. Similarly, while the deluge may threaten destruction to individual books of poetic truth, it does not so threaten the fundamental truths themselves. Indeed, the sea is those truths, and speaks itself everlastingly. As Wordsworth affirms later in this same book,

A gracious Spirit o'er this earth presides,
And o'er the heart of man: invisibly
It comes, directing those to works of love
Who care not, know not, think not what they do
[5.516-19]

—works, specifically, of literature: "romances," "legends," "adventures endless" (5.521, 524); and

> These spread like day, and something in the shape
> Of these, will live till man shall be no more.
> Dumb yearnings, hidden appetites are ours,
> And they must have their food.
>
> [5.528-31]

Thus, if not individual poetic works themselves, yet "the great Nature that exists in works / Of mighty Poets" (5.618-19) would, like great Nature herself—which is here to say, in terms of Wordsworth's own earlier figure, like "old Ocean" himself (5.32)—survive and regenerate; for "yet would the living Presence still subsist / Victorious" within both.

The shell's song, however, has an alternative, darker significance. For our question of what the dreamer hears in the shell has an alternative and more accurate answer: he hears only himself—not the eternal motion of the sea, but the pulsing of his own blood. The shell's prophecy of "destruction to the Children of the Earth" is thus the listener's self-born and self-referential prediction, a personal anticipation of an overwhelming by nature—an intimation of mortality. At the same time, one's own shell is in effect one's own poetry; at this level of the dream's signification, the Arab is himself not only, as "Arab of the Desert," emblematically a representative Ishmaelite "Child of Earth," but also, as "Semi-Quixote," a type of the poet.[6] The Arab's quixotic endeavor, accordingly, is an attempt to preserve his own poetry from the fate of dying with him, to save it so that it may live on after him. To bury it, of course, to save and preserve it, is thus simply to write and publish it. We should remember here that Cervantes himself repeatedly presents Don Quixote as a type of the writer and concludes his history by explicitly paralleling the knight-errant Quixote's and the writer Cide Hamete's undertakings:

> And said the most prudent Cide Hamete to his pen: "Here you shall rest, hanging from this rack by this copper wire, my quill. Whether you are well cut or badly pointed, here you shall live long ages, unless presumptuous and unworthy historians take you down to profane you. But before they touch you, warn them in as strong terms as you are able:

Beware, beware, all petty knaves,
I may be touched by none;
This enterprise, my worthy king,
Is kept for me alone.[7]

The identification at this level of the allegory of the coming deluge as the approach of the *individual*'s death incidentally clarifies a perplexing aspect of the dream, the fact that the "waters of the deep / Gathering upon us" seem after all to be gathering only upon the Arab, somehow harmlessly passing by the dreamer:

He left me: I call'd after him aloud;
He heeded not; but with his twofold charge
Beneath his arm, before me in full view
I saw him riding o'er the Desert Sands,
With the fleet waters of the drowning world
In chace of him.

[5.133-37]

The pursuing sea, at first behind them both, continues to close on the Arab, but is now apparently before, not behind, the dreamer; the sea which is chasing the Arab is chasing only him, because this sea, this time, is the Arab's own approaching death,

whereat I wak'd in terror
And saw the Sea before me; and the Book,
In which I had been reading, at my side.

[5.137-39]

The dreamer's terror is thus sympathetic and vicarious, not personal. And his waking, like the concluding of so much great literature, is restoratively cathartic. The sea is indeed before him, and the Arab must certainly have died beneath it. And truly, this Child of Earth died long ago, in 1616—but not before accomplishing his errand: for the shell he had once striven to save still survives, "buried" literally in the "rocky cave" wherein the reader sits (5.57), and is the book now lying by that awakened reader's side.

Seen in this light, Wordsworth's identification with the Arab bespeaks after all not a selfless but a selfish concern. Like the Arab, Wordsworth is inclined, in his devotion to his poetic vocation, to leave his friend behind him: "I, methinks, / Could share that Maniac's anxiousness, could go / Upon like errand"

(5.159-61).[8] The "great overthrow" he anticipates is his own death, truly an event predictable "by certain evidence." And his great anxiousness, possessing him

> When I have held a volume in my hand,
> Poor earthly casket of immortal Verse!
> Shakespeare, or Milton, Labourers divine!
>
> [5.163-65]

is not simply to preserve Shakespeare or Milton, but to emulate them.

Thus beneath the impersonal, cosmological anxiety of the opening of book 5, two quite personal anxieties lie hidden. First and fundamentally, Wordsworth is, as ever, anxious about the nature of the life to come:

> Tremblings of the heart
> It gives, to think that the immortal being
> No more shall need such garments [as books].
>
> [5.21-23]

But are these tremblings of hope or of fear? In other words, will the "immortal being" merge with or return to "the sovereign intellect" at the very source whence all great books derive their truths, or will it only, like Lucy, merge with the "bodily Image"? Will it no longer need "such garments" because as spirit it will be apotheosized above such needs, or because as matter it will be unconscious of them? Here as in the *Intimations* ode and elsewhere in *The Prelude*, we need to observe and respect the tentativeness of Wordsworth's conjectures.

Rising directly out of this anxiety for the intellect's immortality, Wordsworth's second concern is for its memorialization. If the mind perhaps may not live on in some way after the individual's death, it is all the more important that the mind's finest creations should. Hence Wordsworth's concern with preserving his meditations by recording them. The opening allusion to Shakespeare proves, after all, to be highly relevant and appropriate. For Wordsworth is not so much extending the fears and hopes of Sonnets 63 and 64 as echoing and sharing them—with one major, typical difference: the loved thing Wordsworth fears to lose is not another being, but his own intellectual identity and power.

This memorializing impulse, apparently so similar to that characterizing Wordsworth's poetry of 1800, yet differs from it so fundamentally as to make a comparison particularly instructive. In 1800, concerned for the survival or continuation in some form of the individual's *life*, Wordsworth's reaction was to create monuments in and of life—that is, in and of nature. His poems are themselves types of nature-monument surrogates, intended to imitate, supplement, and extend the memorializing powers of nature's own living presences. In 1804, by contrast, concerned instead for the survival or continuation in some form of the individual's *mind*, Wordsworth's reaction is now to create monuments in and of the mind—that is, in and of works of thought and imagination. Now it is not so much all the lives per se as "all the meditations of mankind" that chiefly interest him, and not so much memorials of life as "holds of truth" (5.37–38) that he hopes to create. If this is but a refinement of his earlier pursuit, it is nevertheless a refinement proceeding from a fundamental reconception of his poetic goals, and one leading, as a comparison of the *Intimations* ode with *To Joanna* or of the Snowdon episode with *Michael* vividly reminds us, to the production of a significantly different kind of poetry.

iii

"This Verse is dedicate to Nature's self, / And things that teach as Nature teaches" (5.230–31), Wordsworth announces in book 5. The "things" to which he is referring here are books, poems, tales, songs, plays—not all, for some works of literature are hollow and dead, but all those "which lay / Their sure foundations in the heart of Man" (5.199–200). His thesis, very simply, is that literature, like the mind which creates it, finds its great analogue and archetype in nature—is in essence and effect another nature.

Even nature, Wordsworth recognizes, though it cannot be killed, can be temporarily blasted and suppressed, reduced to a mere surface, just as individual human minds can be: cataclysmic fire might "wither all / Her pleasant habitations, and dry up / Old Ocean in his bed left sing'd and bare." Just such a withering diminishment and sterility is apparent in much literature and in the Thwackum mentality which sponsors it, "a pest / That might have dried me up, body and soul" (5.228-29). This literature is entirely and literally superficial, like the scorched earth or the reason-extinguished man, a thing of surfaces and appearances only; it is what Wordsworth starkly calls "the dead letter," unsustained by any underlying "spirit of things" (8.432). "Now this is hollow" (5.350), he warns, and its creature is but another type of superficiality, all form and no substance: "Forth bring him to the air of common sense, / And, fresh and shewy as it is, the Corps / Slips from us into powder" (5.352-54).

But nature, Wordsworth knows, is not merely a hollow appearance, the "senseless Idol" (4.304) or "soulless image" (6.454) it may sometimes appear to be; and neither, properly, is literature. Repeatedly Wordsworth himself confronts the seemingly "dead letter"—in the sailor's chalkings, Jack the Giant-killer's inscription, and the blind Beggar's label in London, and most strikingly in "those characters inscribed / On the green sod" (11.301-2) which monumentally record a murderer's name in the first spot of time—and, if he heeds it, finds it infused with life and power. Like nature, good literature is a surface exalted by a substantiating underpresence and creative of defamiliarizing transformations. Its surface, language itself, is like the ambivalent surface of the Snowdon scene: "the letter of the outward promise" shadows forth "the invisible soul" (12.254-55), but conversely "words are but under-agents" of "the language of the heavens" (12.272, 270). In many instances, to be sure, these intimated substantiations are in fact void, these defamiliarizings meretricious: "Full oft the [literary] objects of our love / Were false, and in their splendour overwrought" (5.593-94). But great literature is founded upon "the adamantine holds of truth," and in it we hear, as in a shell, the voice of waters bespeaking the underpresent sea, the underpresent soul.

It is thus with an effect of great naturalness and even inevitability that Wordsworth, in his culminating celebration of literature at the end of book 5, once again unmistakably evokes the Snowdon scene and its multiple significations, and that this book on "Books" which began by acknowledging the sealike underpresence substantiating great literature should end by acknowledging the mistlike defamiliarization emanating from it. Speaking of "the great Nature that exists in works / Of mighty Poets" (5.618-19; cf. 5.219-22, 230-31), and thereby already foreshadowing the analogousness of his visionary reading of nature to a visionary reading of literature, he now brings the emblematization of the Snowdon and Simplon episodes to bear on this new thesis:

> Visionary Power
> Attends upon the motions of the winds
> Embodied in the mystery of words.
> There darkness makes abode, and all the host
> Of shadowy things do work their changes there,
> As in a mansion like their proper home;
> Even forms and substances are circumfus'd
> By that transparent veil with light divine;
> And through the turnings intricate of Verse,
> Present themselves as objects recognis'd,
> In flashes, and with a glory scarce their own.
>
> [5.619–29]

Here as on Snowdon and at Simplon, power thrusts itself forth upon the senses as a defamiliarizing usurpation, wreaking upon the outward face of things transformations which do not obscure or disguise but rather reveal and glorify, veilings which are yet transparent, shadows which paradoxically illuminate. And the analogousness of this vision to those cannot, after all, be surprising to us; for this is but to identify great literature generically as what Wordsworth already recognizes it to be, the work of the imagination, a preservational enshrining (5.48, 11.342) or casketing (5.164) of certain acts of imaginational power performed by higher minds of the past.

Wordsworth's poetic ambition, then, is quite simply, and grandly, the hope

> that a work of mine,
> Proceeding from the depth of untaught things,
> Enduring and creative, might become
> A power like one of Nature's.
>
> [12.309–12]

We may well linger over his formulation here; for scarcely any other poet, and certainly no earlier poet, would or could have expressed his hopes for his work in such a way. That the lines nevertheless hardly give us pause only demonstrates the more strongly how naturally (surely this is the word he himself would have wished!) this highly personal version of the poet's ultimate ambition for poetic immortality—to create something that men will not willingly let die, to build a monument more lasting than bronze—derives from the philosophy of the very poem which proclaims it.

PART IV: AFTER 1805

CHAPTER 8
"Another and a Better World": *The Excursion* and the Transition to Faith

---

i

Just as Wordsworth presents the analogousness of man's and nature's imaginations as his greatest and most profound insight in *The Prelude*, so does he present their cognation as his deepest intuition. His metaphysics is, if anything, more remarkable for its cautiousness and conservatism on the latter point than for its boldness on the former. Blake and Coleridge, in their different ways, pushed beyond similar awarenesses of analogy to assume and insist upon identity; but Wordsworth refuses to leap thus beyond the teachings of his senses. In particular, as I have argued, he carefully, skeptically stops short of extrapolating from his awareness of the mind's power and its analogousness to nature's any faith in the individual mind's immortality. His calling, as he understands it, is exclusively in this world, not in another, or a former, or the next:

> Not in Utopia, subterraneous Fields,
> Or some secreted Island, Heaven knows where,
> But in the very world which is the world
> Of all of us, the place on which, in the end,
> We find our happiness, or not at all.[1]
>
> [*Prelude 1805* 10.723-27]

Increasingly after 1805, however, Wordsworth found himself unable or unwilling to endure without the further consolation of such a faith in the individual's immortality. The immediate impetus to this new attitude was surely, as is generally accepted, the death by drowning of his younger brother John on 5 February 1805. In an anguished letter to Sir George Beaumont a month after the event, Wordsworth presents his newly recognized spiritual dilemma starkly but precisely:

> Why have we a choice and a will, and a notion of justice and injustice, enabling us to be moral agents? Why have we sympathies that make the best of us so afraid of inflicting pain and sorrow, which yet we see dealt about us so lavishly by the supreme governor? Why should our notions of right towards each other, and to all sentient beings within our influence differ so widely from what appears to be his notion and rule, if everything were to end here? Would it be blasphemy to say that upon the supposition of the thinking principle being destroyed by death, however inferior we may be to the great Cause and ruler of things, we have *more of love* in our Nature than he has? The thought is monstrous; and yet how to get rid of it except upon the supposition of *another* and a *better world* I do not see. [*LEY*, p. 556]

"The supposition of the thinking principle being destroyed by death" is the thought that chiefly torments him. Nothing in the natural world he had so long and carefully observed encouraged him to suppose otherwise, but under the direct pressure of John's death Wordsworth found he could not follow the example of his own Pedlar in reconciling himself with equanimity to the finality of death. So instead, hesitantly at first, then more and more outspokenly and dogmatically, he abandons the eschatological tentativeness and skepticism so characteristic of the great *Intimations* ode and *The Prelude*, and chooses to believe, because he cannot tolerate the disconsolateness of unbelief. His ultimate decision is foreshadowed later in the same letter, as he continues to speak of his brother: "So good must be better; so high must be destined to be higher" (*LEY*, p. 556).

But if Wordsworth before 1805 consistently held back from resigning his this-worldly goals for a vague, otherworldly hope, yet the building tension between his humanistic and his transcendental longings which now, after John's death, collapsingly resolves into a dependent faith in an afterlife also frequently surfaces, though always subtly and ambiguously, in that previous work. A striking early example interrupts the Pedlar's narrative of Margaret in *The Ruined Cottage*:

My spirit clings
To that poor woman, so familiarly
Do I perceive her manner and her look
And presence, and so deeply do I feel
Her goodness that a vision of the mind,
A momentary trance comes over me
And to myself I seem to muse on one
By sorrow laid asleep, or borne away,
A human being destined to awake
To human life or something very near
To human life, when he shall come again
For whom she suffered.

[Ll. 614-25]

Here as elsewhere the Pedlar reveals his own all too human vulnerability to "sorrow and despair / From ruin and from change" (Addendum, 11.130–31) which his consoling appreciation of the "one life" nevertheless enables him to rise above. And even this momentary vision is ostensibly naturalistic rather than transcendental in its longings, a wishful fantasy like nothing so much as the story of Sleeping Beauty: the heroine lies long years in an enchanted sleep, frozen in time, but "destined to awake / To human life" when her husband, like a rescuing prince, comes to her at last. But the fairy-tale aura of the Pedlar's musings here cannot disguise his deeper, inexplicit allusion to the apocalyptic Raising of the Dead at the Second Coming, not of him "for whom she suffered," but of Him who suffered for all mankind. Inevitably the allusion to Christian eschatology, even in this seemingly parodic form, implicitly evokes as an alternative to the Pedlar's personal mode of consolation the possibility of a more transcendent hope.

A similar suggestion of transcendental hopes ambiguously infusing and coloring humanistic hopes informs a poem which indeed we have already noted for its otherworldly implications, "It is no Spirit who from heaven hath flown." Earlier I spoke of this poem as an expression of transcendental hope (Chapter 4, section iv); yet I am not at all convinced that Wordsworth consciously intended or even appreciated the transcendental implications of his utterance. The star, as Hartman notes, "at once incites and repels descendental or metamorphic myths"; and Wordsworth's response to it would appear in fact to be correspondingly ambivalent. What seems rather clearly a desire to transcend mortality—

> a thought
> That I might step beyond my natural race
> As thou seem'st now to do; might one day trace
> Some ground not mine; and, strong her strength above,
> My Soul, an Apparition in the place,
> Tread there with steps that no one shall reprove!
> [Ll. 12-17]

—may actually bear a radically opposed reading.[2] Seen as an image of a spirit flown from heaven or a mortal ascended from earth, Hesperus indeed suggests a man transcendently lifted beyond man's "natural race." But seen as the first star of the evening, a star inevitably soon to be followed and joined by a multitude of others, Hesperus does not transcend its natural race but only precedes it. In this sense, it becomes a type not of the soul translated to another life but of the poet somewhat ahead of his own time, as Wordsworth certainly felt himself to be,[3] and anticipates his prayer of the *Prospectus* to *The Recluse* that "my verse may live and be / Even as a light hung up in heaven to chear / Mankind in times to come" (*HG*, 1032-34). So regarded, Hesperus is "most ambitious" as a poet is, ambitious for poetic self-memorialization and immortality, like the Wordsworth whose secret hope and anxiousness in book 5 of *The Prelude* receive open statement shortly afterward in *Personal Talk*: "Oh! might my name be numbered among theirs [that is, among "the Poets," notably Shakespeare and Spenser], / Then gladly would I end my mortal days" (ll. 55-56).

After 1805, however, Wordsworth's immortal longings, no more to be thus delimited by his mortal hopes, begin to break loose from this naturalistic matrix and to seize more explicitly upon a transcendental faith. The change surfaces first in the letters, but soon appears, if but tentatively, in the published work as well.[4] Thus in "Yes, it was the mountain Echo" (mid-June 1806), for example, Wordsworth speaks of mortal man's "echoes from beyond the grave, / Recognized intelligence!" (ll. 15-16).[5] In MS. B of *Home at Grasmere* (late 1806), he similarly—and in this context inappropriately, as he apparently came to see, for the line was later cancelled—prepares to sing of "hope for this

earth and hope beyond the grave" (*HG*, p. 395). More provoca-
tively still, an insinuation of transcendental hope strikingly con-
fuses and charges a passage of *Home at Grasmere* which ostensibly
is but proclaiming once again the poet's self-memorializing am-
bition. Feeling that "unto me ... / ... an internal brightness is
vouchsafed / That must not die, that must not pass away" (*HG*,
ll. 885-87), Wordsworth resolves to forestall such loss by writing
and publishing his insights, by "speak[ing] as I have felt / Of
what in man is human or divine" (*HG*, ll. 908-9). But his inter-
vening statement of his ambition is most curiously ambivalent:

> Possessions have I, wholly, solely mine,
> Something within, which yet is shared by none—
> Not even the nearest to me and most dear—
> Something which power and effort may impart.
> I would impart it; I would spread it wide,
> Immortal in the world which is to come.
> I would not wholly perish within this,
> Lie down and be forgotten in the dust,
> I and the modest partners of my days,
> Making a silent company in death.
>
> [*HG*, ll. 897-906]

In context, the immortality Wordsworth seeks here is clearly
the immortality of poetic fame and the survival into future
generations of his song. But what distinction, then, is he making
here between "the world which is to come" and "this [world]"?
In truth he is making none at all. But the slipperiness of Words-
worth's syntax here and the ringing language of that line,
"Immortal in the world which is to come," almost inevitably
compel our momentary misreading of that coming world as a
transcendent one.

ii

For a few years, Wordsworth hesitates in a tenuous balance be-
tween his humanistic and his transcendental impulses, seeming
to derive consolations from both but pushing the claims of
neither so far as to disturb its precarious equilibrium with the
other. His most notable and successful work of this period, *The
White Doe of Rylstone* (late 1807), may perhaps display the
vagueness of thought to which one critic has objected;[6] but in-

sofar as this be so, it would seem to be the vagueness of a willful camouflage. Wordsworth implies but does not insist upon the otherworldliness of Emily's final consolation, instead allowing her a natural spiritualism much like that of the later books of *The Prelude*: thus while he says she is "by sorrow lifted towards her God," he immediately clarifies moderatingly, "uplifted to the purest sky / Of undisturbed *mortality* (ll. 1851–53; my emphasis). And readers of the poem have not failed to perceive this latitude. So Hoxie Fairchild, discounting the pious language and the supernaturalistic patina of the poem, aptly notes that "the doe is no more necessarily a gift of grace than the ass which softened Peter Bell's hard heart by thoroughly naturalistic means." Similarly, Martin Price argues that "the qualities of the Doe which make her mysterious and provocative in the first canto are given a largely natural explanation in the ensuing narrative. The result is not an explaining away but a deepening of the import of the Doe's influence. A natural explanation of the Doe is an occasion for greater wonder than the 'fancies wild' of the naive worshippers"; and Heffernan agrees that, "presupposed in Canto First, the spirituality of the creature has [by the poem's end] been meticulously established in terms of its relationship with Emily—a relationship whose supernatural influence is firmly rooted in the natural exchange of animal loyalty and human affection."[7]

Within this essentially naturalistic context in *The White Doe of Rylstone*, a familiar Wordsworthian structural device makes one more appearance. In 1808 Wordsworth told Coleridge that the banner and doe "produced their influences and effects, not by powers naturally inherent in them, but such as they were endued with by the Imagination of the human minds on whom they operated" (*LMY* 1:197; and see also *LMY* 2:705). This authorial assertion to the contrary notwithstanding, however, I would argue that the banner and the doe are very different kinds of emblems, standing prominently opposed to one another in this poem much as contrasting emblems or modes of vision do in so many of Wordsworth's earlier poems—*The Borderers*, *The Ruined Cottage, Hart-Leap Well*. The banner, with its "dread emblazonry" (l. 683) of "the sacred Cross" and "the five dear wounds our Lord did bear" (ll. 356–57), is indeed an emblem subjectively endued with its significance (and even given its very being) by men. It emblematizes a mystery, the familiar, fundamental mystery of Christianity, but does not partake of it; the mystery is extrinsic to the sign. The defamiliarizing "mystery" (l. 210) of the doe, however, is intrinsic to the creature, and thus her nature and history prove to afford "substantial motive" (l. 201) for her present behavior. Though liable, like all things, to subjective readings (witness the various "superstitious fancies" [l. 215] of the townspeople who conjecture about her visits to Bolton Priory), she nevertheless has, like natural objects in *The Prelude*, an innate, objective significance, which it is Wordsworth's great purpose in the poem to educe.

The crucial tension informing *The White Doe of Rylstone*, then, is not only between two different attitudes toward emblems, as Hartman has argued, but between attitudes toward two different kinds of emblems. Thus I would push the connection which Hartman suggests between this poem and *Hart-Leap Well* a good deal further than Hartman does himself.[8] Norton's mode of vision, like Sir Walter's, is subjectively emblematic; the townspeople's, superstitious like the shepherd's, is iconic; and the poet's (and ultimately, if perhaps unconsciously, Emily's), like the poet's in *Hart-Leap Well*, is objectively emblematic (see above, Chapter 4, section i). Wordsworth's identification with Emily's ultimate viewpoint here suggests how the poem remains, despite its supernatural trappings, at its heart true to his earlier philosophy. Thus *The White Doe of Rylstone* would appear to be, not Wordsworth's first important transcendental poem, but his last important naturalistic one.

iii

After 1808, Wordsworth no longer holds back from the espousal of a truly transcendental, essentially Christian faith. In the first *Essay on Epitaphs*, for example, he avows as his own and asserts as innately all men's "the faith that Man is an immortal being," refers specifically to man's as not only "a rational, but . . . an immortal Soul," and speaks of "the country of everlasting life" as lying just beyond the bournes of our mortality (*Prose* 2:52–53).[9] In close association with this conversion, moreover, two significant changes of attitude, long developing, now become pronounced in Wordsworth's poetry. First, he experiences and presents an essential change in his mode of vision: abandoning the objectively emblematic mode so characteristic of *The Prelude* and even of *The White Doe of Rylstone*, he now instead consistently tends to see and write in a subjectively emblematic way. Second, and incompatibly, he often presses now to read his emblems again as symbols, assurances of synecdochal identification. These two changes, though simultaneous, must be carefully distinguished, for they produce markedly different effects. The former is essentially a modulation; the latter, however, is inescapably a compromise. The former simply makes Wordsworth a different kind of poet; the latter, sadly, only makes him a weaker one.

Perhaps the easiest way to appreciate the change in Wordsworth's emblematic mode is to consider his new treatment of clouds, the most malleable, transient, and unsubstantial of nature's features. In the objectively emblematic vision of *The Prelude*, as we have seen, Wordsworth values clouds and mists not for themselves—he is well aware how inevitably subjective no less than transient and unsubstantial their appearances are— but for their defamiliarizing power, their power to sensitize him to nature's substantiating underpresences by framing, highlighting, veiling, or even mimicking nature's relatively more enduring appearances. The Solitary's striking cloud vision, which dominates *The Excursion*, works in quite a different way, however, and bespeaks a very different set of values:

> A single step, that freed me from the skirts
> Of the blind vapour, opened to my view
> Glory beyond all glory ever seen
> By waking sense or by the dreaming soul!
> The appearance, instantaneously disclosed,
> Was of a mighty city. . . .
> . . . .
>
> Fabric it seemed of diamond and of gold,
> With alabaster domes, and silver spires,
> And blazing terrace upon terrace, high
> Uplifted; here, serene pavilions bright,
> In avenues disposed; there, towers begirt
> With battlements that on their restless fronts
> Bore stars—illumination of all gems!
> . . . .

Right in the midst, where interspace appeared
Of open court, an object like a throne
Beneath a shining canopy of state
Stood fixed; and fixed resemblances were seen
To implements of ordinary use,
But vast in size, in substance glorified.

[2.830–66 and app. crit.]

Wordsworth himself was not unfamiliar with such visions: the evening of his wedding day, for example, he beheld in the twilit western sky cloud-apparitions of

Grecian Temple, Minaret, and Bower;
And, in one part, a Minster with its Tower
Substantially distinct; a place for Bell
Or clock to toll from. Many a glorious pile. . . .

[*Composed after a Journey
across the Hambleton Hills,
Yorkshire*, ll. 6–9 app. crit.]

But in a responsive sequel to the poem recording this apparition he dismisses such visions, however beautiful or moving, as essentially irrelevant to the nurturing of man's soul:

Nor will I praise a cloud, however bright,
Disparaging Man's gifts, and proper food.
The Grove, the sky-built Temple, and the Dome,
Though clad in colours beautiful and pure,
Find in the heart of man no natural home:
The immortal Mind craves objects that endure.

["Those words were uttered
as in pensive mood," ll. 7–
12 and app. crit.]

The Solitary's response to his own vision, however, characteristic of all the nature readings in *The Excursion*, is entirely different: "That which I *saw* was the revealed abode / Of Spirits in beatitude" (2.873–74). Now nature does not speak of her own inner self, but is made to speak of heaven; and nature's appearances, when revelatory, are not manifestations but illustrations, emblems of a belief already present in the mind of the beholder. As Wordsworth himself remarks in a letter soon after the poem's publication,

> Do not you perceive that my conversations almost all take place out of doors, and all with grand objects of Nature, surrounding the speakers, for the express purpose of their being alluded to in illustration of the subjects treated of? [*LMY* 2:191]

Too often for Wordsworth now, though, the difference between illustration and manifestation tends to disappear under the pressure of his immortal longings. The Wanderer especially, even in the later-written portions of *The Excursion*, cannot rest comfortably in this subjectively emblematic reading of nature, but continually betrays his desire for the absolute assurance of a direct revelation. His quest for such a revelation, however, is characteristically roundabout. Eschewing the enthusiast's or mystic's hope for direct union with God, the Wanderer instead strains to extend his earlier, one-life identification of man with nature into a further, iconic identification of nature with God. He thereby in effect aspires to the ends of enthusiasm without appearing to indulge in its means.

The Wanderer's most sustained expression of this supplementary impulse to iconic vision, his lengthy argument in book 4, also demonstrates how discreetly and even, we might guess, unconsciously Wordsworth is venturing this response to his eschatological anxiety. For in his long disquisition here on the history of religion—more accurately, the history of natural religion—the Wanderer does in fact acknowledge that all these forms of iconic vision, these folk beliefs which populate nature with divinities or govern her through the interventions of divinities, are after all merely superstitious delusions, emblematic projections, the "outward ministers / Of inward conscience" (4.836–37). Despite such an awareness, however, he still celebrates these misreadings of nature for the very iconic, symbolic assumptions which constitute their illusoriness:

> Who would forbid them, if their presence serve,
> On thinly-peopled mountains and wild heaths,
> Filling a space, else vacant, to exalt
> The forms of Nature, and enlarge her powers?
> [4.843–46]

And by the end of his argument his own tacit conversion or regression to an iconic vision becomes apparent in his anecdote of the

> curious child, who dwelt upon a tract
> Of inland ground, applying to his ear
> The convolutions of a smooth-lipped shell;
> To which, in silence hushed, his very soul
> Listened intensely; and his countenance soon
> Brightened with joy; for from within were heard
> Murmurings, whereby the monitor expressed
> Mysterious union with its native sea.
> Even such a shell the universe itself
> Is to the ear of Faith.
>
> [4.1133-42]

As such a shell speaking to the ear of Faith—the Wanderer's ear—then, what the universe expresses is mysterious union, synecdochal identification, with its creator. But how can this by itself be consolatory? The Wanderer's syllogism of faith is in truth an enthymeme; his unspoken assumption is clearly that this mysterious union exists not only for the natural world, but also for the listener—in other words, that there also exists a mysterious union of the ear with the shell. Nor is there the slightest indication, this time, that he is in any way able to regard his own iconic assumption as but one more emblematic projection—even though his chosen image of the shell, which sounds of the sea but actually only echoes the listener's pulse, must inevitably incline us to interpret the Wanderer's own tidings not as original intimations but only as an echo of his own hopes.

That the Wanderer's self-blindness is also Wordsworth's own finds striking confirmation in Wordsworth's curious defense of *The Excursion* to Catherine Clarkson in a letter of early 1815, his fullest private statement on the poem. Writing huffily in response to the relayed criticism of Miss Patty Smith, he asserts:

> She talks of my being a worshipper of Nature—a passionate expression uttered incautiously in the Poem upon the Wye has led her into this mistake, she reading in cold-heartedness and substituting the letter for the spirit. Unless I am greatly mistaken, there is nothing of this kind in the Excursion. . . . She condemns me for not distinguishing between nature as the work of God and God himself. But where does she find this doctrine inculcated? Where does she gather that the Author of the Excursion looks upon nature and God as the same?

But then, only a few sentences later, he juxtaposes a remarkably telling anecdote:

> Oh! that your Correspondent had heard a conversation which I had in bed with my sweet little Boy, four and a half years old, upon this subject the other morning. "How did God make me? Where is God? How does he speak? He never spoke to *me*." I told him that God was a spirit, that he was not like his flesh which he could touch; but more like his thoughts in his mind which he could *not* touch.—The wind was tossing the fir trees, and the sky and light were dancing about in their dark branches, as seen through the window—Noting these fluctuations he exclaimed eagerly—"There's a bit of him I see it there!" [*LMY* 2:189]

It would be difficult to imagine an anecdote less likely to allay Miss Smith's misgivings, or better calculated to confirm her in her reading of *The Excursion*. But our amazement at the signal inaptness of Wordsworth's response should not in turn blind us to the deeper relevance of the anecdote to the poem. Why does Wordsworth relish his son's notion so? The answer, I would venture to suggest, is that it proves, in fact, to recreate the Wanderer's enthymeme of faith. The unexpressed premise here—Wordsworth's, if not his son's—is the familiar one of the correspondent breeze, associating the poet, or more generally man, with nature. The explicit premise, moreover, is again that of the correspondent breeze—this time, however, indicating the correspondence of nature and God. Then emblem collapses into symbol, analogy is taken as identity, and thereby a hope becomes a faith. Thus does young William Wordsworth, Jr., almost perfectly reproduce the Wanderer's avenue to God. This is no straightforward enthusiasm, for he claims no immediate revelation: "Where is God? How does he speak? He never spoke to *me*." But the roundabout quest through nature promises revelation just the same: "There's a bit of him I see it there!"

In too many such ways, the philosophical arguments of *The Excursion*, especially those of the Wanderer, are simply childish and naïve. Thus the example of this poem suggests that Wordsworth's poetic decline after 1807 results not from his loss of youthful spontaneity, his adoption of a transcendental creed, or his conversion to Christian orthodoxy, but from a basic philosophical naïveté and immaturity. But if one part of Wordsworth, like his narrator-Poet, all too uncritically accepts the Wanderer's sermons at their self-proclaimed value, yet another part, like his skeptical Solitary, is not to be so easily persuaded. The Solitary's resistance to the combined and blended arguments of the Wanderer and the Pastor represents a lingering philosophical honesty by which Wordsworth at least preserves, almost despite himself, a strong core of intellectual respectability. Wordsworth's comment, years later, on a possible extension of *The Excursion* helpfully highlights this ambivalence:

> When I reported this promise of the Solitary [to wander again some-time with the other three (9.775-78)], and long after, it was my wish, and I might say intention, that we should resume our wanderings, and pass the Borders into his native country, where, as I hoped, he might witness, in the society of the Wanderer, some religious cere-mony—a sacrament, say, in the open fields, or a preaching among the mountains—which, by recalling to his mind the days of his early childhood, when he had been present on such occasions in company with his parents and nearest kindred, might have dissolved his heart into tenderness, and so to have done more toward restoring the Christian faith in which he had been educated, and, with that, con-tentedness and even cheerfulness of mind, than all that the Wanderer and the Pastor, by their several effusions and addresses, had been able to effect. [*PW* 5:474-75]

Here again we find Wordsworth persisting in his confused at-tempt somehow to blend the teachings of natural and transcen-dental piety, this time with a plan to stage a Christian sacrament or sermon in the open theater of nature (as if he had not already done as much repeatedly in *The Excursion*), and to associate by sheer juxtaposition the promises of Christianity with the joys of early childhood. We may well be grateful, for Words-worth's sake no less than our own, that he never realized this embarrassing intention. But at the same time we must do him the justice of recognizing that what prevented him from writing such a work is precisely and only what prevented him from so restoring the Solitary to contentedness and cheerfulness in the first place—nothing less than his own persistently honest skep-ticism. Though he asserts that this facilely optimistic continua-tion of *The Excursion* "was my wish, and I might say intention," his subsequent description yet too obviously belies the latter claim. For when he says that *"as I hoped,* [the Solitary] *might* witness" some religious ceremony which *"might* have dissolved his heart into tenderness," he is explicitly confessing how purely wishful is such a design, and how unreal. It is as if the skeptical Solitary has a life of his own, beyond the poet's control. And so, in a very real sense, he has. For this Fenwick note makes sense only when we recognize that its speaker is not Wordsworth, but rather his erstwhile persona, the anonymous narrator of *The Excursion*, who lives on after 1814 as Wordsworth's public, pious voice—just as the stubborn Solitary lives on as Wordsworth's more private self, still skeptically resisting the pious blandishments of that public poetry.

Appendix A
The Date of *To H. C.*

To H.C. appears in MS. M (DC MS. 44), which was completed by 6 March 1804. Reed suggests that the poem was "possibly composed between 27 Mar and c 17 June 1802, or, more probably, early 1804, by 6 Mar; fairly certainly between the earliest and latest of these dates" (*CMY*, p. 27). He bases these conclusions on two points: the poem's title and its affinities with the *Intimations* ode. Both points, however, would appear to lend themselves to a different conclusion.

The poem was first published in 1807 under the title *To H. C. Six Years Old*. Reed sees this as evidence that the poem may have been composed after 19 September 1802, Hartley Coleridge's sixth birthday. Noting, however, that in the 1804 MS the poem is entitled simply *To H. C.*, he adds,

> The phrase "Six Years Old". . . may have been subjoined by Wordsworth to the title as a deliberate parallel to the title used by STC on 22 Sept 1803 for his own poem to HC, *The Language of the Birds*—that is, "Extempore—to a Child of Six Years Old" (see *STCL* 2:998)—or simply for its appropriateness to the content. [*CMY*, p. 180 n]

Now, when Coleridge first published the poem to which Reed refers, on 16 October 1802, he entitled it *The Language of Birds: Lines spoken extempore, to a little child, in early spring.*[1] That the poem does probably date from spring 1802 is further supported by Dorothy Wordsworth's mention in her journal entry for 6 May 1802 of receiving "a letter from Coleridge with verses to Hartley"; Moorman notes that these verses are probably

171

this same poem, which indeed is the only likely candidate among Coleridge's extant poetry (*DWJ*, p. 122 and 122 n). In the spring of 1802, however, Hartley was just over five and a half years old—slightly closer to six than to five. Since Coleridge refers to his son as having been "a Child of Six Years Old" at this time, it would seem that Wordsworth's parallel reference "Six Years Old" might similarly mean "almost six years old," and might, as easily and as properly as Coleridge's, apply to the Hartley of spring 1802.

Following a suggestion by Jared R. Curtis in his dissertation on Wordsworth's poetry of spring 1802, Reed notes,

> The close affinities in style and content between stanzas V-VIII of the [*Intimations*] *Ode*, some part of which may have been composed 17 June, and *To H. C. Six Years Old* . . . argue a close connection, perhaps chronological.

Since these stanzas of the ode were more probably composed in early 1804, however, Reed decides that

> early 1804 appears a more probable time of composition for *To H. C.* The poem could have been based on materials composed for the *Ode* at that time with the immediate object of inclusion in MS M, then being made up for STC. [*CMY*, p. 180n]

Against these conjectures, I would argue that *To H. C.* seems even more closely related to *Resolution and Independence* as a statement of fears which the latter poem carefully restates and ultimately resolves (see above, Chapter 4, section iii). *To H. C.* does indeed evince a close thematic relation to the *Intimations* ode—and not simply to stanzas 5-8, but even more significantly to stanzas 1-4, with their comparison of the adult's sense of a lost glory to the child's spontaneous joy. (I see no necessity, however, for concluding, as Reed does, that the ode verses preceded those *To H. C.* rather than vice versa.) And just as *Resolution and Independence* represents Wordsworth's revisionary response to and resolution of his own early *Intimations* ode stanzas, it would seem to relate similarly, and even more pointedly and directly, to *To H. C.* It is very difficult to believe, on the other hand, that Wordsworth could have given way to the particular anxieties of *To H. C.* after he had already resolved precisely those same anxieties in *Resolution and Independence*, and almost inconceivable that he could have written *To H. C.* in early 1804, just when he was reaffirming the philosophy of *Resolution and Independence* in his *Ode to Duty* (see above, Chapter 4, section iv). Therefore I would propose 3 May 1802, when Wordsworth began writing *Resolution and Independence*, as a terminus ad quem for *To H. C.*

Another factor would seem to allow us to advance this date by a month with some confidence. On 4 April 1802, Coleridge wrote as a letter to Sara Hutchinson the first version of his *Dejection*. The draft obviously draws on and responds to the early stanzas of Wordsworth's *Intimations* ode, written on 27 March and certainly shown or read to Coleridge shortly thereafter during the Wordsworths' visit to Greta Hall 28 March–5 April. It also, I would suggest, draws on and responds to *To H. C.* Where Wordsworth had argued that the joyful Hartley knows nothing of injuries and wrongs and could not sustain them, Coleridge rejoins more reasonably that a joyful person is not spared all injuries, but can in his joy rise above them:

> I am not the buoyant Thing, I was of yore—
> When I like an own Child, I to Joy belong'd;
> For others mourning oft, myself oft sorely wrong'd,
> Yet bearing all things then, as if I nothing bore!
>
> Yes, dearest Sara! yes!
> There *was* a time when tho' my path was rough,
> The Joy within me dallied with Distress;
> And all Misfortunes were but as the stuff
> Whence Fancy made me Dreams of Happiness.
> [*STCL* 2:796]

And joy, Coleridge further asserts, is available to the "pure of Heart" (*STCL* 2:798) of whatever age, not to children only.

Thus *To H. C.* would seem to be a part of the continuing poetic dialogue between Wordsworth and Coleridge in 1802, and probably dates from between 4 March (Wordsworth's first visit to Greta Hall since 29 December 1801, and so his first view of Hartley that spring) and 4 April 1802, possibly as late as 3 May 1802.

Appendix B
The Date of "It is no Spirit who from heaven hath flown"

In THE Isabella Fenwick note to "It is no Spirit," Wordsworth dates and comments on the poem as follows:

> 1803. Town-End. I remember the instant my sister, S. H., called me to the window of our cottage, saying, "Look how beautiful is yon star! It has the sky all to itself." I composed the verses immediately.[1] [*PW* 2:518]

Wordsworth's datings of his poems in the Fenwick notes often err by a year or two, occasionally even more. But this particular date is known to be at least approximately correct, and the anecdote Wordsworth relates is so specific as to have encouraged a more precise dating of the poem. Reed notes that Sara Hutchinson was visiting the Wordsworths at Grasmere from sometime after 8 November 1802 to 7 January 1803, and again from 1 to 28 April 1803, and accordingly suggests these two periods as alternative times of composition (*CMY*, p. 29 n).

I would propose that we may date the poem more precisely still. In both the poem and the note Wordsworth clearly seems to be referring to the true evening star, Venus Hesperus. He specifically names the star Hesperus in the poem (1. 4); and that he indeed means Venus, and not simply and imprecisely the first star seen that night, seems evident from the further detail, "First admonition that the sun is down! / For yet it is broad daylight" (ll. 5-6). For ordinarily the first star of the evening will appear in the first areas of the heavens to darken, to the east or towards the zenith; but Venus as an evening star always appears in the western sky, where it is at times so much brighter than any star that it shines clearly even before sunset. Sara Hutchinson's remark in context also implies that the lone star she saw was in the western sky, and so probably Venus; for Dove Cottage then afforded a fine, open view to the west and southwest, across the lake of Grasmere, while the hillside beneath which it stands blocks out the view to the east.

Further, there is a variety of firm evidence elsewhere in Wordsworth's work that he did carefully note and distinguish Venus as the true evening star. *Composed by the Sea-Side, near Calais, August, 1802; To the Planet Venus, an Evening Star* (October 1831); *To the Planet Venus, Upon its approximation (as an Evening Star) to the Earth, January, 1838*; and "The Crescent-moon, the Star of Love" (February 1841) all refer more or less explicitly to Venus, and all date from times when Venus was indeed prominent as the evening star.[2]

In fact Venus passed through its inferior conjunction (that is, between the earth and the sun) on 31 December 1802.[3] Before this time (and since mid-March, 1802), it was the evening star; afterwards (and until mid-October, 1803), it was the morning star. So Sara's and Wordsworth's observation of Hesperus can only have occurred between 8 November and 31 December 1802. (During the last several days of this period, however, Venus was so close to its conjunction, and therefore apparently so close to the sun, as to have been effectively lost to sight.) Furthermore, Venus reached its greatest brightness as an evening star on about 26 November 1802, and for several months before and several weeks after this time it would have been strikingly brilliant, many times brighter than the brightest star, and indisputably the most prominent feature of the western sky after sunset—indeed, a feature which it would be very difficult not to notice. And the moon, which entered its new phase on 25 November 1802, would have left Venus with "the sky all to itself" at sunset on that evening and for those of the preceding three weeks or so, and by very early in the evening of 26 November.

Thus it seems almost certain that Wordsworth composed "It is no Spirit" between 8 November and late December 1802, probably by 26 November.

Notes

Introduction

1. F. R. Leavis, *Revaluation: Tradition and Development in English Poetry* (London: Chatto and Windus, 1936), p. 165.

2. Most critics agree in seeing a change and discontinuity in Wordsworth's philosophy in early 1798. A minority also detect another change, beginning after mid-1798 and *Tintern Abbey* and culminating in the poetry of 1804: see, for example, John Jones, *The Egotistical Sublime: A History of Wordsworth's Imagination* (London: Chatto and Windus, 1954); Jonathan Wordsworth, *The Music of Humanity: A Critical Study of Wordsworth's Ruined Cottage* (New York: Harper and Row, 1969), and "The Growth of a Poet's Mind," *Cornell Library Journal*, no. 11 (Spring 1970): 10–16; Paul D. Sheats, *The Making of Wordsworth's Poetry, 1785–1798* (Cambridge, Mass.: Harvard University Press, 1973), pp. 249–51. Alan Grob, developing this latter view, sees Wordsworth's career from 1797 to 1805 "as a sequence of stages, each possessing a separate and identifiable philosophic character and each falling within reasonably well-defined chronological boundaries": an empirical phase (1797–1800), a transitional phase (1802), and a transcendental phase (1804) (*The Philosophic Mind: A Study of Wordsworth's Poetry and Thought, 1797–1805* [Columbus: Ohio State University Press, 1973], pp. 6–10).

3. Quoted in Henry Crabb Robinson, *Henry Crabb Robinson on Books and Their Writers*, ed. Edith Morley (London: J. M. Dent & Sons, 1938), pp. 87, 158, 482.

4. On Wordsworth as preeminently an imaginative as opposed to fanciful poet, see *STCL* 2:1034; Samuel Taylor Coleridge, *Biographia Literaria*, ed. John Shawcross (London: Oxford University Press, 1907), 2:124.

René Wellek, *A History of Modern Criticism: 1750–1950* (New Haven, Conn.: Yale University Press, 1955-), 2:174. Cf. M. H. Abrams, *The Mirror and the Lamp: Romantic Theory and the Critical Tradition*

(1953; rpt. New York: W. W. Norton & Co., 1958), pp. 168-69, 295. On Coleridge's value judgments, see Coleridge, *Biographia Literaria* 2:202; *STCL* 2:865-66; *Statesman's Manual*, p. 30.

While an investigation of Coleridge's critical theories is at best tangential to my subject, it may be helpful to indicate a few loci of these associations in his works. The following, singly or in combination, are some of the most succinct: *The Statesman's Manual*, in *The Collected Works of Samuel Taylor Coleridge*, vol. 6, *Lay Sermons*, ed. R. J. White (Princeton, N.J.: Princeton University Press, 1972), p. 29 (the Old Testament prophets "are living *educts* of the Imagination," which power "gives birth to a system of symbols, harmonious in themselves, and consubstantial with the truths, of which they are the *conductors*"), p. 30 (allegories "are but empty echoes which the fancy arbitrarily associates with apparitions of matter"); *Miscellaneous Criticism*, ed. Thomas M. Raysor (Cambridge, Mass.: Harvard University Press, 1936), p. 191 (Greek myth is "fundamentally allegorical"); *STCL* 2:865-66 (Greek myth "is but fancy," while Hebrew poetry, wherein "each Thing has a Life of it's own, & yet they are all one Life," is supremely imaginative).

5. Coleridge, *Miscellaneous Criticism*, pp. 29, 102; *Biographia Literaria* 2:124; *Table Talk and Omniana*, ed. T. Ashe (London: Bell, 1909), p. 291 (comment of 23 June 1834); *STCL* 2:866. The occasion for the last remark is a passage from *Comus* which Coleridge proceeds to interpret in extensive detail "as an allegory of Christianity," concluding, "There is a general Ridicule cast on all allegorizers of Poets—read Milton's prose works, & observe whether he was one of those who joined in this Ridicule" (*STCL* 2:866-67).

Perhaps the best discussion of Coleridge's seemingly disparate pronouncements on allegory is that by John Gatta, Jr., "Coleridge and Allegory," *Modern Language Quarterly* 38 (1977): 62-77.

6. Paul de Man, "The Rhetoric of Temporality," in *Interpretation: Theory and Practice*, ed. Charles S. Singleton (Baltimore, Md.: Johns Hopkins University Press, 1969), pp. 190, 191; and see pp. 173-91 passim.

7. This is the fundamental thesis of M. H. Abrams, *Natural Supernaturalism: Tradition and Revolution in Romantic Literature* (New York: W. W. Norton & Co., 1971); see pp. 13, 65-68.

8. While the terms *emblem* and *allegory* are essentially synonymous, I have tended to stress the former in this study simply because the latter connotes narrative or dramatic action, while Wordsworth's usual concern is less with actions than with images.

9. Erwin Panofsky, *Meaning in the Visual Arts* (Garden City, N. Y.: Doubleday & Co., 1955), p. 147.

10. Enid Welsford, *Salisbury Plain: A Study in the Development of Wordsworth's Mind and Art* (Oxford: Basil Blackwell & Mott, 1966), p. 107. Cf. James A. W. Heffernan's very similar formulation that in a Words-

worthian emblem "abstract meaning is not imposed upon an object; it is elicited *from* an object" (*Wordsworth's Theory of Poetry: The Transforming Imagination* [Ithaca, N. Y.: Cornell University Press, 1969], p. 194).

Introduction to Part I

1. Jonathan Wordsworth, *The Music of Humanity*, pp. 200-201.

Chapter 1

1. Wordsworth's imagery here is interestingly reminiscent of *Salisbury Plain*, where the sailor sees, in a "desert" area, a body hanging in a gibbet and attended by a carrion raven. See William Wordsworth, *The Salisbury Plain Poems*, ed. Stephen Gill, The Cornell Wordsworth (Ithaca, N. Y.: Cornell University Press, 1975), pp. 116, 126, and *PW* 1:98 app. crit.; and cf. *Descriptive Sketches* (1793), 402-7.

2. Cf. Matilda's cursing of her father's murderer, ll. 2147-54 and app. crit., where she wills for the guilty man an experience of iconic vision corresponding to his guilty conscience: "Let him *think* he sees, / If e'er he entereth the house of God, / The roof, self-moved, unsettling o'er his head" (my emphasis). And cf. the moving stones pursuing the sailor in *Adventures on Salisbury Plain* (see Wordsworth, *The Salisbury Plain Poems*, p. 127, and *PW* 1:99): Wordsworth's source for this image emphasized the supernatural character of the event, observed not only by the guilty man but also by a corroborating witness (*The Salisbury Plain Poems*, pp. 309-10), but Wordsworth transforms it to the delusion of a guilty conscience, one of "the mind's phantoms."

3. Cf. Geoffrey H. Hartman's observation that for Rivers "there is no Nature that is not established or manipulated by man" (*Wordsworth's Poetry, 1787-1814* [New Haven, Conn.: Yale University Press, 1964], p. 369, n. 8).

4. Frank D. McConnell, *The Confessional Imagination: A Reading of Wordsworth's Prelude* (Baltimore, Md.: Johns Hopkins University Press, 1974), p. 101.

Nature's indifference to man in *The Borderers* is noted by Peter L. Thorslev, Jr., "Wordsworth's *Borderers* and the Romantic Villain-Hero," *Studies in Romanticism* 5 (1966): 84-103, and Sheats, *The Making of Wordsworth's Poetry*, pp. 128-29.

5. Thorslev, "Wordsworth's *Borderers* and the Romantic Villain-Hero," p. 102.

6. Cf. Sheats, *The Making of Wordsworth's Poetry*, p. 158, who terms this "beauty of a distant prospect . . . an emblem of what might have been."

7. No complete version of the 1797 *Ruined Cottage* survives, but a variety of evidence tells us much about the poem's contents. I follow Jonathan Wordsworth's opinion that by the early summer of 1797 *The Ruined Cottage* amounted to some 370 to 400 lines, consisting of "the story of Margaret, already within a dramatic framework, but with very few trimmings," corresponding roughly to lines 312-439, 492-742 of MS. B of the poem, its early 1798 version (*The Music of Humanity*, pp. 9-16). My quotations throughout are from MS. B and its associated additions, corrections, and Addendum, *PW* 5:379-404.

8. Jonathan Wordsworth, *The Music of Humanity*, p. 109.

9. Cf. ibid., pp. 150, 249.

10. Wordsworth's new debt to Coleridge is particularly evident here; see, for example, Coleridge's celebration of God in *Religious Musings* as "nature's essence, mind, and energy!" (l. 49), his assertion in the same poem that "'tis God / Diffused through all, that doth make all one whole" (ll. 130-31), and his description of God, in an early manuscript version of *The Eolian Harp*, as "the universal Soul" (this last is quoted by Jonathan Wordsworth, *The Music of Humanity*, p. 191).

11. Hartman, *Wordsworth's Poetry*, p. 135.

12. On this "dreaming man" motif in *The Ruined Cottage*, see Reeve Parker, "'Finer Distance': The Narrative Art of Wordsworth's 'The Wanderer,'" *ELH* 39 (1972): 90-98.

13. Wordsworth's first draft conclusion to the poem further stresses this engagement:

> The old man ceased: he saw that I was moved.
> From that low bench rising instinctively
> I turned away in weakness, and my heart
> Went back into the tale which he had told.
>
> [*PW* 5:400]

The second draft conclusion similarly refers to "the silence of my grief" (*PW* 5:400). Though Wordsworth struck out these drafts and wrote a different conclusion (the "Addendum"), he soon added a renewed and extended insistence on the narrator's emotional involvement: in an addition to MS. B not noted by Darbishire, Wordsworth inserted after line 110 of the Addendum verses corresponding to *Excursion* 1.917-24, essentially repeating the four lines of the first draft conclusion quoted above and continuing,

> I stood and leaning oer the garden gate
> Retraced that womans story & it seemed
> To comfort me while with a brothers love
> I bless'd her in the impotence of grief.

(I owe my knowledge of this insertion, and the information that it almost certainly dates from before about 5-6 March 1798, to Professor James A. Butler; see William Wordsworth, *The Ruined Cottage and The Pedlar*, ed. James Butler, The Cornell Wordsworth [Ithaca, N. Y.: Cornell University Press, forthcoming].)

14. In MS. D of *The Ruined Cottage*, written in 1799, Wordsworth introduces a few new lines at what corresponds to line 367 of MS. B wherein the Pedlar similarly criticizes himself for this same lapse: "Often on this cottage do I muse / As on a picture, till my wiser mind / Sinks, yielding to the foolishness of grief" (l. 367 app. crit.).

15. As Jonathan Wordsworth notes, "In Wordsworth's terms [the narrator's] extreme grief for Margaret is a failure to perceive the essential beneath the 'forms of things', a judging by appearances only. . . . a misunderstanding of [the natural order]" (*The Music of Humanity*, p. 98).

16. De Man, "The Rhetoric of Temporality," pp. 174, 176-77.

17. The latter line, not given by Darbishire, appears in a contemporary addition to MS. B; see above, note 13.

Chapter 2

1. Charles and Mary Lamb, *The Letters of Charles and Mary Lamb*, ed. E. V. Lucas (New Haven, Conn.: Yale University Press, 1935), 2:127.

2. While P. E. More long ago criticized *Tintern Abbey* as "contradictory" (*Shelburne Essays*, Seventh Series [New York: G. P. Putnam's Sons, 1910], p. 39), William Empson's famous attack in *Seven Types of Ambiguity* (London: Chatto and Windus, 1930), pp. 191-94, on what he regarded as the poem's syntactical confusion and philosophical vagueness has been especially influential. So, more recently, F. W. Bateson has found that the poem "embodies what can only be called a series of concessions to irrationality" (*Wordsworth: A Re-interpretation* [London: Longmans, Green & Co., 1954], p. 141); David Ferry, that "it is hard not to sound captious about the poem, and hard not to mistake for a confusion of feeling what may be a complexity of feeling, a contemplated and contained ambivalence" (*The Limits of Mortality: An Essay on Wordsworth's Major Poems* [Middletown, Conn.: Wesleyan University Press, 1959], pp. 110-11); and Donald Wesling, that the poem "is in conception allowably disheveled, tautological, irregular. For although Wordsworth makes a show of ratiocination, it can hardly be said that he is here following the steps of an argument" (*Wordsworth and the Adequacy of Landscape* [London: Routledge, 1970], p. 25).

3. Arthur Beatty, *William Wordsworth: His Doctrine and Art in Their Historical Relations*, University of Wisconsin Studies in Language and Literature No. 24, 2d ed. (Madison: University of Wisconsin, 1927), pp. 72-96, 107-13, 124-27.

4. Cf. the Pedlar's similar (though younger) age of "appetite" (l. 98) and "yearning" (l. 99) in *The Ruined Cottage.*

5. In line with this particular association of the emotions with "internalized" sensations, Wordsworth tends in his poetry of this period to present such images as "blood" and "heart," or more generally the internal, organic life processes, as analogous to and metaphoric of man's emotional processes. Similarly, such terms or phrases as "appetite," "feeling," "aching joys," and "dizzy raptures" significantly use physiological figures to express emotional experiences. *The Ruined Cottage* and the 1798-99 *Prelude* afford various examples of both sorts. From *The Ruined Cottage*: "the fever of his heart" (l. 237); "There was a heartfelt chillness in my veins" (l. 467); and cf. the grouping of "affections, organs, passions" (Addendum, l. 76). From the 1798-99 *Prelude*: "that giddy bliss / Which like a tempest works along the blood" (1.413-14); "from excess / Of happiness, my blood appeared to flow / With its own pleasure, and I breathed with joy" (2.225-27); "Thus day by day / Subjected to the discipline of love, / His [the infant's] organs and recipient faculties / Are quickened, are more vigorous" (that is, with "gathered passion") (2.280-83); "Along his infant veins are interfused / The gravitation and the filial bond / Of Nature that connect him with the world" (2.292-94). And cf. *Excursion* 9.23-27 and app. crit., "we live by hope / And by desire; they are the very blood / By which we move," a passage probably dating from early 1799-late October 1800 (*CEY*, p. 35).

6. This three-stage pattern of an evolving attitude also characterizes the narrator's spiritual development during the course of *The Ruined Cottage*; see above, Chapter 1, section iv.

7. Similarly, the narrator's education in the brief course of *The Ruined Cottage* essentially parallels the much longer course of the Pedlar's lifelong spiritual development; cf. Neil H. Hertz, "Wordsworth and the Tears of Adam" *Studies in Romanticism* 7 (1967): 31. And analogously the Pedlar, who has already in his maturity attained insight and consolation, must yet work through his recurring grief, as he revisits the site of Margaret's cottage and recites her story, to win his consolation again.

This same ontogeny-phylogeny analogy, it should be observed, informs Hartley's *Observations on Man.* As Beatty demonstrates (*William Wordsworth*, pp. 109-15), Hartley's theory about the growth of man's intellect through the stages of his life parallels, and indeed derives from, an analogous theory about the hierarchy of mental states, ranging from sensations through simple ideas (ideas of sensation) to complex (or intellectual) ideas.

Albert S. Gerard, writing without reference to Hartley, independently demonstrates some notion of the presence of this analogy in *Tintern Abbey.* Gerard suggests a correspondence between the "moments of time" (that is, the three ages) of the fourth paragraph and the "aspects ɔf nature's action" (that is, her effects on the mind) of the second (*English Romantic Poetry: Ethos, Structure, and Symbol in Coleridge, Wordsworth, Shelley, and Keats* [Berkeley: University of California Press, 1978], p. 107).

8. Christopher Salvesen seems to sense that in these lines Wordsworth redescribes an earlier process now spiritualized and reversed: Wordsworth tells us that vivid memories may persist, he writes, "imparting not only 'sensations sweet, / Felt in the blood, and felt along the heart', but working, more spiritually, in the opposite direction," and cites lines 43–46 "Until, the breath . . . a living soul") (*The Landscape of Memory: A Study of Wordsworth's Poetry* [Lincoln: University of Nebraska Press, 1965], pp. 85–86).

9. Herbert Lindenberger, *On Wordsworth's Prelude* (Princeton, N. J.: Princeton University Press, 1963), p. 301.

For explicit examples of allusions to Paradise Lost, see *Prelude 1799* 1.89–90, 373, 2.344 (cf. *Paradise Lost* 12.1–2, 9.27, 249, respectively).

In a study of a copy of *Paradise Lost* owned and annotated by Wordsworth, Bishop C. Hunt, Jr., writes, "A careful study of the handwriting of the marginalia suggests that they probably belong to the years 1798–1800" ("Wordsworth's Marginalia on *Paradise Lost*," *Bulletin of the New York Public Library* 73 [1969]: 168).

10. For a different but compatible and even complementary reading of these lines about the "blind man's eye," see Dennis Camp, "Wordsworth's *Lines Composed a Few Miles above Tintern Abbey*, 22–24," *Explicator* 29 (1970): item 57.

11. Cf. the young Pedlar's vision of the "one life" in all things:

> One song they sang, and it was audible,
> Most audible then, when the fleshly ear
> O'ercome by grosser prelude of that strain,
> Forgot its functions, and slept undisturbed.
> [Ll. 253–56]

The narrator similarly says of the mature Pedlar, "To him was given an ear which deeply felt / The voice of Nature in the obscure wind / The sounding mountain and the running stream" (273–75). And cf. a nearly contemporary fragment from the Christabel notebook:

> The clouds are standing still in the mid heavens;
> A perfect quietness is in the air;
> The ear hears not; and yet, I know not how,
> More than the other senses does it hold
> A manifest communion with the heart.
> [*PW* 5:343]

The tradition of the music of the spheres stems from Pythagoras via Plato's *Republic*, but came to Wordsworth most immediately and influentially, I suspect, from Milton. Especially noteworthy as background to *Tintern Abbey* is Milton's use of this notion in *Arcades*. Here the Genius of the Wood listens to the music of the spheres "when drowsiness / Hath lockt up mortal sense," and notes, following Plato, that this music can

> keep unsteady Nature to her law,
> And the low world in measur'd motion draw
> After the heavenly tune, which none can hear
> Of human mold with gross unpurged ear.
> [Ll. 61-62, 70-73]

12. Hartman, *Wordsworth's Poetry*, p. 392 n. 8, has noted this association.

13. Cf. the opening words of the Pedlar's argument in the *Ruined Cottage* Addendum:

> Not useless do I deem
> These quiet sympathies with things that hold
> An inarticulate language; for the man
> Once taught to love such objects as excite
> No morbid passions no disquietude
> No vengeance, and no hatred needs must feel
> The joy of that pure principle of love
> So deeply that unsatisfied with aught
> Less pure and exquisite he cannot choose
> But seek for objects of a kindred love
> In fellow-natures and a kindred joy.
> [Addendum, ll. 1-11]

It is noteworthy that where the Pedlar's love for his fellow man is all-encompassing, Wordsworth's in *Tintern Abbey*, four months later, is definitely limited to a select circle of compatible spirits (such as Dorothy). This rather abrupt shift seems attributable to Wordsworth's renewed experience of "the din / Of towns and cities." After more than four uninterrupted months of happy rural retirement in Alfoxden, Wordsworth traveled to Bristol on business in May 1798 for a four-day stay, and again for a longer period in June, probably returning to Alfoxden for Dorothy in late June and then going back to Bristol in early July to stay until mid-August (*CEY*, pp. 237, 239, 241). On 3 July 1798 Dorothy wrote to her "Aunt" Rawson, "I am writing in a front room in one of the most busy streets in Bristol. You can scarcely conceive how the jarring contrast between the sounds which are now forever ringing in my ears and the sweet sounds of Alfoxden, makes me long for the country again. After three years residence in retirement a city in feeling, sound, and prospect is hateful" (*LEY*, p. 196).

14. The echo of the Psalm 23 has been noted by Sheats, *The Making of Wordsworth's Poetry*, pp. 240, 244.

15. Cf. ibid., p. 241, and Ferry, *The Limits of Mortality*, p. 110.

16. All citations of the early, two-part *Prelude* in this chapter refer to *Prelude 1799*. Part 1, with which I shall be chiefly concerned here, is the work of October 1798–February 1799; part 2, of May and September–December 1799 (see Jonathan Wordsworth and Stephen Gill, "The Two-Part *Prelude* of 1798–99," *Journal of English and Germanic Philology* 72 [1973]: 507–10, 512–19).

As Wordsworth and Gill note (p. 512), the lines introducing the "spots of time" sequence of part 1 "recall *Tintern Abbey*, but now the 'heavy and the weary weight' is lightened by memories not of landscape 'interfused' by presence of the One Life, but of odd, often guilty, moments, whose power is that of primal experience, never fully explained, but vividly evoking the strength and capacity of the individual human mind."

17. Actually, *The Prelude* explicitly cites only the last of these, the boat-stealing episode, as illustrative of nature's ministry of fear. But in MS. JJ, Wordsworth's earliest extant work on *The Prelude*, one draft passage instead sets up the snare-robbing episode as the specific illustration of this ministry (see *Prelude 1850*, p. 640).

18. Jonathan Bishop, striving to trace a common motif of guilt in these episodes, notes reasonably that the "climbing after the eggs [is] 'plundering'" ("Wordsworth and the 'Spots of Time,'" *ELH*, 26 [1959]: 48; cf. David Perkins, *The Quest for Permanence: The Symbolism of Wordsworth, Shelley, and Keats* [Cambridge, Mass.: Harvard University Press, 1959], p. 16). But this characterization, like some others Bishop cites, is an addition of 1805, when Wordsworth wrote of himself as "a plunderer then" (*Prelude 1805* 1.336); in 1798 he described himself more neutrally as "a rover then" (*Prelude 1799* 1.53).

19. Brief drafts of both *Nutting* and "I would not strike a flower" appear in MS. JJ of *The Prelude* (*Prelude 1850*, p. 641), and in close association with *Prelude* fragments in the Christabel notebook and Notebook 18a (see *CEY*, pp. 325, 327). On the interrelatedness of *Nutting* and "I would not strike a flower," see *CEY*, 331–32; Reed deduces that a long version of the poem included both the present *Nutting* and a version of "I would not strike a flower." Wordsworth's statement about having removed

the poem from *The Prelude*, though referring specifically to *Nutting*, thus would seem to encompass both fragments.

20. David Perkins argues directly the opposite, that "the guilt does not arise primarily from the theft" (*The Quest for Permanence*, p. 16); but here again, the supporting evidence—this time the boy's sense even before the trap-robbing of "be[ing] a trouble to the peace" of the scene (*Prelude 1805* 1.323)—is a later addition, and has no equivalent in the 1798-99 *Prelude*.

21. Hartman, *Wordsworth's Poetry*, p. 215.

22. In the 1805 *Prelude*, where the spots of time are removed from their original location in part 1, only the latter two episodes, now relocated in book 11, are explicitly termed "spots of time"; the first episode is separated from the other two and put into book 5. In the 1798-99 *Prelude*, however, Wordsworth classes all three episodes together as "tragic facts / Of rural history, that impressed my mind / with . . . forms / That yet exist with independent life" (1.282-86) and that "tend . . . / To the same point, the growth of mental power / And love of Nature's works" (1.256-58), indicating that the drowned man episode is then also, in his experience, a true spot of time.

23. This becomes particularly obvious in the final spot of time, the waiting for the horses. As D. G. James notes, "The scene came to have 'visionary dreariness' only after his father's death; his response to it while waiting for the horses was negligible—he was merely impatient to be gone. It became, in all truth, an object to his imagination only after sorrow had come" (*Scepticism and Poetry* [London: George Allen and Unwin, 1937], p. 158).

24. As "memory," see Perkins, *The Quest for Permanence*, p. 57; cf. Lindenberger, *On Wordsworth's Prelude*, pp. 90-91. On "darkness of thoughts," cf. Albert O. Wlecke, *Wordsworth and the Sublime* (Berkeley: University of California Press, 1973), pp. 125-26. Harold Bloom, *The Visionary Company: A Reading of English Romantic Poetry* (Garden City, N.Y.: Doubleday, 1961), p. 157.

25. This same tentativeness, indeed, appears briefly even in *The Ruined Cottage*. Thus the narrator says of the Pedlar,

> To every natural form, rock, fruit and flower
> Even the loose stones that cover the highway
> He gave a moral life, he saw them feel
> Or linked them to some feeling. In all shapes
> He found a secret and mysterious soul,
> A fragrance and a spirit of strange meaning.
> [Ll. 276-81]

See also the immediately following lines, and cf. ll. 102-8.

26. Though Wordsworth speaks at one point of "The gravitation and the filial bond / Of nature that connect [the infant] with the world"

(2.293–94), he nevertheless makes very clear in the preceding verses that this connecting filial bond is in fact the infant's literally filial bond to its mother; see 2.285–90. Cf. Paul D. Sheats, "Wordsworth's 'Retrogrades' and the Shaping of *The Prelude*," *Journal of English and Germanic Philology* 71 (1972): 479–80.

Introduction to Part II

1. See *CMY*, pp. 37, 657, 664–65; *HG*, pp. 16–22; and John A. Finch, "On the Dating of *Home at Grasmere*: A New Approach," in *Bicentenary Wordsworth Studies*, ed. Jonathan Wordsworth (Ithaca, N. Y.: Cornell University Press, 1970), pp. 14–28. We can be especially certain of the 1806 date of the particular lines to which I here refer; for these represent a late addition to the *Prospectus*, appearing for the first time in what is demonstrably the last-written of the three *Prospectus* manuscripts.

2. Robert Frost, "The Need of Being Versed in Country Things," *The Poetry of Robert Frost*, ed. Edward Connery Lathem (New York: Holt, Rinehart, 1969), p. 242.

3. Wordsworth's version of this memorializing impulse is thus remarkably pagan, and particularly evocative of ancient Greek thought. Cf. Orestes' and Electra's conjuration of their dead father:

> *Or.*: Do not wipe out this race of the Pelopidae!
> For if we live you are not dead, even in death.
> For children preserve a man's fame
> after his death; like corks they hold up the net,
> retaining the cord of flax that reaches up from the deep.
> *El.*: Listen! It is for your sake that such laments are uttered,
> and you yourself are preserved if you do honor to our words.
> [Aeschylus, *The Libation-Bearers*, tr. Hugh Lloyd-Jones
> (Englewood Cliffs, N.J.: Prentice-Hall, 1970), ll. 503–9]

As John Jones notes of this passage, "Agamemnon in his grave has the most urgent of reasons to be concerned for the success of Orestes' enterprise: his life depends on it. . . . The price of failure is death—a sinking into cold, hungry oblivion for Agamemnon" (*On Aristotle and Greek Tragedy* [New York: Oxford University Press, 1962], p. 98).

Chapter 3

1. Jonathan Wordsworth, *The Music of Humanity*, p. 212. It is noteworthy that as late as 1804, as he brings *The Prelude* toward its close, Wordsworth still explicitly states his belief in "the life / Of all things and the mighty unity / In all which we behold, and feel, and are" (*Prelude*

1805 13.246-48), even though this is now but a single aspect of his metaphysics.

2. The term is Ferry's, who calls Lucy "not so much a human being as a sort of compendium of nature" (*The Limits of Mortality*, p. 76). See also H. W. Garrod: "In 'Three years she grew . . .' what really is she, except what the things about her make her, or give to her—the floating cloud, the bending willow, the midnight stars, the waters whose sound has passed into the beauty of her face? What is she else?" (*The Profession of Poetry and Other Lectures* [Oxford: Oxford University Press, The Clarendon Press, 1929], pp. 84-85). As Geoffrey Durant observes in response, however, "Lucy is not merged with the forces of nature; she emerges from them" (*Wordsworth and the Great System* [Cambridge: Cambridge University Press, 1970], p. 160).

3. In this respect he is thus, oddly but significantly, the very reverse of Rivers, who sees all things as equally valueless, and so can deem the murder of Herbert an act of no moral consequence:

> Murder!—what, of whom?
> Of whom? of what? we kill a toad, a newt,
> A rat—I do believe if they who first
> Baptized the deed had called it murder, we
> Had quailed to think of it. . . .
> . . . .
>
> Is he not eyeless? He has been half-dead
> These fifteen years.
> > [*The Borderers*, ll. 926-42 and app. crit.]

So Mortimer similarly, when infected with Rivers' philosophy, can respond to the question, "How shall we wash our hands of—of—" (Rivers is alluding to Herbert) with "Oh yes / That mole, that weazle, that old water rat" (l. 1255 app. crit.).

4. I quote the *Prelude* MS. RV version, dating from about September-early December 1799. An earlier version, appearing in *Peter Bell* MS. 2, dates from summer 1799. (For the dates of these passages, see Wordsworth and Gill, "The Two-Part *Prelude* of 1798-99," p. 509.)

5. Even Alan Grob, who holds as I do that Wordsworth's "beliefs of 1802 are not those of 1798 and that those of 1804 depart even further from those held in earlier years," sees a "philosophy firmly held and consistently elaborated" from 1797 to 1800, and argues that "no general and consistent pattern of reassessment of fundamental beliefs occurs until 1802" (*The Philosophic Mind*, pp. 5, 192).

6. Spencer Hall, "Wordsworth's 'Lucy' Poems: Context and Meaning," *Studies in Romanticism* 10 (1971): 172.

7. The passage first appears in MS. D, which was probably written between February and late November 1799 (personal communication from Professor James Butler; see his forthcoming edition of William Wordsworth, *The Ruined Cottage and The Pedlar*).

8. Thus in *Tintern Abbey* Wordsworth similarly acknowledges the partial unreliableness of his own pictorial memory when he sees the Wye valley again after a five-year absence:

> And now, with gleams of half-extinguished thought,
> With many recognitions dim and faint,
> And somewhat of a sad perplexity,
> The picture of the mind revives again.
> [Ll. 58–61]

The "sad perplexity," as Jack Stillinger notes, is "presumably owing to the discrepancy between the 'recognitions dim and faint' and the scene before him (the present 'picture of the mind')" (Jack Stillinger, ed., *Selected Poems and Prefaces by William Wordsworth* [Boston: Houghton Mifflin Co., 1965], p. 516).

9. Quite similarly in the fifth naming poem, *To M. H.*, Wordsworth names for his future wife another secluded and implicitly eternal spot, "made by Nature for herself" (l. 15), but again recognizes that its immortality is not man's:

> If a man should plant his cottage near,
> Should sleep beneath the shelter of its trees,
> And blend its waters with his daily meal,
> He would so love it, that in his death-hour
> Its image would survive among his thoughts.
> [Ll. 18–22]

10. This inscribing, be it noted, is in all probability entirely fictitious; there is no evidence that Wordsworth did actually carve Joanna's name into such a rock.

11. Cf. Geoffrey Hartman, "Wordsworth, Inscriptions, and Romantic Nature Poetry," in *Beyond Formalism*, pp. 206–30, esp. pp. 221–28.

Chapter 4

1. Cf. *Michael*, ll. 367–70, ll. 73–74 app. crit.

2. The relevance of this last passage to *Hart-Leap Well*, incidentally, would seem to have some bearing on the dating of MS. B of *The Borderers*, wherein it first appears. The two most probable dates of MS. B, which is mostly in the hand of Mary Hutchinson, are about late April–December 1799 (when William and Dorothy were staying with Mary at Sockburn) and about the end of February to about 4 April 1800 (when Mary was

visiting William and Dorothy at Grasmere) (*CEY*, p. 330); de Selincourt favors the former date (*PW* 1:344). But Wordsworth first heard the story of Hart-Leap Well, which certainly seems to be in his mind in this *Borderers* passage, immediately *after* leaving Sockburn on 17 December 1799, on his way to Grasmere, and composed *Hart-Leap Well* in early (probably very early) 1800, certainly before Mary departed from Grasmere on April 4 or 5 (see *PW* 2:514; *CMY*, p. 66 n). So it seems likely that MS. B of *The Borderers* dates from the time of Mary's visit to Grasmere, and not from the time of Wordsworth's visit to Sockburn. Wordsworth's renewed work on *The Borderers* would have put into his mind the details from lines 2032–35 contributive to *Hart-Leap Well* lines 41–44, while the story of Hart-Leap Well, learned only in December, conversely would have suggested the thought of *Borderers* lines 2122–24.

3. This new notion of nature as not in itself man's essential home but only a setting for his (socially defined) home surfaces again interestingly in "I travelled among unknown men" (ca. April 1801), which differs markedly from the earlier Lucy poems in its attitude toward nature. In the later poem, Wordsworth regards and presents nature much as he does in *Hart-Leap Well* (but as he did not in the earlier Lucy poems), as a sympathetic and humanized mourner. Frances C. Ferguson's commentary is perceptive and helpful:

> Although the overt memorialization of Lucy occupies only the third and fourth stanzas, it everywhere dictates the terms of the poet's love for England. ... He projects his altered perceptions upon the scene, so that he seems to assume that England would itself say, "And oh, the difference to me!" ... [Nature] mourns for Lucy, so that the poet returning can recognize (that is, imagine) its loss. And the poet loves England for loving and mourning Lucy. ["The Lucy Poems: Wordsworth's Quest for a Poetic Object," *ELH* 40 (1973): 542]

4. Geoffrey Hartman, "False Themes and Gentle Minds," in *Beyond Formalism*, p. 296.

5. At the same time, the Shepherd's obvious sense of a moral life in all features of nature suggests his affinities to the Pedlar, and indicates again how closely related the Pedlar's "one life" philosophy is to iconic vision.

6. There is a curious grammatical indication in the poem that this double-leveled formulation of a spirit beyond or within the presence of nature is indeed precisely what Wordsworth is striving to convey. He writes of Nature that "*she* leaves these objects to a slow decay'" as a lesson to us, but one day again "'shall put on *her* beauty and *her* bloom'"; but he writes also that

"The Being, that is in the clouds and air,
  That is in the green leaves among the groves,
  Maintains a deep and reverential care
  For the unoffending creatures whom *he* loves."
    [Ll. 165–68; my emphases]

This last pronoun would seem not to be a misprint, for it appears not only in all printed texts but also in the one extant manuscript of the poem, Dove Cottage MS. 29 (I am grateful to Professor James Butler for checking this manuscript for me). It seems rather to be Wordsworth's grammatical method of insisting on a distinction between the manifestation ("she") and the essence ("he") of nature. Hoxie Neale Fairchild, *Religious Trends in English Poetry*, 5 vols. (New York: Columbia University Press, 1939–68), 3:177, also notes this point and associates it with a Wordsworthian distinction between transcendent and immanent Nature.

7. Hartman, "False Themes and Gentle Minds," p. 296.

8. Grob, *The Philosophic Mind*, p. 217.

9. On the date of *To H. C.*, see Appendix A.

10. A passage from one of Dorothy's letters some years later interestingly reminds us of the prevalent folk superstition underlying this general notion. Dorothy is writing about her niece and namesake, Dora Wordsworth (William's second child), then fourteen months old:

She has a manner about her—a set of looks that are all her own and I am sure must be genius—but poor darling! we may never get her reared. It is a saying amongst the old wives that a child is "over sensible to live" and I believe there is more truth in this than one would wish to think; I know the tears came into my eyes the other morning when our Servant, looking at Dorothy, said to me suddenly "She has over may pretty ways that Child!" [*LEY*, p. 632]

11. Cf. Ferry, *The Limits of Mortality*, p. 83.

12. Hartman notes this allusion in *Wordsworth's Poetry*, pp. 14, 202.

13. Grob, *The Philosophic Mind*, p. 226.

14. Frederick A. Pottle, "The Eye and the Object in the Poetry of Wordsworth," in *Romanticism and Consciousness: Essays in Criticism*, ed. Harold Bloom (New York: Norton, 1970), p. 275, also notes this divergence of the poem from autobiographical fact.

15. Here again Wordsworth diverges significantly from factual truth. In real life he met the old man not on the moor but on the public road, near Dove Cottage, and Wordsworth's brother John later encountered him in the nearby hamlet of Wytheburn (*DWJ*, p. 42). Wordsworth even ultimately eliminates from the poem any mention of the old man's making a living by selling "godly books." This point,

recorded by Dorothy (ibid.), finds its way into Wordsworth's first draft of the poem—"Yet I procure a living of my own / [Leech-gathering] is my summer work[;] in winter time / I go with godly books from Town to Town"—no doubt because it further testifies to the old man's determined independence. In the next version of the poem, however, Wordsworth eliminates this along with the one other suggestion of the old man's going among men ("From house to house I go from Barn to Barn") and introduces his similes of the huge stone and sunning sea beast; both tactics have the effect of emphasizing the "naked wilderness" (ll. 56/57 app. crit.) as the old man's proper and exclusive milieu.

    The lines from the first draft of *Resolution and Independence* quoted just above are not given in *PW*; I quote them from Jared R. Curtis, *Wordsworth's Experiments with Tradition: The Lyric Poems of 1802* (Ithaca, N.Y.: Cornell University Press, 1971), p. 194.

    16. Commentators have generally passed over Wordsworth's specific description of the "grave Livers" with whom he associates the Leech-gatherer as men "who give to God and man their dues" (l. 98), though Grob interprets "a mode of life that gives to man his due" as one opposed to self-interest and identical with the Romantic poet's way of "genial faith" (*The Philosophic Mind*, pp. 228, 225, 223). I would suggest instead that the phrase alludes to Matthew 22:21, "Render therefore unto Caesar the things which are Caesar's; and unto God the things that are God's." The dues the old man gives to man are those he pays by his labors, "the necessities which an unjust state of society has entailed upon him"; the dues he gives to God are those he pays with his spirit.

    Grob, *The Philosophic Mind*, pp. 227–29, and Edward E. Bostetter, *The Romantic Ventriloquists: Wordsworth, Coleridge, Keats, Shelley, Bryon* (Seattle: University of Washington Press, 1963), pp. 35–36, both point out that consolation in this poem does not come from nature, but in spite of nature; and Albert S. Gerard, *English Romantic Poetry*, pp. 134–35, joins them in emphasizing that the old man's strength comes instead from his reliance upon a transcendent God.

    17. Anthony Conran, "The Dialectic of Experience: A Study of *Wordsworth's Resolution and Independence*," *PMLA* 75 (1960): 74, notes this resemblance but does not seem to regard it as parodic.

    18. For a similar reading of *We Are Seven*, see Grob, *The Philosophic Mind*, pp. 149, 224, 248; and see also Thomas De Quincey, who says that the poem "brings into day for the first time a profound fact in the abyss of human nature—viz. that the mind of an infant cannot admit the idea of death, cannot comprehend it, any more than the fountain of light can comprehend the aboriginal darkness" (*The Collected Writings of Thomas De Quincey*, ed. David Masson [Edinburgh: Adam & Charles Black, 1889–90], 11:301).

19. *The Notebooks of Samuel Taylor Coleridge*, ed. Kathleen Coburn, 3 vols. (New York: Pantheon, 1957-73), 1:1616.

20. On the date of "It is no Spirit who from heaven hath flown," see Appendix B.

Introduction to Part III

1. "Imagination and the light of nature are one": Hartman, *Wordsworth's Poetry*, p. 60. Albert Wlecke takes the same position in stating his thesis that "the 'sense sublime' refers to an activity of the esemplastic power of the imagination during which consciousness becomes reflexively aware of itself as an interfusing energy dwelling within the phenomena of nature" (*Wordsworth and the Sublime*, p. 8).

For my own quite different position that in *The Prelude* Wordsworth presents the imagination and nature as analogous but *not* identical, I find a supporting voice in Patrick Holland: "It is clear that while Wordsworth is far from tending or intending to bestow his own self-consciousness upon nature, he does seek to establish a similitude between imagination and nature.... There is no question ... of Wordsworth's confusing his own consciousness of self with an immanent nature. Nature has its own imagination ...; the poet has *his* imagination" ("Wordsworth and the Sublime: Some Further Considerations," *Wordsworth Circle* 5 [1974]: 22). Similarly, Richard Schell observes, "It seems ... that in identifying the 'breach' as the 'Soul, the Imagination' of the entire scene, Wordsworth is anticipating his later analogy between Nature and the mind of man by locating in Nature a controlling and shaping force, one analogous to the human Imagination, which has wrought this spectacle for man" ("Wordsworth's Revisions of the Ascent of Snowdon," *Philological Quarterly* 55 [1976]: 596).

2. Heffernan, *Wordsworth's Theory of Poetry*, p. 194.

Chapter 5

1. Hartman, *Wordsworth's Poetry*, p. 65; and see pp. 33-69 passim.

2. Some cases in point: Raymond Dexter Havens, *The Mind of a Poet: A Study of Wordsworth's Thought* (Baltimore, Md.: Johns Hopkins University Press, 1941), p. 307; E. D. Hirsch, Jr., *Wordsworth and Schelling* (New Haven, Conn.: Yale University Press, 1960), p. 178; Stuart M. Sperry, Jr., "From 'Tintern Abbey' to the 'Intimations Ode': Wordsworth and the Function of Memory," *Wordsworth Circle* 1 (1971): 46-47; Kenneth R. Johnston, "Recollecting Forgetting: Forcing Paradox to the Limit in the 'Intimations Ode,'" *Wordsworth Circle* 2 (1971): 63; Kenneth R. Lincoln, "Wordsworth's Mortality Ode," *Journal of English and Germanic Philology* 71 (1972): 221-22.

3. Salvesen, *The Landscape of Memory*, pp. 119-20, while he asso-
ciates these *Prelude* book 2 lines with the ode, is careful to note that the
two passages do indeed treat of different, if related, topics. Observing that
"such recollections of pre-existence, and of joy in childhood, are not en-
tirely separate," he decides that "they work in a similar manner and to a
similar end."

4. The lines beginning "A simple child" are, of course, the opening
stanza of *We Are Seven*; and the lines quoted from the ode were added to
it only in 1807.

5. On the relation of the two poems, see Grob, *The Philosophic
Mind*, pp. 247-49.

6. The last two lines are not given by de Selincourt in *PW*, but are
recorded by Paul Sheats, *The Making of Wordsworth's Poetry*, p. 95, from
the manuscripts at Dove Cottage.

7. Cf. Sheats, *The Making of Wordsworth's Poetry*, pp. 20-32, for a
related argument about Wordsworth's claimed experience of a "religious
love" of nature during his later school years:

> We are not, perhaps, entitled to dispute the poet's own memory of a
> 'religious love' for nature. Nor do the poems written at the time fail
> to record occasional 'Sentiments of affection for inanimate Na-
> ture.'. . . But aside from these few explicit and not unconventional
> sentiments, . . . there is little evidence of a primary and conscious
> recognition of nature's value. The poetry suggests rather that in his
> role as an enthusiastic lyric poet, he regarded the natural objects of
> his affection with some condescension and that he consistently
> understood nature in terms of a decorum that was literary. Nature
> enters his poems only when the conditions set by those poems
> permit it. [Pp. 20-21]

8. Arthur Beatty, ed., *Representative Poems*, by William Words-
worth (New York: Odyssey, 1937), p. 661; G. Wilson Knight, *The Starlit
Dome: Studies in the Poetry of Vision* (1941; reprint ed., London: Ox-
ford University Press, 1971), p. 38; Hirsch, *Wordsworth and Schelling*, p.
177; Bloom, *The Visionary Company*, p. 187; Hartman, *Wordsworth's
Poetry*, p. 277.

9. Thomas M. Raysor, "The Themes of Immortality and Natural
Piety in Wordsworth's Immortality Ode," *PMLA* 69 (1954): 865; Florence
G. Marsh, "Wordsworth's *Ode*: Obstinate Questionings," *Studies in Ro-
manticism* 5 (1966): 230, 229; Grob, *The Philosophic Mind*, pp. 251, 261.

10. Wordsworth was later to repeat and further elucidate this same
elaborate cosmological conceit in book 4 of *The Excursion* (written ca.
December 1809-March 1812), there attributing it to the ancient Chaldeans.
The passage is part of the Wanderer's survey of the growth of religious be-
lief:

"—The imaginative faculty was lord
Of observations natural; and, thus
Led on, those shepherds made report of stars
In set rotations passing to and fro,
Between the orbs of our apparent sphere
And its invisible counterpart, adorned
With answering constellations, under earth,
Removed from all approach of living sight
But present to the dead; who, so they deemed,
Like those celestial messengers beheld
All accidents, and judges were of all."
[4.707-17]

While this passage of course postdates the ode by several years, the conceit itself is, as Wordsworth here asserts, an ancient one. One source with which Wordsworth was certainly familiar is Vergil's *Georgics* 1.233-48; another, more general one, obviously is Dante's *Commedia*.

Wordsworth also refers in the ode to heaven, the seat of God, as "that imperial palace" (l. 85); and Salvesen notes the allusion here to "empyreal" (*The Landscape of Memory*, p. 117 n). The Empyrean, of course, the heaven of heavens and the habitation of God, is traditionally the realm of pure fire and light; cf. *Paradise Lost* 3.3-5, 55-57.

11. On "twilight": at about this time, Wordsworth similarly writes in *The Prelude* of infancy as "that twilight when we first begin to see / This dawning earth" (4.537-38).

On "clothing": Cleanth Brooks, "Wordsworth and the Paradox of the Imagination," in *The Well Wrought Urn: Studies in the Structure of Poetry* (New York: Harcourt, Brace, 1947), pp. 126-27, discusses this important motif.

12. Wordsworth's conceit in this last respect is again pointedly Miltonic. See *Paradise Lost* book 7 for Milton's description of how the stars and planets take their light from the sun, the primary receptacle of the world's newly created "liquid Light" (7.362):

Hither as to thir Fountain other Stars
Repairing, in thir gold'n Urns draw Light,
And hence the Morning Planet gilds her horns;
By tincture or reflection they augment
Thir small peculiar. . . .
[7.364-68]

And this passage, we cannot but note, suggests itself most strikingly as a possible and relevant inspiration for Wordsworth's allusion to man's (figuratively a soul-star's) divine source (figuratively a sun) as "the fountain light of all our day" (l. 151).

13. Wordsworth makes a quite similar and explicitly related point in a *Prelude* passage written at about the same time as the ode:

> Our childhood sits,
> Our simple childhood sits upon a throne
> That hath more power than all the elements.
> [*Prelude 1805* 5.531-33]

It is noteworthy that the power here belongs to the *throne* on which childhood is seated, and not to the child himself.

14. See, for example, Epictetus, *Discourses*, 3.24.5-6.

Wordsworth's mention here of "the primal sympathy / Which having been must ever be" (ll. 182-83), asserting more strongly than any other passage of the poem the soul's consciousness of its transcendence, does not, significantly, appear in the 1804 text of the poem, but is a later addition dating from 1806-7.

15. Johnston, "Recollecting Forgetting," p. 60.

16. Havens notes that while "Wordsworth probably had pre-existence in the back of his mind" in this passage, nevertheless "the idea is not necessarily implied in his words" (*The Mind of a Poet*, p. 345). But the image of the yoke as used here is not merely verbally reminiscent of "the inevitable yoke" of the ode (and cf. 5.539-46), but in context strongly suggests the imposition of mortality upon a preexistent strength, the harnessing of a heretofore free energy. Nor does the image of the world as a field in which the soul-seed is sown contradict this implication; here we need only remember Spenser's Garden of Adonis (*The Faerie Queene* 3.6).

17. This passage also, I think, marks an implicit extension or even reinterpretation of the important dual ministries of fear and beauty so strongly emphasized in book 1. In 1798 Wordsworth ostensibly regarded both these ministries, the severe and the gentle, as visitations and interventions of nature (but see above, Chapter 2, section iv). Now in 1804, however, he associates his "milder thoughts" with the natural, mortal world, but his loftier thoughts with the transcendent, immortal one. And the continuation of this passage would seem strongly to encourage our associating this dualism with the twin ministries of book 1:

> Thus musing, in a wood I sate me down,
> Alone, continuing there to muse: meanwhile
> The mountain heights were slowly overspread
> With darkness, and before a rippling breeze
> The long Lake lengthen'd out its hoary line;
> And in the shelter'd coppice where I sate,
> Around me, from among the hazel leaves,
> Now here, now there, stirr'd by the straggling wind,
> Came intermittingly a breath-like sound,

A respiration short and quick, which oft,
Yea, might I say, again and yet again,
Mistaking for the panting of my Dog,
The off-and-on Companion of my walk,
I turned my head, to look if he were there.
                [4.167–80]

First Wordsworth presents a "pastoral quiet," a tranquil scene evocative of those earlier vistas which had been to him the agents of nature's gentler visitations (cf. 1.586–608, 2.342–71—this latter also, like the present passage, an Esthwaite scene). But then he invests this scene with his own sense of an undetermined, unnatural presence, reminiscent of nothing so much as the presences haunting the younger Wordsworth in the snare-robbing and boat-stealing episodes of book 1, agents of nature's "severer interventions."

In effect, Wordsworth in 1804 is moving close to a more conventional association of the fearfully beautiful or impressive with the sublime and with transcendence, the tranquilly beautiful or "lovely" with nature and her lower pleasures. This becomes especially clear in 13.140–58, 204–39, which probably date, like book 4, from the spring of 1804 (part of the former passage, 13.151–58, appears in MS. W).

For general considerations of Wordsworth's notion of the sublime, see W. J. B. Owen, "The Sublime and the Beautiful in *The Prelude*," *Wordsworth Circle* 4 (1973): 67–86, and Heffernan, *Wordsworth's Theory of Poetry*, pp. 154–69.

18. It is true that even in 1798 and 1799 Wordsworth a few times characterized the ultimate power of the world in terms of mind. One example appears in book 2 of *The Prelude*, dating from late 1799, in the famous passage speculating on the growth of the infant's sensibility:

                His mind,
Even as an agent of the one great mind,
Creates, creator and receiver both,
Working but in alliance with the works
Which it beholds,
                [*Prelude 1799* 2.301–5]

Another appears in an Alfoxden notebook fragment dating from early 1798:

And never for each other shall we feel
As we may feel, till we have sympathy
With nature in her forms inanimate,
With objects such as have no power to hold
Articulate language. In all forms of things
There is a mind.
                [*PW* 5:340]

And there is yet another in *The Ruined Cottage*:

> Many an hour in caves forlorn
> And in the hollow depth of naked crags
> He sate, and even in their fixed lineaments,
> Or from the power of a peculiar eye,
> Or by creative feeling overborne,
> Or by predominance of thought oppressed,
> Even in their fixed and steady lineaments
> He traced an ebbing and a flowing mind,
> Expression ever varying.
>
> [Ll. 100-108]

But in all three cases Wordsworth would seem rather certainly to mean by *mind* or *the one great mind* simply the "one life," the "soul of things" (*Prelude 1850*, p. 636, and *PW* 5:402). His attribution in the second and third passages of *mind* to even the inanimate forms of nature encourages such an interpretation; and the second passage does in fact seem to have been intended for Wordsworth's most sustained explication and celebration of the "one life," the Addendum to MS. B of *The Ruined Cottage* (see *CEY*, p. 31; *PW* 5:479; and cf. lines 1-11 of the Addendum). A passage to much the same effect, but with "soul" and "Presence" replacing *mind*, appears in book 3 of *The Prelude*:

> The great mass
> Lay bedded in a quickening soul, and all
> That I beheld respired with inward meaning.
> Thus much for the one Presence, and the Life
> Of the great whole. . . .
>
> [*Prelude 1805* 3.127-31]

(These lines are embedded intrinsically among passages lifted from *The Ruined Cottage*, and probably date from no later than December 1801; see *CMY*, pp. 632-33, and Wordsworth and Gill, "The Two-Part *Prelude* of 1798-99," p. 524.) Further, Wordsworth makes clear in another Alfoxden fragment (dating perhaps from 20 April-16 May 1798 [*CEY*, p. 33]) that, following Locke, he at this time regarded sensational perception itself as a mindlike activity, "creator and receiver both":

> There is creation in the eye,
> Nor less in all the other senses; powers
> They are that colour, model, and combine
> The things perceived with such an absolute
> Essential energy that we may say
> That those most godlike faculties of ours

At one and the same moment are the mind
And the mind's minister.

[PW 5:343]

In this light, the "mind" which is "in all forms of things," the "one life," "the one Presence," "the Life / Of the great whole," and "the soul of things" prove to be simple equivalents.

My argument here in most respects follows Grob, who offers a careful analysis of Wordsworth's sensationalistic epistemology in 1798-99 and locates it in the Lockean tradition (*The Philosophic Mind*, pp. 46-71, especially 64-71, and 114-28, especially 122-26).

Chapter 6

1. The ascent of Snowdon acquires its exceptional status as the climactic episode of *The Prelude* only, we should note, with Wordsworth's great revision. In the earlier, five-book scheme, the final book, beginning with the ascent of Snowdon, was to conclude with the "spots of time" as "a culmination, a pulling-together and placing in a new light, of all that has gone before" (Jonathan Wordsworth, "The Five-Book *Prelude* of Early Spring 1804," *JEGP* 76 [1977]: 21; and see pp. 16-22 passim).

2. The imperfect evidence of MS. W seems to indicate that Wordsworth's last work on the five-book *Prelude* consisted of fragmentary drafts revising and expanding crucial segments of his Snowdon meditations; see ibid., pp. 6, 23-24.

3. In an alternative draft of lines 68-72 in MS. A Wordsworth is even more explicit about extending the emblematic significance of the mist-chasm to this last religious aspect of his mind analogy:

> To my thoughts it gave
> A shadowy image of a mighty Mind
> That while it copes with visible shapes hears also
> Through vents and openings in the ideal world
> The astounding chorus of infinity
> Exalted by an underconsciousness
> Of depth not faithless, the sustaining thought
> Of God in human Being.

[Prelude 1850 13.68-72 app. crit.]

4. *Metalepsis*, the rhetorical trope also known as *transumption*, was called by Quintilian a transition from one trope to another (*Institutio oratoria* 8.6.37-39; cited in Richard A. Lanham, *A Handlist of Rhetorical Terms* [Berkeley: University of California Press, 1968], p. 66). I use the term in this book to mean a trope of a trope (in this particular case, a metaphor of a metonymy). Thus far I follow Harold Bloom, whose *A Map*

of Misreading (New York: Oxford University Press, 1975) points out how important metalepsis is for Milton and his successors (Bloom defines metalepsis as "the trope of a trope" on p. 74).

5. Hence his repeated evocation of spiritual depths in man and nature: "Under-Powers" (1.163), "the under soul" (3.540), "under-countenance" (6.236), "under-thirst" (6.489), "under-sense" (7.712), "under-agents" (12.272), "underpresence" (13.71).

6. Wordsworth's last trope here becomes retrospectively clearer and more significant in Book 8 when he describes the moment he first passed beyond London's suburbs and entered the city proper:

> Never shall I forget the hour
> The moment rather say when having thridded
> The labyrinth of suburban Villages,
> At length I did unto myself first seem
> To enter the great City. . . .
> . . . .
>
>   . . . At the time,
> When to myself it fairly might be said,
> The very moment that I seem'd to know
> The threshold now is overpass'd, Great God!
> That aught *external* to the living mind
> Should have such mighty sway! yet so it was
> A weight of Ages did at once descend
> Upon my heart; no thought embodied, no
> Distinct remembrances; but weight and power,
> Power growing with the weight. . . .
> . . . .
>
> All that took place within me, came and went
> As in a moment, and I only now
> Remember that it was a thing divine.
>   [8.689-710]

Thus to pass from the suburbs into the city proper of the mind is to rouse the true imaginative Power and to touch the very soul.

7. I take *another* in l. 221 to mean "another Cripple" and not simply "another individual": Wordsworth has just before this been describing "a travelling Cripple, by the trunk cut short, / And stumping with his arms" (7.219-20).

A vivid and illuminating description of the kind of scene Wordsworth is sketching here appears in Herman Melville's *Redburn*, a semi-autobiographical novel written in 1849 but based in part on Melville's own

1839 voyage to Liverpool. Redburn devotes an entire chapter of his narrative to "The Dock-Wall Beggars" of Liverpool, and offers among others the following reminiscences:

> I remember one cripple, a young man rather decently clad, who sat huddled up against the wall, holding a painted board on his knees. It was a picture intending to represent the man himself caught in the machinery of some factory, and whirled about among spindles and cogs, with his limbs mangled and bloody. This person said nothing, but sat silently exhibiting his board. Next him, leaning upright against the wall, was a tall, pallid man, with a white bandage round his brow, and his face cadaverous as a corpse. He, too, said nothing; but with one finger silently pointed down to the square of flagging at his feet, which was nicely swept, and stained blue, and bore this inscription in chalk:—
>
> > *"I have had no food for three days;*
> > *My wife and children are dying."*
>
> Further on lay a man with one sleeve of his ragged coat removed, showing an unsightly sore; and above it a label with some writing.
> In some places, for the distance of many rods, the whole line of flagging immediately at the base of the wall, would be completely covered with inscriptions, the beggars standing over them in silence.

[Herman Melville, *Redburn*, ed. Harrison Hayford, Hershel Parker, and G. Thomas Tanselle (Evanston and Chicago: Northwestern University Press and the Newberry Library, 1969), pp. 186-87]

8. Perhaps, indeed, Wordsworth had already heard this "voice of waters." Both episodes date from the same period: Wordsworth's residence in London actually spanned February–November 1791; his excursion to climb Snowdon was in the late spring of 1791, and thus may have occurred either shortly before or shortly after his encounter with the blind Beggar.

9. Wordsworth's unexpected use of *blank* here for what is, after all, not an absence of signs but a confusion of too many signs points suggestively to the Miltonic precedent for his larger trope:

> . . . from the cheerful ways of men
> Cut off, and for the Book of knowledge fair
> Presented with a Universal blanc
> Of Nature's works, to me expung'd and ras'd,
> And wisdom at one entrance quite shut out.
> [*Paradise Lost* 3.46-50]

10. Jonathan Wordsworth, *The Music of Humanity*, p. 229.

11. See John 2:4, 7:6, 7:30, and 8:20; and cf. Matt. 24 and 25, especially 24:36 and 25:13.

It is noteworthy that De Quincey, in his *Literary Reminiscences* of Wordsworth, applies this Biblical phrase—ostensibly after Wordsworth's example, though De Quincey was quoting from memory a manuscript poem he had not seen in years—to Wordsworth himself:

> Wordsworth, though not idle as regarded his own pursuits, was so as regarded the pursuits of the place [Cambridge]. With respect to them he felt—to use his own words—that his hour was not come; and that his doom for the present was a happy obscurity, which left him, unvexed by the torments of competition, to the genial enjoyment of his life in its most genial hours. [*Collected Writings* 2:265]

This would seem to be a memory of *Prelude 1805* 3.80-82, another passage with scriptural overtones.

12. Hartman, *Wordsworth's Poetry*, p. 184; see also p. 60.

13. Victor Shklovsky, "Art as Technique," in *Russian Formalist Criticism: Four Essays*, ed. Lee T. Lemon and Marion J. Reis (Lincoln: University of Nebraska Press, 1965), p. 18; see also p. 12.

It is perhaps Shelley who formulates the Wordsworthian and Romantic position most succinctly (though of course "naked and sleeping beauty" is hardly a Wordsworthian phrase): "Poetry . . . strips the veil of familiarity from the world, and lays bare the naked and sleeping beauty which is the spirit of its forms" (Percy Bysshe Shelley, "A Defence of Poetry," *Shelley's Prose*, ed. David Lee Clark [Alburquerque: University of New Mexico Press, 1954; corrected ed. 1966], p. 295; cf. p. 282). See also Coleridge, *Biographia Literaria*, 2:6.

Wordsworthian defamiliarization differs from that recognized by the formalists in one further respect, a tenet already noted. In the usage of formalism, *defamiliarization* refers to a tone of perception, or to the artistic imitation of such a tone. Wordsworth, however, insists also that the perceived object, nature herself, sometimes actually defamiliarizes herself, transforming her appearances, and thereby thrusting them upon our notice, solely by "her own naked work / Self-wrought, unaided by the human mind" (*Prelude 1850*, p. 624; MS. W). The Snowdon scene itself is one such instance; others explicitly include the apparitions of the rainbow amid the storm on Coniston and the immobile, silhouetted horse, seemingly "an amphibious work of Nature's hand, / A Borderer dwelling betwixt life and death, / A living Statue or a statued Life" (pp. 623-24), scenes Wordsworth originally cited in MS. W to illustrate this very point about nature's imaginative expressiveness but omitted from the finished poem. On these occasions, nature herself truly operates "as if with an imaginative power" (13.78/79 app. crit.; MS. W). To repeat Hartman's observation, Wordsworth indeed says and believes that "there exists an imagination in nature analogous to that in man. . . . He does not consider what he sees as a projection of his mind on nature" (*Wordsworth's Poetry*, p. 184).

14. As it does briefly at 7.696, so here also Wordsworth's language suggests his Miltonic precedent—essentially the same precedent, for he draws in both instances from the same passage:

> But cloud instead, and ever-during dark
> Surrounds me. . . .
>
> . . . .
>
> So much the rather thou Celestial Light
> Shine inward, and the mind through all her powers
> Irradiate, there plant eyes, all mists from thence
> Purge and disperse, that I may see and tell
> Of things invisible to mortal sight.
> [*Paradise Lost* 3.45-55]

15. Wlecke, *Wordsworth and the Sublime*, p. 27.

16. Doubtless this reading calls for some defense. Did the scene near Penrith Beacon really seem ordinary to the boy? I realize that I raise a lonely voice in suggesting that it did. Critics customarily portray the child as not only frightened by being lost and separated from his guide, but superstitiously terrified as well by the gibbet site. Thus Hartman speaks of the child's "dread-inspiring impression of place" and asserts, "It is quite clear that the child does not know that what he sees and feels is an effect of the power of his imagination" (*Wordsworth's Poetry*, pp. 214-15). This traditional reading, of course, associates the Penrith experience with such incidents as the snare-robbing and boat-stealing episodes, from which I instead would wish to distinguish it—episodes where the child's intense emotion (specifically in these cases his sense of guilt) heightens, colors, and even distorts his perceptions.

It will never do, of course, to argue that the child is unmoved by his predicament; but I would argue that his terror has been exaggerated—not least, perhaps, by the elderly poet himself. Wordsworth in fact is extremely vague about what the boy fears, and how deeply. Certainly the child "through fear / Dismount[s]" (11.286-87); but this, surely, is merely a fear of being unable to manage his horse unaided—"at a time / When scarcely (I was then not six years old) / My hand could hold a bridle" (11.279-81)—and is effectively allayed by his dismounting to lead the horse. Too, he is lost; but for how long? And is he really so badly frightened by the gibbet site? Both these questions, as it happens, turn on Wordsworth's revision of the passage in 1839. In the 1850 *Prelude*—typically cited by those who see here a badly frightened and bewildered boy—Wordsworth very definitely does portray the child's experience as a compounding of fear upon fear: the boy becomes lost; he strays onto the gibbet site, with its memorial inscriptions on the turf: "A casual glance had shown them, and I fled, / Faltering and faint, and ignorant of the road" (*Prelude 1850* 12.246–47). In 1805, however, Wordsworth's presentation and implications are strikingly different: the boy becomes lost; "Faltering, and ignorant where I was, at length / I chanced to espy those characters inscribed / On the green sod: forthwith I left the spot" (11.300–302). There is a very strong implication here, I think, that when the boy sees those letters he recognizes and utilizes the place as a landmark, now suddenly realizing both where he is and where that is. He may still be separated from his guide, but now he is no longer lost. The beacon, which he now locates, serves a similarly orienting and guiding function. And is this really fortuitous, or might not he now know just how to find the beacon? *Forthwith I left* may well imply that he now has a sense of direction, not that he flees blindly in fear. Here as in so many other passages, Wordsworth in his much later revision of *The Prelude* has not clarified, but has actually changed the implications of his earlier poetry.

Two further points would seem to afford this interpretation additional support. First, there is the implicitly parallel example of the second spot of time, the waiting for the horses. Here as at Simplon the defamiliarization postdates the perception (it comes with the death, some days later, of his father), and thus, as even the child realizes, unquestionably derives not from the natural scene but from the mind. Second, there is Wordsworth's characterization of the spots of time as "passages of life in which / We *have had* deepest feeling that the mind / Is lord and master" (my emphasis); both tense and phrasing here indicate that this feeling, despite Hartman's assertion to the contrary, does indeed date from the original experience. Significantly, Wordsworth changes this implication, too, in his later revision, eliding his temporal reference in the vague, timeless restatement, "passages of life that give / Profoundest knowledge to what point, and how, / The mind is lord and master" (*Prelude 1850* 12.220–22).

17. On Snowdon's mist, cf. the second spot of time, where "the mist / Gave intermitting prospect" (11.362–63).

"I was lost as in a cloud": Hartman also notes this parallel (*Wordsworth's Poetry*, p. 218).

A passage in book 3 mediately suggests a further linking of "breathing-place" and "hiding-places": "Points have we all of us within our souls, / Where all stand single; this I feel, and make / Breathings for incommunicable powers" (3.186–88).

18. Cf. 6.527, where Wordsworth similarly speaks of the Imagination as a "Power."

19. *Personifying nature and naturalizing persons:* this is the practice that De Quincey was noting in his praise of the Boy of Winander passage, where the visible scene, as De Quincey quotes (somewhat inaccurately) from memory, "was carried *far* into his heart, / With all its pomp, and that uncertain heav'n received / Into the bosom of the steady lake." "This very expression, 'far,'" De Quincey continues, "by which space and its infinities are attributed to the human heart, and to its capacities of re-echoing the sublimities of nature, has always struck me as with a flash of sublime revelation" (*Literary Reminiscences* [Boston: Ticknor, 1851], 1:310; this passage does not appear in the revised version of *Literary Reminiscences* in *Collected Writings*).

Lindenberger discusses various aspects of this Wordsworthian technique as "the rhetoric of interaction" (*On Wordsworth's Prelude*, pp. 41-98).

On the "corresponding breeze," cf. M. H. Abrams, "The Correspondent Breeze: A Romantic Metaphor," in *English Romantic Poets: Modern Essays in Criticism*, ed. M. H. Abrams (New York: Oxford University Press, 1960), pp. 37-54.

Chapter 7

1. Cf. his prayer for the schoolchildren of Hawkshead: "May books and nature be their early joy!" (5.447).

2. It is perhaps necessary to emphasize here what is already quite explicit in the poetry, that the cataclysm Wordsworth is brooding upon involves the destruction of civilization but *not* of mankind—"what he may lose, / Nor be himself extinguish'd." Wordsworth is not, as has been suggested, conjuring a threat here of "a very literal Apocalypse . . . the violent fate of Nature and implicitly of natural man" (Thomas Weiskel, *The Romantic Sublime: Studies in the Structure and Psychology of Transcendence* [Baltimore, Md.: Johns Hopkins University Press, 1976], p. 186).

3. Cf. *Prelude 1805* 5.164, "poor earthly casket of immortal Verse!"

4. Wordsworth carefully avoids this association in part, I would suggest, because already the knowledge that crystals *grow*, almost as if they were living matter, was widespread, and he had no wish to introduce any such quasiorganic implication into his emblem of abstract mathematical truth.

5. Patrick Holland, "Wordsworth and the Sublime," p. 21, notes the first two of these three potential meanings of 5.46.

6. Jonathan Bishop, "Wordsworth and the 'Spots of Time,'" p. 65, also notes the point that the dreamer hears only himself.

As an intimation of mortality, the shell's prophecy is thus analogous to the "ancestral voices prophesying war" which Kubla Khan hears in the tumultuous sounds of the life-imaging river Alph. Indeed, this entire dream is extensively analogous to "Kubla Khan," another allegorical presentation of poetic creation and memorialization which is itself, Coleridge tells us, the matter of a dream. Implicitly, we should remember, Wordsworth's friend who recounts this Arab-Quixote dream is Coleridge himself—"a Philosophic Friend" (*Prelude 1850* 5.49-50 app. crit.), "a studious friend" (5.51), as later revisions term him.

David Perkins, *Wordsworth and the Poetry of Sincerity* (Cambridge, Mass.: Harvard University Press, 1964), p. 105, calls the Arab a poet.

7. Miguel de Cervantes Saavedra, *Don Quixote*, tr. Walter Starkie (New York: New American Library, 1957), pp. 1049-50. Cide Hamete's farewell to his pen comically and movingly parodies a knight's farewell to his sword, and his monitory verses cast an enchantment upon it in the best chivalric tradition.

8. And surely in the opprobrium of this unfeeling act—

> "It is," said he, "the waters of the deep
> Gathering upon us," quickening then his pace
> He left me: I call'd after him aloud;
> He heeded not
>
> [5.130-33]

—we find the explanation of Wordsworth's curious and clumsy revision in the 1850 *Prelude* whereby he makes the dream not his friend's but his own. By presenting himself in 1850 as the abandoned man, Wordsworth manages to oppose himself to the Arab with whom he will subsequently identify, and thus temper an unflattering characterization of himself as one who would be ready to abandon others. He accomplishes this, of course, at no little expense to the tautness (not to mention the honesty) of his verse; for after revision the friend has nothing to do but listen, and his presence in the poem becomes painfully extraneous.

Chapter 8

1. The allusion to "subterraneous Fields," surely the Elysian Fields, makes clear that Wordsworth is referring here to worlds of life after death as well as to Utopian schemes. Thus "some secreted Island, Heaven knows where" could allude to More's island Utopia, but could also refer to a type of Heaven itself—the Hesperides, the Islands of the Blessed—or again to the Arthurian isle of Avalon. Cf. the substantiating parallel reference of the *Prospectus* to such realms:

Paradise, and groves
Elysian, Fortunate Fields—like those of old
Sought in the Atlantic Main—why should they be
A history only of departed things,
Or a mere fiction of what never was?
For the discerning intellect of man,
When wedded to this goodly universe
In love and holy passion, shall find these
A simple produce of the common day.
[Ll. 47-55]

2. Geoffrey Hartman ("Evening Star and Evening Land," in *The Fate of Reading and Other Essays* [Chicago: University of Chicago Press, 1975], p. 157-58), while definitely reading the poem as a transcendental statement, also seems to sense the presence and force of an opposing inclination: "The final verses . . . quietly merge the idea of ground and heaven. Their subject is transcendence, but this is depicted as a *stepping*, and compared to the ghostly apparition of the soul in a place (that is, heaven) not its own. Yet Wordsworth preserves . . . a sense of distance: the soul is not of the place but appropriates it "strong her strength above."

3. Cf. *LEY*, p. 355: "A great Poet . . . ought to travel before men occasionally as well as at their sides." And cf. also MS. 1 of the *Prospectus*, wherein he describes himself as "in part a Fellow citizen, in part / An outlaw, and a borderer of his age" (*HG*, p. 261).

4. Beyond the evidence of Wordsworth's letter of 12 March 1805 to Beaumont, cited above, and his statement of 16 April 1805 to his brother Richard, "[John] went a brave and innocent Spirit to that God from whom I trust he will receive his reward" (*LEY*, p. 583), there is also the relevant testimony of Dorothy's contemporary letters—relevant (though of course not definitive) because Dorothy throughout their life together shared, echoed, and upheld (even as she to a degree shaped) the opinions and tenets of her brother. Before John's death she had displayed no more concern for an afterlife than had William; after it, however, she wrote to Lady Beaumont, in harmony with William's letters to Sir George Beaumont and Richard Wordsworth,

> True it is that the agony which follows on the death of those in whom our hope has been could only close in settled gloom and heaviest disappointment, were it not for those elevating thoughts of a better life, and a more glorious nature which the contemplation of the virtues of the departed raises up in us with a strength unknown before. [*LEY*, pp. 575-76]

And again:

Yes, my dear Friend, if we had not a faith that the best are selected for sorrow and affliction as to the "post of honour," to be thereby rendered the more perfect in another state, how could we bear to live here after the first pleasure of youth is gone! [*LEY*, pp. 591-92]

5. While Wordsworth speaks of "such rebounds" heard by "our inward ear" as dear because they are "of God," nevertheless an echo is, of course, by its very nature a highly ambivalent figure for an intimating voice. Cf. the quite similar figure of the shell in *Prelude* 5.80-109 and *Excursion* 4.1132-47, and see my discussions above, Chapter 7, section ii, and below, Chapter 8, section iii.

6. John Jones, *The Egotistical Sublime*, p. 153.

7. Fairchild, *Religious Trends in English Poetry*, 3:206; Martin Price, "Imagination in *The White Doe of Rylstone*," *Philological Quarterly* 33 (1954): 198 (cf. Hartman's assessment in *Wordsworth's Poetry*, pp. 327-28); Heffernan, *Wordsworth's Theory of Poetry*, p. 223.

8. Hartman, *Wordsworth's Poetry*, pp. 326-27.

9. The essay dates from December 1809-February 1810, but the former phrase, probably Wordsworth's most explicit affirmation herein of man's personal immortality, was added only in 1814 (*Prose* 2:52 n).

Appendix A

1. Samuel Taylor Coleridge, *The Complete Poetical Works of Samuel Taylor Coleridge*, ed. Ernest Hartley Coleridge, 2 vols. (Oxford: Oxford University Press, Clarendon Press, 1912), 1:386 n.

Appendix B

1. "S. H." is Sara Hutchinson, Wordsworth's sister-in-law; "Town-End," the address of Dove Cottage, the Wordsworths' home in Grasmere.

2. Similarly noteworthy and accurate are *Prelude 1805* 6.380, a memory of the summer of 1790, and Dorothy Wordsworth's letter of 25 March 1804 to Catherine Clarkson, referring to an evening star shining over Silver How (the mountain directly across the lake of Grasmere from Dove Cottage) which again can only have been Venus, now shining as Hesperus for the first time since 1802 (*LEY*, p. 461).

3. For the contemporary astronomical data, I have referred to [Ming's] *Hutchins' Improved . . . Almanack and Ephemeris . . . 1803* (New York, [1802]), and *The [Old] Farmer's Almanack, 1802* and *1803* (Boston, [1801] and [1802]); for general astronomical information, to Robert H. Baker and Laurence W. Fredrick, *Astronomy*, 9th ed. (New York: Van Nostrand, 1971), pp. 202-3.

Index

Abrams, M. H., 177 n.4, 178 n.7,
205 n.19
*Address to the Scholars of the
Village School of* ——, 54
Aeschylus, *The Libation-Bearers*, 187
n.3
Aesop, 86
Allegory, xvii-xx, 75-76, 79, 96,
178 nn. 4-5, 178 n.8. *See also*
Emblematic vision
Anecdote for Fathers, 56
Arcades (Milton), 184 n.11
"A slumber did my spirit seal," 53-
54

Baker, Robert H., 208 n.3
Bateson, F. W., on *Tintern Abbey*,
181 n.2
Beatty, Arthur: on Hartley, 182 n.7,
194 n.8; on the *Intimations* ode,
104, 181 n.3; on *Tintern Abbey*,
30
Beaumont, Lady, 207 n.4

Beaumont, Sir George, 158, 207 n.4
Biographia Literaria (Coleridge),
177 n.4, 178 n.5, 202 n.13
Bishop, Jonathan, 185 n.18, 205 n.6
Blake, William, 45, 157
Bloom, Harold, 186 n.24, 191 n.14,
194 n.8; on the *Intimations* ode,
104; on metalepsis, 199 n.4; on
Tintern Abbey, 45
Borderers, The, xx-xxi, 3-13, 14,
16-17, 19, 42-43, 162; dating of,
189 n.2; emblematic vision in, xx-
xxi, 3, 9-13, 50, 95-96; *and Hart-
Leap Well*, 77-80; iconic vision in,
xx, 3-4, 9, 43, 50, 179 n.2; mor-
ality in, 3, 9, 12-13, 19, 58,
188 n.3; and *Resolution and In-
dependence*, 88
Bostetter, Edward E., on *Resolution
and Independence*, 192 n.16
Brooks, Cleanth, 195 n.11
Brothers, The, 49, 64-67, 71, 76
Burns, Robert, 86-87

Butler, James A., 181 n.13, 189 n.7, 191 n.6

Camp, Dennis, 183 n.10
Carroll, Lewis, 88
Cervantes, Miguel de, 147-48; *Don Quixote*, xviii, 144, 147-48, 206 n.7
Chatterton, Thomas, 86-87
Christ, 123
Clarkson, Catherine, 102, 167, 208 n.1
Coleridge, Hartley, 83, 171-72
Coleridge, Samuel Taylor, 13, 45, 84, 89, 112, 139, 157, 162, 171-73; on allegory versus symbol, xvii-xviii, 178 nn. 4-5; carving initials, 68; influence on Wordsworth, 3, 16; on *Intimations* ode, 105; on Lucy poem, 53; on "one life," xx. *Biographia Literaria*, 177 n.4, 178 n.5, 202 n.13; *Dejection*, 84, 173; *The Eolian Harp*, 180 n.10; *Kubla Khan*, 206 n.6; *The Language of Birds*, 171; *Miscellaneous Criticism*, 178 n.5; *Religious Musings*, 180 n.10; *The Statesman's Manual*, 178 n.4
Complaint of a Forsaken Indian Woman, 78
Composed after a Journey across the Hambleton Hills, 165
Composed by the Sea-Side, near Calais, August, 1802, 175
Conran, Anthony, 192 n.17
"Could I the priest's consent have gained," 55
Curtis, Jared R., 172, 192 n.15

Danish Boy, The, 62, 80
Dante, 195 n.10
Darlington, Beth, 187 n.1
Defamiliarization, 125-26,

202 n.13; associated with mist in *The Prelude*, 125, 131, 133, 151, 164; of Boy of Winander, 130; in great literature, 151-52; in ministry of fear, 132; on Snowdon, 125; in spots of time, 133, 204 n.16; in *The White Doe of Rylestone*, 163
Dejection (Coleridge), 84, 173
De Quincey, Thomas, 142; on *The Prelude*, 202 n.11, 205 n.19; on *We Are Seven*, 192 n.18
Descriptive Sketches, 179 n.1
Don Quixote (Cervantes), xviii, 144, 147-48, 206 n.7
Durant, Geoffrey, on Lucy poems, 188 n.2

Elijah, 5, 6, 88
Emblematic vision, xx, 3-4, 9, 26, 96; objective mode of, xxi, 81, 95-96, 163, 178 n.10; subjective mode of, xx-xxi, 13-14, 162-63. *See also* Allegory; *The Borderers*; *The Excursion*; *Hart-Leap Well*; the *Intimations* ode; *Lines Left Upon a Seat in a Yew-Tree*; *The Prelude* 1799; *The Prelude* 1805; *The Ruined Cottage*; *The White Doe of Rylstone*
Empson, William, 30, 181 n.2
Enthusiasm, xxi, 166, 168; defined, xx; as mode of symbolic vision, xx-xxi
Eolian Harp, The, (Coleridge), 180 n.10
Epictetus, 196 n.14
Essay on Epitaphs, 69, 102, 105, 163
Essence: of literature, 150-51; of mind, 114-16, 118-23; 129-35; of nature, 114-16, 120-22, 134-35. *See also* Substantiation
Evening Walk, An, 103